Cultural Politics in the Age of Austerity

In 2008 another economic crisis emerged in the long history of capitalism which created a period of 'austerity economics' across many nations. *Cultural Politics in the Age of Austerity* examines how austerity has impacted upon cultural politics in relation to understanding how established power is both maintained and challenged.

The book begins by detailing the meaning of cultural politics before exploring themes such as media discourse, austerity narratives, class, cultural hegemony/government policymaking, social movements and the European Union, and left responses to austerity. It also includes chapters tracing cultural politics in Spain, with a focus on anti-austerity movements and the relationship between austerity and Spanish football.

Cultural Politics in the Age of Austerity assesses the impact of a range of cultural/political forms concerning the dynamics of society and relations of power during times of crisis. As such, it will appeal to scholars of culture, media, politics, philosophy, sociology and social psychology.

David Berry is Senior Lecturer in Media, Communication and Culture at Southampton Solent University, UK, and the author of *The Romanian Mass Media and Cultural Development* and *Journalism, Ethics and Society*. He is the co-author of *Public Policy and Media Organizations*, the co-editor of *Radical Mass Media Criticism: A Cultural Genealogy* and *British Marxism and Cultural Studies: Essays on a living tradition,* and the editor of *Ethics and Media Culture: Representations and Practices* and *Revisiting the Frankfurt School: Essays on Media, Culture and Theory.*

The Cultural Politics of Media and Popular Culture
Series Editor: C. Richard King
Washington State University, USA

Dedicated to a renewed engagement with culture, this series fosters critical, contextual analyses and cross-disciplinary examinations of popular culture as a site of cultural politics. It welcomes theoretically grounded and critically engaged accounts of the politics of contemporary popular culture and the popular dimensions of cultural politics. Without being aligned to a specific theoretical or methodological approach, *The Cultural Politics of Media and Culture* publishes monographs and edited collections that promote dialogues on central subjects, such as representation, identity, power, consumption, citizenship, desire and difference.

Offering approachable and insightful analyses that complicate race, class, gender, sexuality, (dis)ability and nation across various sites of production and consumption, including film, television, music, advertising, sport, fashion, food, youth, subcultures and new media, *The Cultural Politics of Media and Popular Culture* welcomes work that explores the importance of text, context and subtext as these relate to the ways in which popular cultures work alongside hegemony.

For a full list of titles, please visit: https://www.routledge.com/ The-Cultural-Politics-of-Media-and-Popular-Culture/book-series/ ASHSER-1395

Also available in the series:

Post-9/11 Heartland Horror
Rural horror films in an era of urban terrorism
Victoria McCollum

Belligerent Broadcasting
Synthetic argument in broadcast talk
Michael Higgins and Angela Smith

Cultural Politics in the Age of Austerity
Edited by David Berry

Cultural Politics in the Age of Austerity

Edited by David Berry

Routledge
Taylor & Francis Group

LONDON AND NEW YORK

First published 2017
by Routledge

2 Park Square, Milton Park, Abingdon, Oxfordshire OX14 4RN

52 Vanderbilt Avenue, New York, NY 10017

Routledge is an imprint of the Taylor & Francis Group, an informa business

First issued in paperback 2018

British Library Cataloguing-in-Publication Data
A catalogue record for this book is available from the British Library

Library of Congress Cataloging-in-Publication Data
A catalog record for this book has been requested

ISBN: 978-1-4724-3488-3 (hbk)
ISBN: 978-0-367-08537-7 (pbk)

Typeset in Garamond
by codeMantra

Contents

Notes on contributors

Maggie Andrews is Professor of Cultural History at the University of Worcester and author of a range of publications, including *The Acceptable Face of Feminism* (2015), and co-editor of *Lest We Forget: Remembrance and Commemoration* (2011). Maggie is Co-Investigator for AHRC funded 'Voices of War' and 'Peace First World War Community Engagement Hub' and historical consultant for the first series of a new BBC Radio 4 drama *Home Front.*

David Berry has published since 2000 and will continue into the future. He has a PhD.

Philip Bounds holds a PhD in Politics from the University of Wales and has published widely on the intellectual history of the British left. His books include *Orwell and Marxism* (2009), *British Communism and the Politics of Literature* (2012) and *Notes from the End of History* (2014).

Emma L. Briant specialises in political communication at the University of Sheffield. Her research interests are propaganda and US, and British governmental adaptation to a changing media and conflict environment. Her PhD (University of Glasgow, 2011) examined Anglo-American counter-terrorism propaganda strategies since 9/11, the subject of her latest book *Propaganda and Counter-terrorism.*

Steven Harkins is an ESRC-funded PhD candidate at the University of Sheffield's Department of Journalism Studies. His research examines news coverage of poverty and inequality. He is also part of the Joseph Rowntree Foundation's Expert Communications Group, and his research can be found in *Critical Discourse Studies*, *Critical Studies on Terrorism* and the *British Medical Journal.*

Mark Hayes is Senior Lecturer in Politics and Criminology at Solent University. He has published widely on a range of topics.

His latest book is *The Ideology of Fascism and the Far Right in Britain* (2014).

Sallie McNamara is Senior Lecturer at Southampton Solent University. Publications include 'Lady Eleanor Smith and the Society Column, 1927–1930' in *Women and the Media: Feminism and Femininity in Britain, 1900 to the Present* (2014) and 'Mask and Mascara: The Female Masquerade in Women's Historical Romances of the 1930s and 1940s' in *Beauty: Politics, Poetics, Change* (2014).

Jim O'Brien is Senior Lecturer in Journalism and Sports Journalism at Southampton Solent University. He has previously held posts in the Netherlands, Greece and the United States and has written extensively on the historical, political and cultural contexts of Spanish football in recent years.

Glen Parkinson is an independent-minded individual.

Joan Pedro holds a PhD in Communication, Social Change and Development from Complutense University, Madrid, Spain. He is an Associate Professor in Media and Communication at Saint Louis University-Madrid Campus. Joan is interested in the theory and practice of social change through communication, education and culture.

Preface

David Berry

This book is a collection of essays on various themes and perspectives within the context of the period known as the 'Age of
Austerity'. This period began in 2008 with the collapse of commercial enterprises and increases in sub-prime mortgages in the US
spreading to banking systems and nation-states within Europe and
beyond. 'Age of Austerity' is a curious term in the sense that austerity economics are nothing new within the historical structures
of capitalist development. In fact, it's fair to argue that austerity
has been and will continue to be a central feature of said development; it is as Marx would have it, the inherent contradiction of
the system itself. Austerity is no more than a reaction imposed by
elites to the re-emerging crisis of capitalism, and its impact and
consequences are traditionally/historically more brutally imposed
upon the working class and the poorest communities. One essential
difference of this current phase of crisis is that austerity has also
impacted upon the middle class, which further alters the dynamics
of cultural politics.

Despite the fact that the period from 2008 onwards is but
another crisis, this present 'Age of Austerity' does have some unique
features that separate it from previous forms. One, in Europe it
was formed post-fascism and post-communism (1989 political
revolutions); two, the enlargement and incorporation of former
fascist and Stalinist states into the European Union; three, the expansion of China and Russia into global markets; four, the hegemonic position of global capital (the End of History theory) and five,
in the United Kingdom the perverse idea forwarded by the former
leader of the Tories, David Cameron that 'we are all in it together'
which defined austerity, in the UK, in purely ideological terms.

The overall objective of this book is to assess the relationship
between austerity and cultural politics which briefly can be measured in terms of resistance and /or imposition of established norms
which is exactly what Cameron's phrase was meant to create (i.e.
an attempt to rationalize, normalize and legitimize the status quo).

The fact that Labour Party members unanimously supported Jeremy Corbyn to become the leader in September 2015 is testament to the fact that such attempts by Cameron – and the majority of Parliamentary MPs including Labour – to impose austerity was not only a rejection of austerity economics but more importantly a rejection of the staid and turgid established Parliamentary system which is meant but failed to represent ordinary people; this is direct evidence of the relationship between austerity and cultural politics in the 'Age of Austerity'. There are other political examples including the emergence of Syriza in Greece and Podemos in Spain amongst others. But the relationship is not simply a political process; it also operates within the fine contours of culture and media which collectively produce complex and often competing cultural narratives that interact within the political context, and they often merge making cultural politics not only a fascinating area to observe but more importantly an extremely complex system to understand.

1 Cultural politics, austerity and responses

David Berry

The *nexus* of cultural politics

In 2008, another systemic economic crisis in capitalism emerged, this time beginning in the US with the collapse of Lehman Brothers and the sub-prime mortgage market[1] coupled with a crisis in the banking industry. In 2009, what became known as the Eurozone Crisis[2] was measured by the inability of a number of European nations to service debts with banks, which were accused of 'bad lending' within global markets on a grand scale. The response across Europe, the US and Canada, to varying degrees, was for governments to introduce austerity policies in order to control the crisis, to reduce government debt and control deficit. The debate among economists over whether austerity policies were effective and indeed necessary as a response to the crisis have been heated and vigorous with deep divisions emerging as to what was the most economically appropriate way to address the crisis caused by an unregulated banking industry but impacting mostly on ordinary citizens with huge cuts in public spending, including welfare, social benefits, confiscation of housing due to enforced non-payment, reduced spending on health, reduction or freezing of wages, increase in student fees and in parts of Europe – most notably Greece and Spain – substantial rises in unemployment. Economists and politicians that supported 'economic austerity' were claiming that they based austerity policies on pure economic decisions in relation to what Weber referred to as 'calculated rationality', principally governed by neo-liberalism that fêtes the free market as the dominant economic rationale. This, in my view, includes ideological and moral perspectives despite any arguments negating these two points on behalf of said economists, which they would claim play no role in cold, calculative thinking.

However varied the consequences of austerity measures across Europe, one common theme is shared, and that is the fact that ordinary working people were not responsible for the crisis, but ordinary working people, as opposed to elites who caused the crisis, suffered the most as governments sought to reduce public spending. In the case of the United Kingdom, austerity policies were not simply based on 'calculated rationality'; in fact, austerity economics became an opportunistic-ideological excuse to shrink the size of the state, reduce public spending in the longer term and rely on the market and private sector to increase investment. Whatever national context we wish to analyse, austerity economics have had a profound impact on various societies, thus it is in this context that I wish to pose the following question: what impact has austerity economics had on cultural politics within nation-states?

This chapter serves as a theoretical basis for the scholarly essays that follow by presenting a discussion on cultural politics and austerity, both as economic rationality and as an ideological construct that permeates various narratives under the latest crisis in capitalism and neo-liberal philosophy. Raymond Williams' concept of 'cultural materialism' is a useful conceptual framework to study the processes of cultural politics. For instance, in his little but extremely condensed book *Marxism and Literature,* Williams draws upon three concepts that are central for understanding cultural production and power; these are 'dominant', 'residual' and 'emergent'. 'Dominant' is self-evident, and 'residual' has echoes of the anarchist focus on 'memory' of a past-historic lived culture that resides in the present. Such ideas, beliefs and values, which can be termed as 'tradition', can sometimes conflict with the modern. The most obvious ones are religious beliefs (morality) and working class culture, but it is a murky field, because conservatism, a dominant ideology (ideas, beliefs and values) also draws upon the past to be lived in the present, which converge with the modern.

What this ultimately means is that the 'emergent' contains contradictory ideas, beliefs and values, and at the very least those ideas that dominate perhaps use methods of 'containment' through various types of intervention to stem what Williams referred to as 'oppositional' in his analysis of culture. Hall (2007) later used the 'containment-resistance' model to argue exactly that (i.e. the site of popular culture – not to be confused with commercial culture masquerading as the popular – has the potential to edge out, threaten, even overthrow the dominant ideology); dominant may equal establishment, but these values, ideas and belief systems permeate into working class culture. This makes the space of cultural politics very complex and difficult to analyse, and perhaps in times of 'prosperity' we may be forgiven to say that the establishment has the whip hand, because times are good or at least seen to be good derived from various political and media representations.

Like Williams, Richard Rorty viewed cultural politics not simply as a form of linguistic practice – although this is extremely important for both – but equally as a space of *practice as action*:

> Interventions in cultural politics have sometimes taken the form of proposal for new roles that men and women might play; the ascetic, the prophet, the dispassionate seeker after truth, the good citizen, the aesthete, the revolutionary. Sometimes they have been sketches of an ideal community – the perfected Greek Polis. … Sometimes they have been suggestions about how to reconcile seemingly incompatible outlooks … .
>
> (Rorty, 2007: ix–x)

The moral and political dimensions of this statement are clear vis-à-vis the complex processes of cultural politics, thus placing the word 'nexus' prior to cultural politics in the section title above is to highlight the complexity of the term; for what exactly are the *connections* between concepts, narratives and ideas that shape cultural politics, and once again what impact does austerity have on cultural politics? Something is missing from Rorty's statement: the absence of economic policy and its impact on thinking and thus the 'interventions' Rorty highlights. I don't wish to revisit the debate on economic determinism as *the* force for thinking and acting, but for our purposes, it is worth bearing in mind the economic basis (rationale) and neo-liberal justification for attempting to normalize the idea of economic austerity as a rational act of judgment within the constraints of capital.

Rorty was influenced by John Dewey's pragmatic philosophy (pragmatism) and whilst not entirely in agreement, Rorty offered contentious and specific interpretations of Dewey's work and fully understood that Dewey's basis for thinking about democracy was instinctively a moral judgment regarding cultural politics.[3] This partly explains the use of the word 'intervention' because Dewey rejected its absence detailed in 'spectator theory',[4] but Rorty's usage was not entirely dependent on morality. For Stuart Hall, such 'interventions' into a space of cultural politics was more specifically referred to as 'popular culture' detailed in his work titled 'Notes on deconstructing the popular' (2007). Hall had argued that popular culture was not the authentic sphere of peoples' production but rather the space whereby resistance to dominating ideologies emerged. Hall maintained that dominating ideologies – what Horkheimer ridiculed as (bourgeois) 'reason' – clashed with alternative narratives, ideas and actions of the people which emerge as a form of popular culture; this, in essence, is the core of cultural politics because quite rightly this, for Hall, rests on the containment-resistance axis. In other words, political elites seek to contain resistance and normalize society by whatever means are at their disposal and pass it off as 'reason', and this is why Horkheimer is equally important to include, because the title of his book of which he offered a scathing attack of 'bourgeois reason' – as absolute rationality – *The Eclipse of Reason* rests upon interventions at all levels of society.

This current collection of scholarly contributions is an attempt to understand how the period of austerity shapes cultural political spheres and how interventions help form a social process under conditions aligned to neo-liberalism. Such interventions include what Emma Briant and Steven Harkins refer to as 'nudging' in their chapter partly titled 'The cultural politics of neo-liberal nudging', referring to processes of 'social interventionism' and by using Gramsci's theory of hegemony further detailing how state-led interventions operate in civil society in order to influence the dynamics of cultural politics. In Sallie McNamara's essay, we see how media discourse as a cultural intervention operates, using examples such as *Breaking Bad* and *Girls* (US) and *Downton Abbey* (UK) to demonstrate the various types of 'austerity narratives'[5] in play within culture and how such narratives are multi-dimensional in meaning and context.

Broadly speaking, where oppositional narratives to austerity are evident, they may constitute a cultural dispute with the types of 'nudging' displayed by government agencies discussed by Briant and Harkins. Public responses to both media and governmental-led political discourse are notoriously difficult to quantify, but if cultural politics is anything it is the discursive relationship between production of discourse/narratives, consumption and response. Certain forms of opposition and resistance to dominant cultural-political hegemonic forces have been and continue to be seen as threats to the prevailing order. For instance, in Glen Parkinson's chapter concerning the riots that occurred in England in 2011, he states in relation to Erich Fromm that 'cultural deviancy necessarily implies a sickness of the individual rather than of the society'; this was demonstrated at the 2015 Tory conference in the UK where Prime Minister David Cameron lambasted the leader of the opposition, Jeremy Corbyn, as a 'threat' to society. Cameron's speech, also peppered with claims that the Tories were now the 'party of labour', clearly demonstrated the desire to connect between and govern two opposing poles of the social spectrum (i.e. establishment and labour) which is how hegemony operates with regards to seeking the consent of the ruled.

When Rorty argued that 'The term "cultural politics" covers, among other things, arguments about what words to use' (2007: 1), he was in part referring to the varying 'linguistic practices' in process; however, the phrase 'among other things' clearly demonstrates a broad, not narrow, view of cultural politics – in other words, something beyond narratives. Linguistic practices in circulation such as austerity narratives define the practice of cultural politics and relate to what Raymond Williams referred to as hegemonic and counter-hegemonic production, basing his thoughts on Gramsci's contribution for understanding relations of power. Such practices are evident throughout Europe where political forces of resistance to hegemonic powers are Syriza (Greece); Podemos (Spain); Five Star Movement (Italy); Bloco de Esquerda (Portugal); the shift to the left by the British Labour Party under the leadership of Jeremy Corbyn; the emergence in the US 2015/16 of Bernie Sanders' challenge to Hilary Clinton for the leadership of the Democratic Party which generated significant grassroots support; and the election of Justin Trudeau in Canada, 2015, on an anti-austerity agenda.

Such opposing narratives serve as a battle of words and ideas that compete for our attention as Milan Kundera once eloquently argued; such competing discourses underpin cultural politics which are defined by narratives and counter-narratives, relations of power and morality; Foucault argued just this. Jackson (1991: 200) argued that cultural politics is 'the domain in which meanings are constructed and negotiated, where relations of dominance and subordination are defined and contested'. Ten years earlier, Hall's emphasis on the study of popular culture was based on the 'containment-resistance' dialectic – this is the process of cultural politics and movement. In an illuminating piece concerning cultural politics in relation to human geography, Clive Barnett (1998: 633) criticized Jackson's formulation – and by association Hall – because 'it tends to attribute a high degree of unity and intentionality to the exercise of power in order to be able to represent the active work of everyday meaning-making as so many acts of popular resistance'. Barnett is correct because establishment power blocs do not require 'unity' in order to convey discourse, and resistance is not always unified either, it's often contested within groupings particularly on the left; furthermore, media discourses are equally multifarious, which is why cultural politics and the struggle over hegemony is not only complex but also ongoing – a sort of 'permanent revolution', to borrow Leon Trotsky's term.

In Michèle Barrett's (1982: 37) work titled 'Feminism and the definition of cultural politics', she begins by stating that 'Cultural politics are crucially important to feminism because they involve *struggles* over meaning' (my emphasis); 'struggles' are based on the interventions Rorty referred to in the process of cultural political practice, engagement and the formation of ideas via linguistic practice. The production of linguistic practice in relation to power relations is clearly evident in Chapter Three of this book presented by Maggie Andrews. For instance, in the section 'Remembrance and the working class soldier hero in austerity Britain', Andrews presents a variety of narratives which are evident in relation to various television programmes and political commentary, including 'war narratives' and 'technological narratives'. Under the sub-section titled 'All Tommies are heroes', Andrews states how 'the complex interweaving of past and present ... constitutes the construction of *historical narratives* in the centenary of the First World War combatants, particularly Tommies, of that war and more contemporary conflicts ...' (my emphasis). Andrews also states that 'programmes are the products of a particular cultural moment', which in this present context is austerity based.

Similarly McNamara's use of the term 'austerity narratives' describes how drama conveys a linguistic practice in the context of austerity within the production of cultural politics, not oppositional but reaffirming: 'We have to keep going, whatever happens. We have to help each other keep going' is the rallying call to staff during World War I at *Downton Abbey* (ITV) by the Earl of Grantham. McNamara shows us the relationship between this statement and the ideological rallying call and perfunctory statement of David Cameron, the leader of the Tory Party during the period of austerity which is, 'we're all in it together'.

Linguistic practice as a relationship of power and its concomitant engagement by subjects underpins the dynamics of cultural politics and whatever form this takes. Cultural politics – the act of thinking and response – is in the first instance a site of intellectual struggle concerning the vision and direction of society, and clearly an embryonic form of cultural positioning is in play on which response depends, and quite clearly in the wider context of society, the cultural hegemony of power and counter-hegemonic movements provide us some evidence of the struggle over the legitimacy of linguistic practice and narratives.

A moral dimension central to the notion of cultural politics is the pursuit of social justice and how social justice is achieved, and how the struggle between often opposed interests are effectively played out (dramaturgy) is central to the struggle between class difference, despite its post-modern rejections. Class and relations between levels of power are intrinsically linked in the space of cultural politics, even if only as a subtle form of false consciousness. Scott Fitzgerald's *The Great Gatsby* spoke in part of the illusion of class barriers and an illusion of class difference – or at the very least spoken in deferential terms; the idea of a classless society was fermented as ideology in the US and has seeped into the consciousness of Europeans, conditioning prevailing norms. The negation of the idea of class as a central form for movement is in itself an insistence of other categories that formulate cultural politics which may determine the shape of things to come, but the outlook isn't delicious.

In Mark Hayes' chapter, he is critical of such illusions where under the sub-heading 'The reality of class ... ' he argues: 'Not only is class in Britain an enduring social phenomenon, the inequality between the classes has increased dramatically in recent years, with differences in income, wealth and status more pronounced'. Using Hall's containment-resistance dichotomy in relation to Hayes' statement, the process of cultural politics is not so much the annihilation of class but rather to present it by elites as an illusion where in times of austerity – as already stated in relation to Andrews and McNamara – the reactionary, 'we're all in it together' context is how containment, or the attempt to *contain resistance*, operates.

The term 'cultural politics' is not to be confused with 'political culture', although the two are closely interwoven. If we take Gabriel Almond as our lead, followed closely by another American writer, Walter Lippmann, political culture is primarily governed by the ruling elite. What eventually became known as the 'Almond-Lippmann Consensus' was the belief that public opinion had little if no impact on political decision making. This view has always been a contentious issue to argue that, in the US at least, citizens were generally unable to understand the complexities of politics so were broadly ignored by elites that governed public policy and, what's more, negates Rorty's thinking on 'interventions' and upholds the notion of 'spectator theory' of which Dewey despised.

Cultural politics assumes the opposite to the Almond-Lippmann Consensus, and it does not recognize the problematic notion of 'public opinion', because by its definition cultural politics is fragmented, dispersed with all types of narratives and actions. In reality public opinion cannot exist as a totality – whilst cultural politics can often, but not always, atomize into a thousand fragmented pieces. Cultural politics in Western systems, for example, embraces all the contradictions one wishes to observe witnessed by the growth of anti-globalization, anti-capitalist movements such as Occupy and the Million Mask Marchers. Within each of these groupings, we witness the contradictory tumult between various ideas within the totality of movement. The only real material thing people have in common is being part of a collective group without the production of an agreed agenda for change; all else melts into air! The politics of opposition placed its emphasis on the negative 'anti' – the positive 'pro' materialized in a loose confederation of atomized objectives. In the wider sense in the US, the cultural political space remains governed by the political culture of the Almond-Lippmann Consensus.

If we truly seek to understand the dynamics of the continued dominance of capital and the political cultures which espouse its logic to varying degrees, we need also to locate cultural politics as a process in the contemporary period of late capitalism and the neo-liberal project in relation to the monumental events that occurred throughout Europe and Russia in 1989. The political revolutions which brought down Stalinism throughout the region has had less attention compared to other significant revolutionary periods in relation to their respective impact. This is despite the fact that across Europe the prevailing political cultures pursue the logic of capital in various forms. It is a fact that no new ideas were indigenously developed within the former regimes – they simply absorbed the neo-liberal project in its entirety, becoming mirror images of the West – but nevertheless the ideological affect for rationalizing neo-liberalism has been profound. This in some way explains the way in which neo-liberalism has impacted within the sphere of culture as a new rationality across the European landscape. The tumultuous year 1989, entrenched Central and Eastern Europe into the neo-liberal project embedding itself as the dominant mode of thinking and rationalizing economics throughout the EU. The economic ideology of neo-liberalism and its impact on the shaping of capital outcomes prevails with its hegemonic position in the sphere of cultural politics; this dominant form of ideology, despite the crisis of capital since 2008, remains intact despite the challenges to its authority evidenced in the European elections in 2014.

Despite any abstractions, cultural politics, as empirical reality and the manner in which cultural politics proceeds, can be properly understood only in terms of conjectural analysis of which history and tradition bears down upon the present; cultural politics and relations of power therein represents the dialectics of social and economic development. If history has ended, stagnated or entered into a reverse mode containing micro-dispersed nationalisms, then cultural politics turns into a form of simplistic, barbaric, limited, subtle alterations of capitalist development that merely redefines the economic and political framework of late capitalist development. Up to the moment of the collapse of Stalinism in 1989, cultural politics, in various waves, was a space of inherent subversion with *ideas* pitted against domination, but now the former is lax, particularly in Central and Eastern Europe, because what else is there? Without radical alternatives to what currently exist, cultural politics appears redundant as a site of opposition to the established order. You can have your ideas, Fukuyama once said, but let them remain as a form of Hegalian idealism and not turned into a Marxist materialist reality of historical development; one can shout loudly and protest vigorously, but what is on offer as an effective alternative? If 1989 represented anything it is the absence of alternatives particularly when we consider the expansion of the European Union subjected to neo-liberal principles.

Austerity

Depending on which country we observe austerity measures will vary in terms of the types of fiscal policies governments implement. Overall, austerity is a neo-liberal economic response to the crisis in capital, but it is also ideological in terms of its overall intentions which, once more, vary according to which state we observe. As discussed above, in the UK, for example, the ideological intentions to substantially reduce the size of government is akin to what Robert Nozick referred to as a 'minimalist state'. Furthermore austerity measures are a form of imperialistic domination to control economies external to a core power, the latter clearly demonstrated in the relationship between core European powers – primarily led by Germany – and Greece where austerity economics is imposed by one over the other. However, similarities between the two examples include reduction in spending, less emphasis on the public sector, more privatization and in Greece therefore a shrinking of the State as in the UK but enforced externally. This is perhaps ironic in the present Greek context considering that the governing party, the left-wing Syriza Party, embraced a larger state and sought to support public spending as a core principle of its ideals.

Austerity in Spain has had similar outcomes to Greece in terms of high levels of unemployment but also across other sectors of society. For instance, in Chapter Eight Joan Pedro details how austerity has negatively impacted on social housing through forced 'privatization' that, for Pedro, 'limits human rights'. Pedro also argues that austerity has equally impacted negatively on the educational sector by arguing that 'the politics of austerity work as a method to augment the corporate and political control of knowledge to the detriment of its subversive edge and emancipatory value for the common good'. But it doesn't end there because, as Jim O'Brien demonstrates in Chapter Nine, austerity in Spain has impacted on football, which is deeply embedded in Spanish culture. O'Brien argues that 'in the post-2008 era the extensive and accelerated use of visual and social media as the prime mode of mediatized communication has been a key facet in linking the iconography of football with the contemporary processes of mass political communication adopted by Podemos and other forces of change', which for our purposes is a clear example of the production of cultural politics.

The fact that austerity economics exist, post-2008, is proof of the continued volatility of the markets and instability of capital despite the best efforts of the former UK Chancellor of the Exchequer Gordon Brown of 'New Labour' to convince citizens that no more 'boom and bust' would occur. The context of Brown's statement is one in which the universal truth of political failure to eradicate poverty collapses into a culturally specific narrative which sought to alter cultural politics within the UK; however, the inference of Brown's thinking was the exportation of his ideas on a global scale. To a large extent Brown's theory was an attempt to re-theorize the world-systems theory forwarded by Immanuel Wallerstein, in which 'core', 'semi-core' and 'peripheral' countries are bound by an unequal relationship. Brown's statement therefore was an attempt to rescue and rectify the ideal nation within the broader context of global capital, and it was equally an attempt to maintain some form of hegemonic rule within the UK. Thus, from 1997 to 2007, New Labour sought to consolidate and legitimize its position as a party that not only championed the free market but also would build a new utopia 'on the bedrock of prudent and wise economics management'. Brown in his speech in May 1997 to the CBI said, 'The British economy of the future must not be built on the shifting sands of boom and bust. …'

Brown made numerous speeches between 1997 and 2007 to the Confederation of British Industry (CBI; May 20, 1997), the British American Business Council (April 28, 1990), the Mansion House (June 10, 1999), the British Chamber of Commerce (April 5, 2000), Mansion House speech (June 20, 2001), the Transport and General Workers Union (TGWU; March 28, 2002), CBI (November 18, 2003), British Chamber of Commerce (April 21, 2004), the Trades Union Council (TUC; September 13, 2005) and the CBI's President's Dinner (June 05, 2006). Almost ten years to the day on May 5, 2007, Brown said this:

> I am … speaking to you … to say that we need to forge that same shared national purpose for the years ahead … to meet and *master* the new and … profound challenges ahead – *mastering* the pace of change and … competition we face from every part of the world.
>
> (*The Guardian*, September 11, 2008; my italics)

This was Brown recasting himself as a political 'he-man' related to the film *Masters of the Universe*; no lessons learnt from Marx here, who detailed the inherent instability and contradictions of capitalism, an economic system that excels in boom and bust and is largely uncontrollable particularly in its neo-liberal free-market form of which it naturally developed. In fact Brown's statements were a direct refutation of socialism and not that far removed from Fukuyama's claims in his book that we are at *The End of History*; 'for what else can we envisage?' other than the free market in light of the collapse of Stalinism in the former USSR.

The economic slumps and crises so indicative of capitalism reverberate violently into the realm of political life where elected governments make adjustments to the economy in order to maintain legitimacy, not only at the level of governing but in the very system itself. We shouldn't underestimate the role of public policy in this context and therefore governments' attempt at quelling dissent; public policy is after all based on notions of the 'common good' and how best society develops and acts as a corrective or adjustment to crisis; this is exactly the underpinning logic and rationale of *austerity as public policy*.

Clearly, Brown was deluding himself, because the period since late 2008 has been characterized as an 'age of austerity' in light of the financial deficits within nations, and its impact on cultural politics is yet to be fully realized and documented. That said, the emergence of left-leaning social movements across Europe – most notably in Greece, Spain, Italy, Portugal and the United Kingdom with the election of Jeremy Corbyn as leader of the Labour Party – indicate change and opposition to austerity politics, economics and ideology, as I detail in Chapter Seven. However, it's important to note that this development is coupled with the emergence of far-right groups in Greece, Hungary, Switzerland, Austria, France and Germany over the influx of refugees and immigration during the period of austerity; the outcomes of each are yet fully known but emergent and indicative of the complexities associated with cultural politics.

The ubiquitous use to positively promote the word 'austerity' as perfected rationale within political discourse and media is designed specifically to rationalize, normalize and legitimize its meaning within popular vernacular and is an act of ideological intent which attempts to rationalize austerity economics. It is also an example of the type of dominant linguistic practices in circulation to justify such rationality, as detailed by Rorty, Williams, Hall, etc. The first point to raise, however, and in spite of the ubiquitous use of the word 'austerity' is that there is nevertheless no absolute agreement amongst economists over its actual meaning, over and above dictionary definitions, which are restricted to bare minimum explanations such as 'enforced or extreme economy' or 'a situation in which there is not much money and it is only spent on things that are necessary' (Merriam-Webster). Fiscal policy and public policy are therefore governed by political interpretations and 'value judgments' particularly upon the word 'necessary', and this in turn is governed by political philosophy and ideological perspectives equally conditioned by free-market, neo-liberal structures.

The key point and contradiction in terms of governments and media that support free-market ideology is that austerity politics is state-led and thus a degree of state intervention into the market is actualized and the overall beneficiaries continue to be at the upper end of the class system. Contradictions aside, any defence of such governing actions are often related to the idea of 'minimalist state intervention' as Robert Nozick once argued in *Anarchy, State and Utopia*, where 'rights of individuals' and businesses are the prioritizing economic right and entitlements over public expenditure. Ernest Mandel's (1975) work concerning the three main functions of the state is useful for understanding how the state not only exists within such a contradictory condition – or deception if you prefer – but also how the state seeks to control society and economy in times of austerity to ensure private production of wealth and defend so-called rights of the individual to pursue profit:

i   Provision of those general conditions of production which cannot be assured by the private activities of the members of the dominant class.
ii Repression of any threat to the prevailing mode of production from the dominated classes or particular sections of the dominant classes, by means of army, police, judiciary and prison-system.
iii Integration of the dominated classes, to ensure that the ruling ideology of the society remains that of the ruling class, and that consequently the exploited classes accept their own exploitation without the immediate exercise of repression against them (because they believe it to be inevitable, or the 'lesser evil', or 'superior might', or fail even to perceive it as exploitation) (Ibid.: 475).

In the UK ideological austerity has been governed by the Tories where, as Atkinson, Roberts and Savage (2013: 4) stated within weeks of the Tory-led coalition coming to power:

an 'emergency budget' was put together seeking, it was said, to reign-in the excessive spending recklessly pursued by Gordon

Brown's short-lived administration, slash the bloated budget deficit and steadily navigate the choppy tides whipped up by world-wide recession.

When we contextualize this statement in the context of using the crisis to purposely shrink the state and radically reduce public spending, we may see how this tallies perfectly with Mandel's writing on the functions of the state. Moreover, Paul Krugman highlighted how austerity economics was a front for more ideological intentions in his document titled 'The case for cuts was a lie: why does Britain still believe it? The austerity delusion'. It's an interesting question particularly for critical theorists and social psychologists interested in persuasion, and it reflects the linguistic practices referred to in the first section whereby cultural politics is defined by hegemonic powers determined to rationalize ideology – austerity – and counter-hegemonic forces which seek to undermine dominating austerity narratives; Krugman's intervention belongs to the latter. Krugman reminds us that in 2010, 'elites all across the western world were gripped by austerity fever' which became the predominating logic of our time. Krugman refers to 'austerity ideology' particularly the ideas forwarded by the so-called 'austerians' – a term first coined by fellow economist Rob Parenteau – and further states:

> The 'primary purpose' of austerity, the Telegraph admitted in 2013, 'is to shrink the size of government spending' – or, as Cameron put it in a speech later that year, to make the state 'leaner … not just now, but permanently'.

And this is why Krugman was correct to refer to austerity as *ideology* because in reality it is unnecessary in relation to workers making financial sacrifices and enduring cuts in public spending.

Responses

Across Europe fiscal policies via austerity logic has impacted on the poorest within working class communities but crucially across class structures, also impacting on the middle class, a section of society normally protected from crisis and austerity to a large extent, or certainly less effected. This impact across class is extremely relevant for our understanding of how austerity is helping to redefine modern-day cultural politics. Indeed, Goran Therborn (2012) notes that this present historical period is characterized by a global growth in the middle class but crucially sharing characteristics of the traditional working class which may impact on the way they define their position vis-à-vis austerity. In relation to the research of Abhijit Banerjee and Esther Duflo (2007), Therborn states:

> Their most remarkable finding is that this 'middle class' is no more entrepreneurial in its approach to savings and consumption than the poor who fall below the $2 threshold. The defining characteristic of its members is that they have a steady wage. One could thus describe them as occupying a stable working-class position rather than belonging to a nebulous middle class.

This shift is coupled with a new radical social consciousness developed in the UK when Junior Doctors in the National Health Service voted 98 per cent in favour of industrial action in November 2015, taking industrial action early in 2016. On the BBC's *Daily Politics* show (Wednesday, November 18, 2015), the chief organizer of the Junior Doctors dispute and demonstrations, Dr Anna Carrington, criticizing austerity measures, said: 'Let's look at the broader picture here. We are in times of austerity'. Headlines from the BBC (February 13, 2016) such as 'Junior doctors' dispute could become a war, union warns' indicate the shifting terrain of cultural politics under austerity.

In Greece the left-leaning party Syriza won the support of middle-class voters who had previously voted for mainstream political parties, and Podemos in Spain is a cross-class political movement. In the US a report by the National Employment Law Project (NELP) titled 'The low-wage recovery: industry employment and wages four years into the recovery' in 2014 provided data that employment/hiring of the middle class was low despite an 'economic recovery'. In 2012, the US-based Pew Research Center produced a report titled 'Fewer, poorer, gloomier: the lost decade of the middle class'. Under the sub-title 'Party and ideology', the report states:

> While both parties present themselves as champions of the middle class, neither has closed the deal with a majority of the middle class itself. Only about a third of all middle-class adults identify with the Democratic Party (34%), while a smaller share are Republicans (25%). About a third (35%) say they are independents. These breakdowns are virtually identical to the partisan divisions among all adults.

The data provided by the Pew Research Center partly demonstrate responses by middle-class voters to austerity economics. In the US, the race for the Democrat leadership saw the emergence of the Socialist outsider, Bernie Sanders, who, like Jeremy Corbyn in the UK, represents a left-leaning alternative not only to austerity but also to the vision of the future. The NBC/Marist Poll (US 2015) demonstrated that amongst independent voters, Sanders was way ahead of his rival, the establishment figure Hilary Clinton. This headline from the Huffington Post, with poll data, also demonstrated the support for Sanders: 'HUFFPOLLSTER: Bernie Sanders wins focus groups and social media, but Hilary Clinton wins post debate polls'. In February 2016 Sanders won the New Hampshire primary with 60 per cent of the vote. Perhaps more significantly was the election of the Canadian Liberal Party in 2015 on an anti-austerity programme led by Justin Trudeau with Larry Summers stating:

> ... in an era of extraordinarily low interest rates and slow growth, it is becoming increasingly clear that progressives do best when they reject austerity and embrace public investment. The British Labour Party and the Canadian NDP sought to demonstrate their soundness by embracing budget balancing as an objective. Their results were terrible.

Summers' statement reflects the popularity of Trudeau, Sanders and the Corbyn-led Labour Party which was reflected by a substantial increase in membership after Corbyn was elected. Furthermore, Corbyn's victory was a resounding rejection of the Labour Party's position prior to Corbyn, which as Summers states simply sought to embrace 'budget balancing'. Other responses vary from the creation of citizen social movements such as Podemos in Spain, the emergence of Bloco de Esquerda in Portugal, the election to government of Syriza in Greece, the rejection by the House of Lords to the Tory proposal to cut tax credits to the needy in 2015, to critical responses by economists such as the influential Paul Krugman, to the creation of a new pan-European movement (DiEM25) by the former Syriza economist Yanis Varoufakis, to the writings of Paul Mason.

Whatever the motives for imposing austerity economics, the crisis of capital and its concomitant narratives and economic policies concerning austerity, also appear to be reshaping European thought which former BBC Economics Editor Paul Mason enthusiastically endorsed in his book titled, *Why It's All Kicking Off Everywhere: The New Global Revolutions*. In his blog, Mason produced twenty reasons 'why it's all kicking off' that went viral gaining a substantial audience in the process.

Mason spoke of the 'collapse of neo-liberalism' which was the first crucial factor for ending free-market ideology and provides a quotation from the former Chairman of the Federal Reserve of the United States Alan Greenspan in order to justify and give credence to his *belief* that the established order was 'collapsing'. The 'factors' Mason provides for the apparent collapse of the old and introduction of a new order are, first, a 'revolution in technology' which provides the ammunition for 'activism' and 'protest', and second, 'a change in human consciousness'. For our purposes the second point is vitally important vis-à-vis changes within cultural politics and, in my mind, the former less so because technology is the means by which cultural politics may flow. This isn't to underestimate technology, but without the latter, the former is redundant vis-à-vis 'resistance'. But here's the question: was Mason right on the second point? Mason based the latter on Castell's idea of 'the networked individual'. There's even a reference to Hegel and his comments after the French Revolution:

> Our epoch is a birth-time. The spirit of man has broken with the old order of things, and with the old ways of thinking, and is in the mind to let them all sink into the depths of the past and to set about its own transformation.
>
> (*Phenomenology of Mind*, 1807)

And this: 'What we are seeing is not the Arab Spring, the Russian Spring, the Maple Spring, Occupy, the *indignados*. We're seeing the Human Spring'. In a lecture Mason gave in 2013, he also said this in relation to the so-called 'Arab Spring' in North Africa:

> Two years on from the Arab Spring, I'm clearer about what it was that it inaugurated: it is a *revolution*. In some ways it parallels the revolutions of before – 1848, 1830, 1789 – and there are also echoes of the Prague spring, the US civil rights movement, the Russian 'mad summer of 1874' ... but in other ways it is unique. Above all, the relationship between the physical and the mental, the political and the cultural, seems to be inverted. There is a change in consciousness, the intuition that something big is possible, that a great change in the world's priorities is within people's grasp (New Left Project; my emphasis).

One needs only to observe Egypt today under the repressive Sisi-led government to deduce that, on this issue at least, Mason was wrong, but what Mason was observing elsewhere in Europe and the US were that groupings were rebelling and mostly in an anarchic fashion, without 'leadership' and agreed programmes for change. Bearing in mind Mason's views on changing consciousness, it's worth noting Žižek's arguments in the *New Statesman*

(2013) acknowledging that the field of cultural politics continues to be dominated by the logic of capital, coupled with chaotic and dis-unified opposition; this led Žižek to call for a 'new master' to lead us towards socialism. The said piece was titled 'The simple courage of decision: a leftist tribute to Thatcher' stating: 'What we need today is a Thatcher of the left: a leader who would repeat Thatcher's gesture in the opposite direction, transforming the entire field of presuppositions shared by today's political elite' and,

> The function of a Master is to enact an authentic division – a division between those who want to drag on within the old parameters and those who are aware of the necessary change. Such a division ... is the only path to true unity.

Žižek isn't as enthusiastic as Mason, because Žižek is arguing that the *people* remain generally reluctant to see beyond the current ideological horizons and seek socialist alternatives. Further it is worth noting that John Kampfner wrote a fairly stinging criticism of Mason's views:

> Mason is a half-full sort of guy. I'm far more sceptical. For every optimistic assertion that he makes, such as: 'People know more than they used to', I posit the counterpoint. Yes, but has all that information actually made us more able to engineer change or influence outcomes? Indeed, little that's happened in the five years since the banks sent us to our knees suggests to me that we've learned the lessons. Only a few weeks ago at Davos, the financial titans were exhorting one another to stop wittering on about the sins of the past and get back to making money.

Was Mason wrong and Kampfner right? Is it a fact that the field of cultural politics remains largely influenced by hegemonic forces tied to capital and largely, but not entirely, devoid of radical forces of resistance in the age of austerity? Certainly, like many media commentators, Mason wrongly referred to the 'Arab Springs' as 'revolutions' or at least did not attempt to differentiate between various types of revolutions such as 'political revolutions' and 'social revolutions' in any effective way, and this in my view led to a misunderstanding and overenthusiastic approach to the civil unrests in Greece and Spain. Despite the crisis and fragility of capital since late 2008 the sphere of cultural politics continues to be conditioned and dominated by the management of crisis most notably through the imposition of economic austerity and austerity as an ideological weapon to enhance powerful hegemonic interests; cultural politics therefore is a sphere dominated by the established 'political cultures' of capital, and large parts of the public across Europe subscribe to austerity narratives and measures as a rational response to crisis; it's ideal crisis management for many. Perhaps it is in this context that Philip Bounds states in the final chapter of this edition, the following: 'It could even be argued that the left has massively overstated the extent to which ours is genuinely an age of austerity'.

Certainly, responses to austerity have been varied ranging from the Occupy Movement, Anti-Capitalist and Anti-Globalization Movements, the Million Mask Movement to various media and artistic narratives, but generally speaking such response is a form of 'decentred resistance' creating new forms of decentred cultural politics that help to define this period of late capitalism. That said, there are perhaps less obvious but no less interesting opposition and responses to austerity and the global market economy in general, for instance, from within the Catholic Church documented by Pope Benedict XVI's encyclical *Caritas in Veritate* where the Pope attacked free-market capitalism for its neglect of the Aristotelian notion of 'common good'; above all else, the assault is focused on the negation of morality where the Church sees capitalism turning economics into a form of human nature. In 2014 Pope Francis wrote his *Apostolic Exhortation, Evengelii Gaudium* stating in relation to free-market ideology that

> some people continue to defend trickle-down theories which assume that economic growth, encouraged by a free market, will inevitably succeed in bringing about greater justice and inclusiveness in the world. This opinion, which has never been confirmed by the facts, expresses a crude and naïve trust in the goodness of those wielding economic power and in the sacralized workings of the prevailing economic system.

This critique of rampant, unregulated capitalism is also present within Judaism (see *Radical Then, Radical Now*, by former Chief Rabbi Jonathan Sacks) and Islamic texts, and similar to the writings of Pope Francis they represent a defence of the poor. In the UK the Anglican Church in March 2013 publicly denounced the Conservative Coalition-led government's policies on welfare following on from an article titled 'Archbishop pours scorn on Cameron's "big society"' (*The Observer*, June 24, 2012). The attack was on the idea of the Big Society for shrinking 'the state' and neglecting 'responsibilities' and 'civic identity and dignity' in times of 'austerity'. Archbishop Vincent Nichols, the leader of the Catholic Church in England and Wales, revisited this critique in February 2014 by informing the *Daily Telegraph* that the 'safety net' of the welfare system had been 'torn apart', further stating that 'it no longer exists'. Religious criticism is centred on reform and redistribution of wealth that combines capitalist production with social needs in a period where no major political party can effectively control banks or enforce what the Green Party calls a 'Robin Hood Tax' on the wealthy to be redistributed within society.

Final thoughts on cultural politics

The interrelation of culture and politics as a space of action and meaning departs from the notion that all culture is political. The politicization of culture is therefore specific in context. If we imagine a space known as culture inclusive of the various dynamics ranging from everyday conversation (gossip) to the fragmentation of communities due to an economic downturn, we can at least acknowledge, if not agree upon, the vastness of content and context of cultural moments; from the benign to the political.

When Stuart Hall wrote 'Notes on deconstructing the "popular"', he perceived popular culture as a space where the embryonic signs of socialism *may* evolve. This idea was based on the struggle between the elite and the people based on what Hall referred to as the dichotomous relationship between domination and resistance to power. Hall would have been fully aware that this struggle ordinarily becomes more acute in times of capitalist crisis. As Marx noted, capitalism is prone to boom and slump and periodical crisis, fluctuations in investment in new technology as profits are sought after – a reduction in investment, wage decreases to protect profit margins.

The public relations efforts by governments to rationalize and legitimize austerity is both an attempt to enforce bureaucratic authority in the Weberian sense and intervene directly into civil society – a space quite unlike the Gramscian ideal. Perry Anderson in the *Antinomies of Antonio Gramsci* was absolutely correct then to argue that, by definition, the political intervention into civil society meant corruption of freedoms; the fact is the imposition of public policy based on austerity is exactly that. This is not to argue that resistance to dominating ideologies is futile – far from it; it's just currently not effective and perhaps Syriza's eventual compliance towards German-led austerity policies best indicate this. Here we see the convergence of European bureaucratically led political culture and cultural politics and how the dominant ideas prevail, thus shaping dynamics of cultural politics. The conquest of austerity as ideology and lack of overall opposition therefore signifies in my view that cultural politics and the changing cultural landscapes is the negation of critical popular culture presided over by the events of 1989.

The economic and political transition from liberalism to neo-liberalism in Western social-democratic systems has brought with it a system of thought and being unprecedented in human history. The relationship between varying sections of society reflect a complex web of thought towards a system that has produced wealth, technological and communicative advances hitherto unknown in history, advances worth preserving in many cases. Yet despite the 'consent' sought to rule by powerful political and business elites, and in spite of the collapse of economies throughout Europe and the US, the project of neo-liberalism continues.

Political adjustment and public policy is a clear example of exercising 'bureaucratic authority' – an attempt to control and subdue society, which becomes particularly acute in times of austerity, as governments seek to reorganize economic criteria through political intervention. The reforming/adjusting of the political economy is only unstable in so far as the outcomes of public policy are unknown in the sphere of cultural politics – because the sphere of cultural politics is the site or meeting place between representative government, public policies and the people; a mass of people with differing responses to austerity. Cultural politics is in this context the sphere where bureaucratic authority, the establishment and the peoples' 'consciousness' that Mason spoke of are formed. Missing from Mason's account, however, is the issue of how the 'consent' of the people is carefully crafted and sought after in order to continue its rule and for rationalizing the very system that causes crisis and austerity politics in the first place; Gramsci taught us this and it is a pivotal moment in the dialectical process so indicative of the containment-resistance moment that Hall spoke of in relation to cultural politics.

Notes

1 Sub-prime mortgages were mortgages lent to people with low credit ratings, including ex-prisoners. Many people were unable to repay their debts which contributed towards the housing crisis in the US. In sum this was a result of bad lending by banks plus poor regulation of the housing market.
2 Also referred to as the European Debt Crisis or the European Sovereign Debt Crisis.
3 The moral dimension of Dewey's thinking is detailed in his work 'The ethics of democracy'.
4 For Dewey the individual within democracy should be more than a mere 'spectator' waiting to be 'governed' by political elites, thus 'intervention' into the democratic process was a moral obligation as well as a political necessity.

5 It's important to note that 'austerity narratives' aren't simply narratives which promote austerity economics or ideology but rather are also forms of narrative that are created out of the conditions of the latter two. In this sense, they are also responses, sometimes critical and oppositional as in *Girls* but not always as in *Downton Abbey* which as Marcuse would argue offered an 'affirmative' form of cultural expression.

Bibliography

Atkinson, W., Roberts, S. and Savage, M. (eds) (2013). *Class Inequality in Austerity Britain: Power, Difference and Suffering*. Basingstoke: Palgrave Macmillan.

Barnett, C. (1998). 'Cultural twists and turns. Environment and planning'. *Society and Space*, 16(6): 631–34.

Barrett, M. (1982). 'Feminism and the definition of cultural politics'. In: R. Brunt and C. Rowan, eds., *Feminism, Culture and Politics*. London: Lawrence & Wishart.

Brown, G. (2008). 'No return to boom and bust: what Brown said when he was chancellor'. *The Guardian*, September 11.

Hall, S. (2007). 'Notes on deconstructing the popular'. In: J. Storey, ed., *Cultural Theory and Popular Culture: A Reader*. London: Pearson.

Huffington Post. Poll Data. Available at: http://www.huffingtonpost.com/entry/post-democratic-debate-poll-clinton-wins_5620e1dbe4b06462a13b948b.

Kampfner, J. (2013). 'Why it's still kicking off everywhere by Paul Mason – review'. Available at: http://www.theguardian.com/books/2013/feb/17/paul-mason-kicking-off-review.

Kouvelakis, S. (2011). 'The Greek cauldron'. *New Left Review*, (72) November–December: 17–32.

Krugman, P. (2015). 'The case for cuts was a lie. Why does Britain still believe it? The austerity delusion'. Available at: http://www.theguardian.com/business/ng-interactive/2015/apr/29/the-austerity-delusion.

Mason, P. (2013). 'Why it's still kicking off everywhere'. Available at: http://www.newleftproject.org/index.php/site/article_comments/why_its_still_kicking_off_everywhere.

National Employment Law Project (NELP) (2014). 'The low-wage recovery: industry employment and wages four years into the recovery'. Available at: http://www.nelp.org/content/uploads/2015/03/Low-Wage-Recovery-Industry-Employment-Wages-2014-Report.pdf.

NBC/Marist Poll. Available at: http://maristpoll.marist.edu/wp-content/misc/IApolls/IA150923/NBC%20News_WSJ_Marist%20Poll_Iowa%20Nature%20of%20the%20Sample%20and%20Tables_October%202015.pdf#page=1.

Pew Research Center (2012). 'Fewer, poorer, gloomier: the lost decade of the middle class'. Available at: http://www.pewsocialtrends.org/files/2012/08/pew-social-trends-lost-decade-of-the-middle-class.pdf.

Pope Francis (2014). 'Apostolic exhortation, evengelii gaudium'. Available at: http://w2.vatican.va/content/francesco/en/apost_exhortations/doc-

uments/papa-francesco_esortazione-ap_20131124_evangelii-gaudium.
html#No_to_an_economy_of_exclusion.

Summers, L. (2015). 'Canadian election proves an anti-austerity message
is a winning one'. Available at: http://blogs.ft.com/larry-summers/2015/
10/20/canadian-elections-prove-an-anti-austerity-message-is-a-winning-
one/.

Szeman, I. and Kaposy, T. (2011). *Cultural Theory: An Anthology.*
Chichester: Wiley Blackwell.

The Observer (2012). 'Rowan Williams pours scorn on David Cameron's
"big society"'. Available at: https://www.theguardian.com/uk/2012/
jun/23/rowan-williams-big-society-cameron.

Therborn, G. (2012). "Class in the 21st century". New Left Review, (78)
November–December. Available at: https://newleftreview.org/II/78/
goran-therborn-class-in-the-21st-century.

Žižek, S. (2013). 'The simple courage of decision: a leftist tribute to
Thatcher'. *New Statesman*, April.

2 Unmasking the golem

English riots, media and the social psychology of madness

Glen Parkinson

Erich Fromm paves us a remarkably insightful path toward cultural edification in his 1955 work, *The Sane Society*, by arguing that culture itself can become symptomatic of serious pathological disorder, not perhaps within relativist contexts but certainly if analysed in concordance with its capability to meet human fundamental needs. One of the greatest mistakes of contemporary psychological practice is, according to Fromm, the supposition that cultural deviancy necessarily implies a sickness of the individual rather than of the society. If the values and practices of culture oppose the conditions of human natural state of being, then from an objective standpoint they institutionalize neuroticism; adherence to them can therefore, as a matter of consequence, only conventionalize neuroticism within the individual.

Since psychologists themselves could be operating under an erroneous characterization of normalcy, their cornucopian encyclopaedia of known social dysfunction might predominantly then document the manifestation of normal (or at least reactionary) behaviour within an abnormal culture. To use a relevant contemporary illustration, the British media's reporting of the 2011 riots,[1] for example, has largely dehumanized the participants as opportunist 'yobs' (*Daily Mail*, 2011a; *The Telegraph*, 2012a), thus inferring that a large parade of spontaneous, angry and unified social disorder still evidences a pathology of the individual rather than the society which that individual is part of. But how can this be if the anomaly is simultaneously spread across a wide platform of individuals? Surely, we cannot believe that every one of those people has precisely the same behavioural deficiency. The phenomenon becomes explainable only in terms of a reaction to a social *environment* which is neurotic – otherwise, we are left resolving why thousands of different people all suddenly began exhibiting identical symptoms of psychological illness.

To follow reason would instead be to propose that social unrest in general evidences a semi-logical reaction – resistance – to social variables oppressive to the human condition. Even under terms of conventionalist understanding, group psychoses such as 'shell shock' and 'Gulf War syndrome' are attributable to external environmental conditions, yet in the case of the English riots, little effort has been undertaken by the media to investigate properly the full extent of their relationship with oppressive socioeconomic circumstances and the pervading domestic climate of austerity.

The comminatory, self-qualifying approach of the media has been heavily criticized by academics such as Gus John, who spoke out at the Media and the Riots conference held by the London College of Communication in 2011: 'The media appeared to have embarked on a moral crusade, setting down benchmarks by which the "rioters" should be judged in the court of public opinion'. This evangelistic and denunciatory perspective, keenly adapted by the British press, is clearly exhibited by the historical record. *The Telegraph* (2012b) abandons reason entirely and expresses the problem as one of coloured skin: 'A year after the riots in England, our political class has shamefully shied away from tackling the problems of race and a destructive black street culture'. *The Mirror* (2011a), equally bizarrely, in an article supposedly about why the riots happened, rather seems to have them mixed up with the iron grip of Stalin: 'The Britain that we knew, the Britain we loved, died on our streets this week. It went in an orgy of mindless wanton murderous violence'; while further on, 'the apocalyptic images of fear are etched in our minds ... too many have been burned from their homes. Too many have seen their children weep in terror. And too many have seen their loved ones die'.

Perhaps we should relish, though, in the outrageous blatancy of such establishmentarianist prepossession, since the *Daily Mail* (2011b) goes a stage further and tries to legitimize its clear predilections with selectively chosen words from a professional study: 'The riots which swept across England this summer offered young people "a day like no other", a chance to get "free stuff" and were likened to a "rave", a report has found'. The irony should not be lost that here selection bias is used to rationalize conformist bias. The sentence seduces the reader into feelings of resentment toward the rioters and hence misdirects them from the true reaction of reasoned understanding by means of temptation into indignation and disgust. *The Telegraph's* (2012a) 'Businesses pay £4,000 for yob culture' can be similarly critiqued as evidence of an abnormal social model, in which the most important fact from a mainstream news perspective is not cost to life, justice or order but rather the financial cost to non-biological business apparatus. Fromm (2008: 121) emphasizes this point succinctly:

> Man has created a world of man-made things as it never existed before. He has constructed a complicated social machine

to administer the technical machine he built. Yet this whole creation of his stands over and above him. He does not feel himself as a creator and center, but as the servant of a Golem,[2] which his hands have built.

It is precisely this golem which these newspapers fear to question or excoriate and whose beneficial impact upon man they always presuppose to be a ubiquitous and de facto truth. However, given that the riots were initially catalysed by the shooting of Mark Duggan and pervaded throughout by an obdurate animosity toward the police as a symbol of state power (LSE/*Guardian* 2011), there exists irrefutably a polarized view which has been passionately underrepresented by these sources. In all of these articles, the process of reasoning is asphyxiated by the fallacy that such manifestations of social psychosis need explication not in terms of understanding but of blame. Jennie Bristow writes of the media reaction for Sociological Research Online (2013): 'destabilising, "parent-blaming" initiatives tend to be welcomed in the absence of any other ideas'. Effectively, any analysis which negates the need for critical understanding of the relationship between the golem and the rioters is entertained because of a germinal, psychoneurotic idea that the psychology of the golem must necessarily be sound. As Nancy Snow (2003: 13) says similarly of Britain's long-term ally, the US: 'As I grew up in the land of the free, I began to see that freedom did not mean a full range of choices but was narrowly defined as what was generally acceptable within a dominant framework'. It is thus acceptable for the media to question race, adolescence, parenting, even materialism, but only within the parameters of the premise that the golem is healthy and must never constitute a first cause. The severity of this prejudice is further compounded of course by the fact that the riots occurred in one of the gloomiest periods of austerity in British economic history, yet chronic economic pressure must be stricken from the itinerary of discussion because it inexorably leads back to inquisition of the golem.

But knee-jerk media reactions aside, if we are to assume the event symptomatic of discord between society's capability to meet the needs of the individual, as opposed to vice versa, why then did the reaction exteriorize itself not in the form of political action but in violence, destruction and looting? Some reason may be found for discrediting the feasibility of the former by referencing the age of the participants involved. According to a critically appraised study of the riots conducted by *The Guardian* in conjunction with the London School of Economics in 2011, *Reading the Riots* claims that of 270 interviewees, 'Almost 30% were juveniles (aged 10–17) and a further 49% were aged 18–25'. Hence, almost a third were too young for direct political involvement, and speaking of the disposition of young people in general toward politics, Quintelier (2007) says:

> In almost every election young people are the least likely to vote, and these participation rates are continuously declining; the youth membership of political parties is dropping; young people are less concerned with politics, less politically knowledgeable, do not participate in social or political activities, are more apathetic, and have low levels of political interest.

We should not consider this cynical verdict of youth politics to be a recent one either. The Roper Center for Public Opinion Research makes similar comments (1996): 'The conventional wisdom has it that young people are a "TV Generation" that doesn't pay much attention to day-to-day politics. ... [Recent] survey findings, shown here, generally support this assessment'. Kimberlee (2002) writes of the British youth in particular: 'Pre/post-election surveys following the 1997 general election do reveal some evidence for an increase in the rate of youthful non-participation'.

However, attacking the practicability of a political solution to the dysphoria doesn't tell us much about the larceny and violence which actually occurred. Here, we are instead faced with the seemingly daunting task of correlating complex social factors with a criminally discordant reaction in a particular demographic which did not decisively better its social or political situation. Indeed, given that Britain now has one CCTV camera for every eleven people (*The Telegraph* 2013a) reason would stipulate that criminal damage and theft would be highly contradictory to a person's best interests. Mass descent into violent criminality commands logical plausibility only if austerity measures were so crippling that people were verbatim starving; under any other circumstances, it cannot be seen how political devolution into outright anarchism exhibits any form of common sense. Similarly, while the death of Mark Duggan might be a tenable catalyst for the initial outbreak of riots in Tottenham, it quickly loses credibility as a determinant in explaining similar lawlessness in Birmingham, Bristol, Manchester and Liverpool (BBC 2011).

The seductive 'false' logic of consumerism

In the end, it is *precisely* the spontaneity and ill-judged logic of these behaviours that betray them as a psychological *reaction* to environmental factors rather than a calculated or rational form of dissent. In keeping with our opening paragraph, we must elect that the social subconscious galvanized the conscious to reject state-sanctioned conditions of socioeconomic oppression. To candidly scoff away that young people just wanted 'free stuff' defies logic even as a reductionist argument because young people always want free stuff! We programme them to want stuff, and all the better if it's free; however, rarely do they take to the streets as an organized force and loot for it. Rather, the riots were a social reflex; a paroxysm of subconscious resistance, expressed consciously in terms exclusive to the dysfunctional paradigm of reason traditionalized by culture.

The subconscious mutinied, but the conscious directed that mutiny into irrational channels of materialism and violence chiefly because the reason of society has been confined to an ideological prison in which the chase for increasing levels of material acquisition and power are its only real forms of exercise. To illustrate the point, rioters 'complained about perceived social and economic injustices', 'the increase in tuition fees', 'the closure of youth services and the scrapping of the education maintenance allowance' (*The Guardian/* LSE 2011), yet they applied reason to these remonstrations only to the extent that they became self-justifications for violence and theft. Loyalty to initial grievances was bargained away by people in exchange for a momentary reversal of power over the system which had radicalized them into action. While no lucid effort was made to institute solidarity and intransigence in terms of the specific political issues, instead the defective psychology of the social personality sought to establish itself by precisely those same warped core principles which constitute identity within consumer culture in the first place – acquisition and authority. Yet further support for this argument can be found in the following statement: 'The evidence suggests rioters were generally poorer than the country at large' (*The Guardian/*LSE 2011), since now we have fractioned down our demographic from loose juvenility specifically to the economically deprived underclass of juvenescence. These were the 'have-nots' in a culture which perpetually inculcates us into the notion that to be is to have; thus, they tried to take their identity direct from sports stores and the police line. To put it into Fromm's (2008: 90) terms: 'Capitalism is based on the principle that is to be found in all class societies: the use of man by man'. During the riots the *used* momentarily became the *users*. Those hunted out and punished by the inequitable grip of austerity found themselves the hunters.

We might perhaps extract profound wisdom then, from the words of the late Will Durant (1935: 2):

> A people may possess ordered institutions, a lofty moral code, and even a flair for the minor forms of art, like the American Indians; and yet if it remains in the hunting stage, *if it depends for its existence upon the precarious fortunes of the chase*, it will never quite pass from barbarism to civilization (emphasis mine).

If we philosophise our argument in terms of Durant's observation, it is not the social conduct or demeanour of isolated pockets of culture which expose us as avaricious, belligerent philistines, but rather the very fundamental principles upon which that culture is based. As we peel back the multitudinous layers of defence – from austerity to apologism to authority – we see the deconstruction of our logic lead the way home to sheer contemptible lunacy: the perpetual chase for human identity in material property. We are a society of treasure hunters, hacking, slashing and weaving our way through the torrid jungles of an abstractionist economy in search of what we can never find. We can never find it because we search in the wrong place. By externalizing social identity into a new pair of trainers, or a track suit, or a plasma TV, the rioters – indeed, society in general – succeeds only in diluting it among those things which they have acquired. Hence, the stimulus of our culture serves and idolizes an inverse square relationship to genuine social identity, while in a simultaneous context consumerism forces us to search for personal distinguishability – that which makes us original – in the indistinguishability of our desire for power. However, our desire for power is but *itself* a psychotic aberration of the true Platonic principle of desire for recognition, which again leads us back to *identity*. Capitalist consumerism has encouraged humans to search for identity in false symbolizations of power over fellow humans rather than in a ubiquitously cooperative power over nature – and that is precisely where he has abandoned reason. It is our cause to know ourselves and master nature, yet capitalist culture has twisted it that we merely need to know nature for the rudimentary purpose of mastering our fellow human.

For late Brazilian revolutionary and educator Paulo Freire, this pathological consumerist pollution of reason contaminates society by virtue of a poison latent within the public education system. Other didactics, such as parental instruction, media and advertising, play only secondary roles, in that they are invariably executed by others who have earlier been infected by the same cultural index case. In terms specific to the argument that the riots were a sociological reaction to economic misery, the reciprocation of elite oppression by the underclass was a mistake Freire (2005) sedulously implored people not to make. Had he not been writing over forty years earlier in fact, we might be fooled into thinking he was warning the rioters themselves in saying:

> Sectarianism in any quarter is an obstacle to the emancipation of mankind. The rightist version thereof does not always, unfortunately, call forth its natural counterpart: radicalization of

the revolutionary. *Not infrequently, revolutionaries themselves become reactionary by falling into sectarianism in the process of responding to the sectarianism of the Right.* This possibility, however, should not lead the radical to become a docile pawn of the elites. Engaged in the process of liberation, he or she cannot remain passive in the face of the oppressor's violence (Ibid.: 35) (emphasis mine).

If we understand Freire's enslavement to 'sectarianism' as a metaphor for the polarization of bigotry and resentment, then the reactions of the rioters were every bit as symptomatic as their subsequent lambasting by the media. It is equally important for us to note that when Freire speaks of 'the oppressor's violence', he does not necessarily refer to violence of the body but rather also of the mind and/or spirit. For Freire any subjugation of one will by another constitutes violence. State-enforced preconditions of austerity constitute violence – meaning through Freire's eyes the rioters did not strike the first blow. However, let us expand and move our discussion toward the conspiratorially cryptic admonition about becoming a 'docile pawn of the elites'. The best way to analogize Freire's meaning here in terms of our own case is by elaborating how incidents such as the riots perpetuate and sophistically justify increasingly Orwellian legislation to British parliament. The Anti-social Behaviour Crime and Policing Bill, which was passed through the House of Commons in 2013, for example (National Council for Civil Liberties 2014),

> Proposes to replace existing orders (such as ASBOs) with a new generation of injunctions which are easier to obtain, harder to comply with and have harsher penalties. The Bill would also introduce unfair double punishment for the vulnerable, as social tenants and their families will face mandatory eviction for breaching a term of an injunction.

Hence, the screws of class poverty are further tightened by reactionary legislation, and the beggared are exposed to checkmate by their own move. Freire's metaphor of the 'docile pawn' extends well, since in reaction to the manoeuvring of more powerful pieces an isolated pawn can do very little – yet united as a *structure*, and with a reasoned *strategy*, a chain of pawns can eventually overthrow a king. But let us abandon momentarily Freire and his dramatic warnings about sectarianism because a far more decisive point is to be had. The vicious circle of class aggression is not a tit-for-tat game, since while the reactions themselves might equally oppose each other, the externalizations of those reactions clearly do not. We live in a class hierarchy, and therefore economic power is disproportionately balanced in terms of liquid capital, company holdings and property. Since the engine of capitalism is economic rather than political, this dominion of power cannot help but spill over into the political domain – and of course it frequently does in the form of political think tanks, excessively funded election campaigns, lobbyist projects and 'cash for questions' scandals (*The Guardian*, 2010; *The Telegraph*, 2013b). Only a fool could possibly think then that the underclass has an equivalent level of quality control over the direction of new legislation as does the economic class. Moreover, since the socioeconomic aspirations of these two classes diametrically oppose each other in the first instance, any legal ground seized by one must necessarily be taken from the other. If we return once more to Durant (1935) and the earliest beginnings of civilization: 'Law comes with property, marriage and government; the lowest societies manage to get along without it' (Ibid.: 72). Since the concept of law in our culture is predominantly fixated upon property, even to the extent that a human life is a type of property – evidenced in the concept of paying financial compensation to the families of the deceased in cases of death by professional or state negligence – it stands to reason that those with property (or capital, in its liquid form) benefit more from the rule of law than those with little or no property. Where legal rights are concerned, they generally augment the first principle of property and therefore represent state-sponsored ingeminations of an initial socioeconomic divide which stratifies the human experience. Of course, nothing is morally wrong with the concept of possession, per se, but rather with the inauguration of its natural counterpart in *non-possession*. During conditions of scarce resources, such as prolonged periods of austerity, the former often evokes bold illustrations of the latter. Where resources are finite and under pressure, one human's legal right to survive can hence become another human's legal barrier to that same survival.

Class and the cultural politics of identity formation: oppression and resistance

So let us now use this idea to venture the proposition that the oppression versus resistance cycle as a reductionist understanding of class struggle is fought out within a perpetually tightening bureaucratic net. Its development is governed by a law of entropy in which the system that surrounds it cannot over time become less, only more, legislatively totalitarian. While throwing stones at police and smashing shop windows cannot ever serve as anything but a short-term release from underclass oppression enforced and exacerbated through state-imposed austerity, legal ramifications which derive their logic from such crises can have a *cumulative* long-term negative effect upon civil liberties. This is subsequent to the privileged economic class perennially enjoying the simultaneous factors of being favoured by law and having a more powerful influence upon social policy. The process can be understood as self-perpetuating because once policy is enacted into legislation it becomes law and any non-conformity validates establishmentarian use of the socially ostracising brand, 'criminal'. Discovering themselves overwhelmed with a puzzling statistical increase in criminal behaviour, police then request new powers to bring it under control, prompting yet further calls for new legislation, and so on. The sum and substance is that reactionary law clumsily intended to patch up the social system can and has invoked broad and sweeping powers over civil liberties in Britain, but if this leads to yet more reactionary and hence self-defeating resistance, it will prompt yet further expansion of state power. This is precisely the trap Freire warns resistance not to fall into.

Inexorably then, economically stratified societies generally, and perhaps Britain in particular (*The Australian*, 2009; Prowle, 2013), are plagued by an internal pull toward totalitarianisms enacted legitimately through the legal justice system. Law is stacked upon law in the interminable bid to eliminate dissent precipitated upon underclass remonstration against class privilege. The political protection of class interests of course further extends to general public policy instrumentation during phases of implemented austerity. Our case is certainly supported at least by the Anti-social Behaviour Crime and Policing Bill 2013, which further expands and loosens restrictions upon powers granted under the Anti-social Behaviour Act 2003. Part four of the initial 2003 act (Crawford and Lister 2007),

> Gives the police in England and Wales new powers to disperse groups of two or more people from areas where there is believed to be persistent ASB and a problem with groups causing intimidation. Within a designated zone a police constable or community support officer (CSO) may disperse groups where their presence or behaviour has resulted, or is likely to result, in a member of the public being harassed, intimidated, alarmed or distressed.

At a superficial glance, this policy might seem innocent and sensible enough, but as pertinently summarized by legendary comedian and social critic George Carlin (*The Progressive*, July 2001),

'By and large, language is a tool for concealing the truth'. Since the behaviours which expedite feelings of 'alarm' and 'distress' are relativized by a multiplex of social factors, there is nothing in theory to prevent this legislation being used as a state-sponsored artillery weapon against individual civil liberties. At risk of being accused of selectivism, let us consider for example the cases of Sabrina Cross, 'banned from setting foot on motorways across England and Wales', and Norman Hutchins, 'banned from every hospital in the country' (*Mirror*, 2011b). The language propping up the 2003 Anti-social Behaviour Act is however but *itself* derivative of the Public Order Act of 1986, which has an entire section (5) devoted to the ruthlessly subjective phraseology of 'harassment, alarm or distress'. It is precisely this vague ambiguity which capacitated the following (National Council for Civil Liberties 2008):

> On 10th May 2008, a young person was issued a summons by the City of London Police for refusing to remove his sign which read: 'Scientology is not a religion, it is a dangerous cult'. The boy was taking part in a group protest outside the Church of Scientology's central London headquarters and the police said that his use of the word 'cult' violated section 5.

The latest Anti-social Behaviour Crime and Policing Bill of 2013 makes yet further provisions for the expansion of state power, predicated upon a veritable glossary of potential abuses capable of being derived semantically from its nonsensical language. Though recently voted down in the House of Lords – tellingly because of the equivocality of its terms – the preferred counterproposal merely retracts the definition of 'anti-social behaviour' back to its initial and wildly enigmatic intimation of anything which facilitates feelings of 'harassment, alarm or distress' (BBC 2014). In a report from the House of Lords/House of Commons Joint Committee on Human Rights dated October 2013, we are told: 'The current drafting of the Bill in relation to the prohibitions and requirements that can be attached … is far too broad'.

Yet the misdirection of this argument becomes vivid under consideration that the baseline from which the opinion has been derived is itself too broad! In its original form, the bill sought to yet further mythologize the concept of 'alarm and distress' to 'nuisance and annoyance' (government factsheet, 2013; BBC, 2014). If such draconian impact can be had upon civil liberties through the medium of ambiguous legal phrases like 'harassment, alarm or distress', one would almost dread to contemplate the social dystopia which might spawn from terms like 'nuisance and annoyance'. Perhaps being the only British paper still at least ostensibly prepared to question these issues, *The Guardian* (2014a) writes:

> Advertisers, who cause plenty of nuisance and annoyance, have nothing to fear; nor do opera lovers hogging the pavements of Covent Garden. Annoyance and nuisance are what young people cause; they are inflicted by oddballs, the underclass, those who dispute the claims of power.

Indeed, as the great H.G. Wells allegedly said (1934): 'Advertising is legalized lying'. But under terms of economic capitalism, media *itself* has a symbiosis with advertising, oxygenating the very heart of which is an exchange of cultural for economic capital. Furthermore, the media commands real, tangible political power. Once the new precedent has been established, the media's function is to be found in saturating the British public with information which either overtly or clandestinely validates the new bureaucratic reality. The dominant parameters get slightly tighter, and the media normalizes the new standards to satisfy pretexts of economic and political purpose. Over time, the entire paradigm of culture is shifted to accommodate the new baseline as point zero. *The Guardian* only evidences the point further, since it skilfully frames the problem as being with this particular piece of legislation, rather than the cycle of oppression and resistance which permitted it to ever evolve in the first place. Under this uncompromising light, the media's true and duplicitous identity as a wholesale pacifier of the underclass reveals itself. How can capitalist media credibly be expected to remain critical of a system in which its own prosperity and survival are intertwined? Disassociation is a fundamental requirement of neutrality and the British media's calumniatory attacks during and after the riots evidence quite a conflicting picture in terms of the austere social context in which they took place. Whatever the problem happens to be in the selectionist eyes of the British media, it absolutely must not be the critical faults integral to the system itself. Fromm's golem is permanently vacant from the table of discussion. To remind ourselves briefly of the vested interest conventionalist media has in the political class struggle, let us quickly turn to those great assassins of propaganda, Herman and Chomsky (1994: 14):

> In sum, the dominant media firms are quite large businesses; they are controlled by very wealthy people or by managers who are subject to sharp constraints by owners and other market-profit-orientated forces; and they are closely interlocked, and

have important common interests, with other major corporations, banks, and government.

So the parochial and often self-contradictory sentiment of privatized media becomes perfectly understandable given that its financial operations and institutional relationships are all reticulated within that same system it is expected to be critical of. It is part of the golem, and if the golem is not psychologically well, then we cannot expect the components to behave in a rational manner either. The truly important point, however, is that media also acts *intelligently* in that it instinctively seeks to safeguard and aggrandize its own power. A pathogenic individual might interact objectively with the outside world in terms of a defective belief structure, but subjectively, in the manner in which that individual seeks to serve his or her own self-interests, the behaviours remain non-deviant. On the scale of the society, this analogy juxtaposes itself with striking clarity. As organs of the golem, the media and the political system will intelligently attempt to survive and prosper within the environmental confines of that system, but what they will not be able to do is extrovert themselves rationally if the preconditions of that system are psychologically defective to begin with.

Let us stay with the media for the moment and superimpose our idea that an irreducible, incessantly tightening legislative structure is a by-product of the capitalist class struggle. Media itself exhibits its own reactionary behaviours to the pressures of capitalism which are as simple to evidence as merely referencing the Leveson Inquiry. Crushed under the weight of readership expectation, 'drive to be the first to break the story' (Allan and Zelizer, 2004: 8), profit margins, and often just pure competitive capitalist ego, media sometimes abandons the rules, too. The brazen irony is that media itself then becomes one of Freire's 'docile pawns' as these infractions then lead to legal protections against state media interference gradually being eroded away by legislative apparatus. A pertinent example would be the Deregulation Bill of 2013–14. Speaking for The Society of Editors in early 2014, Gillian Phillips, Director of Editorial Legal Services, Guardian News and Media Ltd writes:

> A threat to the protections given to journalistic material is lurking in the … Deregulation Bill. Clause 47 … removes the statutory procedural safeguards set out in Schedule 1 of PACE. … The removal from parliamentary scrutiny of such a fundamental free speech protection is worrying.

Indeed, it is petrifying, but the point unspectacularly missed by Phillips is that it is a necessary consequence of the preconditioned cycle of oppression and resistance which pervades the original madness of our society. Underclass resistance to the parameters of the system in the real world begets an abstract legal reaction from the elitist class which either tightens those same parameters or loosens restrictions upon how they are to be enforced – ultimately engendering the precise same erosion of personal freedom. Eventually, either the culture must become a textbook totalitarianism or explode into civil action following the systematized garrotting of civil liberties over a broad but indefinite expanse of time. Contradictorily, as far as the media is concerned, there can never be a fundamental problem with the sanity of the golem or the behavioural incentives which drive it; the cold-blooded outrage is always to be found in future legislation, or 'yobs', or rap, or any one of a million other clues which betray the same root cause.

Of course, the particular amendments under discussion have a clear pretext in the British phone hacking scandal, but whichever opinion we might hold about the behaviour of the British press specific to those circumstances, we must not fall into yet the same trap the press itself fell into after the 2011 riots in wagging fingers of blame at each other. People's phones were hacked because the expectations placed upon media by the same convoluted system it characteristically defended during the riots – by sophistically blaming broken parts – perpetually pressurize it for information it often does not have, and cannot obtain legally without excruciating difficulty and/or cost. Rigorous analyses of behavioural anomalies within subculture as are offered by the Leveson Inquiry, or the LSE's *Reading the Riots*, are in general but cruel and epic acts of misdirection since the stimuli underlying those behaviours rather than the behaviours themselves are defective in the first instance. The schizophrenic individual behaves oddly because she/he is schizophrenic; hence, without a prior understanding of schizophrenia, scrutinizing the schizophrenic's behaviour – or even the contextual environment in which it took place – gives us little information about how to solve the underlying problem which facilitates the behaviour. Dysfunctional actions are caused by dysfunctional belief; they are symptoms and not the disease itself. To extrapolate the point further, let us consider the wording of a Media Standards Trust report submitted to the Leveson Inquiry dated June 2012:

> Over two dozen national newspapers and magazines were found to have commissioned over 17,000 transactions, many of them alleged to be in breach of the Data Protection Act, to gather *personal information* (emphasis mine).

It is of paramount importance that we note the specific reference to personal information, since this discloses for us that the implicated data concerned individual personalities (i.e. celebrities) and not groups, institutions, political parties or corporations. The readership pounds the door of British media not for exposés of further domestic austerity plans or for insider knowledge about corporate consolidation but rather to know the colour of Gordon Brown's toothbrush or which year Alex Ferguson will finally retire! This fixation upon the celebrity, upon that which we are drawn to believe is the apotheosis of capitalist existence, is both a sedative against the monotony of our everyday existence and part of the same cult mentality which permits us to ever endure it in the first place. As *The Independent* (2006) writes:

> Being a celebrity has topped a list of what children under 10 believe to be the 'very best thing in the world' in a survey carried out for National Kids Day. Those who believe we live in an increasingly shallow culture will not be surprised to learn that at numbers two and three in the poll of 2,500 children were 'good looks' and 'being rich'.

If we dare confront the grotesqueness of its appearance, this particular demographic can sketch out a profound illustration of the monster lurking deep within the psychology of our culture, since it has been exposed to predominant elements and values of society (i.e. advertising, celebrity, education, trade, etc.) yet lacks the personal experience to frame them into terms of any type of partisan political bias. Young children make no claims about what could, would or should be and are instead concerned only with what they see as their immediate reality – the reality we have presented to them as a cultural blueprint for happiness. But can we in any way remonstrate with the sheer *sociopathy* of this blueprint? Of believing these false gods of celebrity, beauty and wealth administer logical directives in any human quest toward greater ambitions of peace, scientific discovery or intellectual understanding? These factors are all human/time relative and represent almost liquidly trite acquisitions which only exhibit further the logically egregious, deep-rooted narcissism of the social personality. There is little or no concern with objective mastery over the universe; over conquering the fundamental monotony of day-to-day existence for the human race; only with a make-believe feeling of security ostensibly derived from being a revered subject of *admiration* within culture or subculture; *we are thus back to the cultural politics of identity*. Were we not so cognitively impaired from the psychosis of Fromm's golem and the convention of propaganda which barricades it from view, from such a young age in our lives, we might question why we ever have to pray for identity in the first place. These prizes lauded by the posterity are drugs, and they are the only things capable of making us feel marginally better within a society which robs us of our identity, only to forcefully preoccupy us with spending our entire lives looking for it again.

To reiterate, social identity cannot be self-validated merely at the community level anymore because the structure which governs us is far too large for that. Wherever industrialization has emerged, as Dahrendorf puts it (1978: 302), 'Everywhere it displays those conditions of social structure which give rise to social conflict in terms of class theory'. Hence, at the very root of social conflict is a ruthless battle for identity precipitated upon the extrication of an old order and the sudden release of labour and capital. Were we to question children from a twelfth century peasant village about their most secret aspirations, doubtless we would elicit shy responses about becoming kings and queens, lords and ladies. It is thus only to the same false symbols of power, of wealth, of identity to which we still aspire in a precise reciprocation of feudal thinking; the economic placebo of industrialization has done nothing for society in terms of its most serious psychological health problems – other than to arguably prolong them by releasing some of the practical apparatus by which people might achieve the former ends in terms of labour and capital. At the heart of class conflict is a fight for which of us gets to know that we exist again, which of us gets to palpably experience the illusion of purpose, and which of us gets to sit in the front of the train as it plunges toward the cavernous abyss of logical redundancy.

Let us pause for a moment to gather our thoughts. If we consider what wealth, power and beauty represent in a pragmatic sense, it is security – freedom from pressures of austerity; freedom from Durant's 'precarious fortunes of the chase'. But they are not *genuine* forms of security since they are not objective acquisitions against the competing power of the universe to eliminate us. Rather they are but religious symbols of eudemonia, consummately subjective to a culture which is plagued with delirium. The value of wealth fluctuates even when it is static, power is always relative to other power, and beauty is ceaselessly eroded by the physical law of entropy. It matters not if we talk about the 2011 riots, the legislative response to subversion or the British phone-hacking scandal: the free fall descent of culture into neurotic rejection of its objective insecurity and the replacement of that objectivity with a subjective, quasi-religious worship of false symbols of control is simultaneously guilty as an embryonic first cause.

It is precisely this arrogant religiosity which precipitated the sensational economic crash of 2008, and yet in a strict policy response of national austerity all we have really encountered is dissatisfaction with the fundamental outcome – not the warped, subliminal mechanics of the social personality which careered British society into the bumper of near-economic ruin in the first place. As has been said by so many people, so often that it has become a mere unascribable platitude: doing the same things over and over again but expecting different results is the very definition of madness. Appropriately, just as the already-poor British rioters in 2011 reacted psychotically to the alienating, repressive environment of state-imposed austerity, so too did the political elite react with coterminous deviance to the ice-cold reality of an economy constipated from a diet of elitist exuberance. By ever proposing that institutionalized spartanism could offer a genuine long-term socioeconomic solution to the people of Britain, all ministers begrudgingly acknowledged was the temporary need to strap the golem down to a chair and feed it a sedative.

In both contexts, the cultural orthodoxy of neuroticism remained constant, and only the strategy applied to protecting the values of the neuroticism changed. For the rioters, it became about stealing things; for the coalition government, it became about neglecting the public sector, repealing civil liberties and kicking people off benefits (*Guardian*, 2012; BBC, 2013; Burton, 2013: 67). However, our true common denominator here is this: these irrational class reactions to paralyzing yet by no means insuperable core problems in British society betray a corresponding reversal of object and subject. Rather than Fromm's golem being the object and the social components the subjects, the aggregation of these themes infers an ideology has been rationalized ubiquitously throughout the political class system that the economy itself is the subject and man is the object to be acted upon! To put it another way, when the economy falters, we must repair ourselves and our habits – not that which has faltered. We must be less passive in the face of the economy's aggression. The complexity of our psychosis is simply staggering, since we are now revealed to have surrendered control to even those few things which *are* ours, which we *can* objectively control, simply because of our pathological desire to terminate responsibility for accepting those which we can't.

Perhaps the most prolific damage of all to our long-term social health, though, is inflicted by politicians themselves: those same people to whom society surrenders the task of steering the human ship. Politicians represent mere buffers to true cultural edification in that their own political identity exists only relative to the system which validates it. Similar to our earlier understanding of the mainstream press, their interests are not credibly neutral. Thus, a politician will always in the end be found to be misdirecting attention away from the intrinsic sickness within the social personality into smaller, less relevant sub-problems to preserve and protect their own interests of identity. Diminutive ideological differences are inflated and dichotomized into a deliberately false cartography of the political landscape (Blair, 2010: 119), while the fundamental delusiveness of capitalist civilization remains forever inexpressible in real political terms. Let us consider just how skilled politicians are at concealing the facts by looking briefly at the 2010 Conservative Party election manifesto – that which won the Conservatives majority power in a coalition government. David Cameron writes:

> Our economy is overwhelmed by debt, our social fabric is frayed and our political system has betrayed the people. But these problems can be overcome if we pull together and work together. If we remember that we are all in this together.
>
> Some politicians say: 'give us your vote and we will sort out all your problems'. We say: real change comes not from government alone. Real change comes when the people are inspired and mobilised, when millions of us are fired up to play a part in the nation's future.
>
> Yes this is ambitious. Yes it is optimistic. But in the end all the acts of Parliament, all the new measures, all the new policy initiatives, are just politicians' words without you and your involvement.
>
> How will we deal with the debt crisis unless we understand that we are all in this together?

Who can argue that this is a breathtakingly persuasive piece of writing? It almost pangs of the Shakespearean *Henry V* speech on the Eve of St. Crispin's Day! But it is persuasive because its cause *is* persuasion, and its author is a professional persuader. Let us instead look in slightly more detail.

First, we should consider that omnipresent theme of oppositional party election-time literature: 'change'. Despite clear preconditions of the 2008 economic crash, appealing to change represents but a standard political rubric in fishing for that portion of the electorate which will always be discontent with the long-term decisions government has made. It would be quite plainly unremarkable in terms of our own case were it not for the incriminating auxiliary language concomitantly appended. 'Real change comes when the people are inspired and mobilised, when millions of us are fired up to play a part in the nation's future', supports our earlier revelation by inferring that 'change' is something the people are going to have to do (in becoming 'fired up', 'inspired and mobilised') rather than something the structure or its product are going to have to do ('the nation's future'). We get to 'play a part' in the future of the golem rather than the authentically logical inversion (which would open for criticism the dialectical validity of its role in *our* future). Somewhat contemptibly, the Conservative Party's *'Invitation to join the government of Great Britain'* begins then by boldly acknowledging the problems of society head on, only to immediately – and deceptively – reverse cause and effect. Man becomes the object, the ideology becomes the subject, and the delicate ground is thus laid out that it is not the ideology which has failed but man and man's needs to become more 'inspired', more 'mobilised' or have more 'involvement'. The problems are not problems intrinsic to the ideology but are instead 'your problems'. Indeed, the very title of the manifesto encourages voters to 'join' the state – the very institute which failed in its duty to protect the people – rather than change it.

Second, in what can only be a calculated act of repetition, we are somewhat pertinaciously informed both in beginning and con-clusion that 'we are all in this together'. Challenging the sheer absurdity of this statement should not be circumvented since we began this chapter by establishing the grim disagreement of the underclass of the rioters. Eighty-six per cent of those interviewed during the initial *Reading the Riots* study claimed that poverty was either an 'important' or 'very important' factor, while as we discovered antecedently: 'Evidence from several sources suggests rioters were generally poorer than the country at large'. Clearly the objective fact is that we do not live in an economically egalitarian society. Thus, while the assiduous theme that 'we are all in this together' is not strictly in itself an outright falsity, it is a textbook act of deception in that it fails to stipulate the underlying small-print that 'we are all in this' to significantly different extents and have significantly different apparatus at our disposal to get out of it. It swerves quite beautifully from any acknowledgment of the economic ripple effect, ineluctable as belts systemically tighten throughout the hierarchy to cope with sudden pressures of auster-ity (CBS, 2008; *Washington Times*, 2014). If corporate executives can retain a judicious profit strategy by eliminating extraneous personnel, then of course they will do just that; hence, it becomes a self-refuting idea to propose that we can ever all be in this to-gether, since minor reactions at the top will indubitably cause sig-nificant hardships at the bottom. The physical impact of poverty speaks for itself and, as the Joseph Rowntree Foundation puts it (2013): 'Stress, depression, low self-esteem and lack of hope high-light the mental impact of austerity measures'.

Finally, by virtue of the first two points, our excerpt from the 2010 Conservative election manifesto is neither 'ambitious' nor 'optimistic' but rather regurgitates precisely the same sophistic rhetoric it has become almost a banality to associate with politicians during election time. Let us finish up the discussion by rather sardonically juxtaposing the Conservative eagerness for everyday people to become more involved in 2010 with this excerpt from *The Guardian*:

> The transparency of lobbying, non-party campaigning and trade union administration bill – a.k.a. the gagging bill – which the coalition government has insisted on pushing through parliament, is intent on severely hindering third-party campaigning (2014b).

Conclusion

To close the chapter with some rough conclusions then, we are effectively confronted by a social experience in which the information reflected back to us through both the media and political systems is normalizing a kind of warped ideological pietism. To question or reject the system is to question or reject God. Resistance to God is never to be suffered because the wisdom and mercy of God are self-evident and do not need to be explored further – indeed, to do so is considered a sacrilege in and of itself. Since God is omnipotent and man is flawed, man's problems are caused by man. Any rejection of God by man must necessarily evidence man's ingratitude and lack of understanding; never must we be tempted to question the architect or validity of the agenda. Hence, we are blown a long way away from Fukuyama's belief (1992: 185) that it is true reason which drives humanity within the consumerist framework, and instead find ourselves reverberating Fromm (2008: 62) that it is mere animal intelligence which satisfies the demands of the materialist culture. By squeezing reason through the parameters of consumerism, man is able to act both *intelligently* and *irrationally*.

The infamous English occult practitioner Aleister Crowley, educated at Cambridge, was doubtless intelligent, but are we genuinely to say he was also a man of *reason*? We would be scorned by Fromm for synonymizing these terms. A human can be considered intelligent if she/he understands the precise system in which they are immediately involved and how to benefit from it; but without the capacity to reason, human is unable to critically question the validity of the system or the behaviour it elicits from them. She/he can succeed only within the very limited parameters of their own environment. Intelligence teaches man how to get things, and reason teaches man why she/he is trying to get them. Intelligence is practical, and reason is abstract. Intelligence can have parameters, but reason – by its very existence as an intelligence *of* the abstract – cannot. If we are to believe that reason is being emancipated rather than restricted by consumerist desire, how do we reconcile this with the reduction of serious sociological problems to economic cost and/or wanton finger-pointing by the British media, or with inveterate long-term economic vulnerabilities (Blair, 2010: 44; *The Economist*, 2014) being ad hoc band-aided by temporary measures of austerity? Indeed, if reason were just about satisfying human material desire, we could not even say Hitler's Germany lacked reason! So then, if we are to finish with this line of thought, has man been fooled into incarcerating this transcendental intelligence of – reason – for the sake of overdevelopment of material intelligence?

Well, the industrialization of modern man has expedited yet larger and larger social constructs which have plucked man out of a localized agricultural reality and instead environmentalized man into conditions whereby man must now theoreticize the greater part of man's social function. Rationalizing man's effort today depends on faith that the rest of the system is operating adequately and to man's benefit – a matter of much greater scope and depth than man's individual awareness can determine empirically. Hence, society besets itself with large-scale confirmation bias as a self-defence mechanism against the objective reality of its own insecurity, despite (or rather because of) individual components never having any knowledge of that system outside of isolated existence as a single element. This reactive fallacy is a mere evolution of the same natural need for security in man, which saw man explain man's condition away in gods and devils. Its manifestation can be seen within our earlier context of the 2011 riots as a harmony of outraged journalists, red-faced because of the pernicious impact sedition has upon socioeconomic apparatus, concerned only with the damage done to the system, not by it. Such vilification is quite analogous to the reaction of a medieval monk to desecration of the holy cross. The perpetrators of the riots are dehumanized – demonized as blasphemers and heretics – but the objective reality is that their actions disrespect what is in both cases only the symbology of a system of faith-based thinking. Henry Thoreau put this new world of ours into perspective as far back as 1863 when he wrote: 'If a man was tossed out of a window when an infant, and so made a cripple for life, or scared out of his wits by the Indians, it is regretted chiefly because he was thus incapacitated for – business!' The unfettered reality is that consumerist capitalism has satisfied the needs of man only in the same way the Catholic theocracy of medieval Europe did: by convincing man they are part of God's greater plan. The new God is business, politicians are its priests and mainstream media is for all intents and purposes the new Bible – the text which translates for us the difference between good and evil.

Notes

1 See David Berry's (2013) account of the English riots in Chapter Two 'Public Policy' particularly pages 43–61 in *Public Policy and Media Organizations* co-authored with Caroline Kamau.
2 For the original use of 'golem' further research into Jewish literature is wise.

Bibliography

Allan, S. and Zelizer, B. (2004). *Introduction – rules of engagement: journalism and war reporting. Reporting war journalism in wartime.* London: Routledge.

BBC (2011). 'UK riots: trouble erupts in English cities'. Available at: http://www.bbc.co.uk/news/uk-england-london-14460554 [Accessed February 22, 2014].

BBC (2013). 'Life when the Jobcentre says you broke the rules'. Available at: http://www.bbc.co.uk/news/uk-24829866 [Accessed February 18, 2014].

BBC (2014). 'Government suffers defeat over anti-social behaviour bill'. Available at: http://www.bbc.co.uk/democracylive/house-of-lords-25656511 [Accessed February 15, 2014].

Blair, T. (2010). *A journey.* London: Hutchinson.

Bristow, J. (2011). 'Reporting the riots: parenting culture and the problem of authority in media analysis of August 2011'. *Sociological Research Online*, 18(4). Available at: http://www.socresonline.org.uk/18/4/11.html [Accessed February 7, 2014].

British Government Factsheet (2013). 'Anti-social Behaviour, Crime and Policing Bill'. Available at: https://www.gov.uk/government/uploads/system/uploads/attachment_data/file/251312/01_Factsheet_Replacing_the_ASBO_-_updated_for_Lords.pdf [Accessed February 16, 2014].

Burton, M. (2013). *The politics of public sector reform.* Basingstoke: Palgrave Macmillan.

Cameron, D. (2010). 'Invitation to join the government of Great Britain'. Conservative Party 2010 election manifesto. Available at: http://media.conservatives.s3.amazonaws.com/manifesto/cpmanifesto2010_lowres.pdf [Accessed February 19, 2014].

CBS News (2008). 'The economic ripple effect gone awry'. Available at: http://www.cbsnews.com/news/the-economic-ripple-effect-gone-awry/ [Accessed February 19, 2014].

Crawford, A. and Lister, S. (2007). *The use and impact of dispersal orders*. Bristol: The Policy Press.

Dahrendorf, R. (1978). *The authority structure of the industrial enterprise: The sociology of modern Britain*. Glasgow: William Collins and Sons Co. Ltd.

Durant, W. (1935). *The story of civilization: our oriental heritage*. New York: Simon and Schuster.

Freire, P. (2005). *Pedagogy of the oppressed*, 30th anniversary edition. New York: Continuum.

Fromm, E. (2008). *The sane society*, 2nd ed. Abingdon: Routledge Classics.

Fukuyama, F. (1992). *The end of history and the last man*. New York: Macmillan.

Herman, E.S. and Chomsky, N. (1994). *Manufacturing consent: the political economy of the mass media*, 2nd ed. London: Vintage.

House of Lords/House of Commons Joint Committee on Human Rights (2013). 'Legislative scrutiny: Anti-social Behaviour, Crime and Policing Bill. Fourth report of session 2013/14'. Available at: http://www.publications.parliament.uk/pa/jt201314/jtselect/jtrights/56/56.pdf. [Accessed February 16, 2014].

Joseph Rowntree Foundation (2013). 'Austerity in the UK: deprivation, depression and demonisation part of daily struggle'. Available at: http://www.jrf.org.uk/austerity-birmingham [Accessed February 19, 2014].

Kimberlee, R. (2002). 'Why don't British young people vote at general elections?' *Journal of Youth Studies*, 05(1). Available at: http://www.tandfonline.com/doi/abs/10.1080/13676260120111788?journalCode=cjys20#preview [Accessed February 10, 2014].

London School of Economics and Political Science/The Guardian (2011). *Reading the riots*. England: Guardian Books.

Media Standards Trust (2012). 'A free and accountable media. Reform of press self-regulation: report and recommendations'. Available at: http://www.levesoninquiry.org.uk/wp-content/uploads/2012/07/Submission-by-Media-Standards-Trust.pdf [Accessed February 17, 2014].

National Council for Civil Liberties (2008). (a.k.a. Liberty). 'Policing and protest: Liberty's response to the joint committee on human rights'. Available at: http://www.liberty-human-rights.org.uk/pdfs/policy08/response-to-jchr-re-protest-2.pdf [Accessed February 15, 2014].

National Council for Civil Liberties (2014). (a.k.a. Liberty). 'Anti-social Behaviour, Crime and Policing Bill 2013–14. Policy and lobbying'. Available at: https://www.liberty-human-rights.org.uk/policy/bill-tracker/anti-social-behaviour-crime-and-policing-bill-2013-14.php [Accessed February 12, 2014].

Phillips, G. (2014). 'Another backdoor attempt to restrict essential protections'. Society of Editors. Available at: http://www.societyofeditors.co.uk/pageview.php?pagename=News&parent_page_id=0&news_id=6899&numbertoprintfrom=1 [Accessed January 1, 2014].

Prowle, M. (2013). 'Are We Sleepwalking Into a Totalitarian Society?' *Huffington Post*. Available at: http://www.huffingtonpost.co.uk/malcolm-prowle/are-we-sleepwalking-into-totalitarian-society_b_2996968.html [Accessed February 14, 2014].

Quintelier, E. (2007). 'Differences in political participation between young and old people'. *Contemporary Politics*, 13(2). Available at: https://lirias. kuleuven.be/bitstream/123456789/183907/2/CP_Youth+and+Politics.pdf [Accessed February 9, 2014].

Snow, N. (2003). *Information war: American propaganda, free speech and information control since 9/11*. UK: Turnaround Publisher Services Ltd.

The Australian (2009). 'Thought police muscle up in Britain'. Available at: http://www.theaustralian.com.au/opinion/thought-police-muscle-up-in-britain/story-e6frg6zo-1225700363959 [Accessed February 14, 2014].

The Economist (2014). 'The inevitability of instability'. Available at: http://www.economist.com/news/finance-and-economics/21595010-welcome-burst-new-thinking-financial-regulation-inevitability [Accessed February 20, 2014].

The Daily Mail (2011a). 'UK riots: "a curse on Britain's yobs and slobs"'. Available at: http://www.dailymail.co.uk/femail/article-2028993/UK-riots-A-curse-Britains-yobs-slobs-says-Joan-Collins.html [Accessed February 2, 2014].

The Daily Mail (2011b). 'Riots were like "a rave" and a chance for young people to get "free stuff"'. Available at: http://www.dailymail.co.uk/news/article-2057492/England-riots-2011-chance-young-people-free-stuff.html [Accessed February 6, 2014].

The Guardian (2010). 'Conservatives spent twice as much as Labour on election campaign'. Available at: http://www.theguardian.com/politics/2010/dec/02/conservatives-spent-twice-labour-election-campaign [Accessed February 12, 2014].

The Guardian (2012). 'Report warns government against neglecting regeneration projects'. Available at: http://www.theguardian.com/local-government-network/2012/sep/27/work-foundation-government-neglects-regeneration [Accessed February 18, 2014].

The Guardian (2014a). 'At last, a law to stop almost anyone from doing almost anything'. Available at: http://www.theguardian.com/commentisfree/2014/jan/06/law-to-stop-eveyone-everything [Accessed February 16, 2014].

The Guardian (2014b). 'The gagging bill looks designed to undermine trade unions'. Available at: http://www.theguardian.com/commentisfree/2014/jan/29/lobbying-bill-trade-unions-law [Accessed February 19, 2014].

The Independent (2006). 'Children say being famous is best thing in world'. Available at: http://www.independent.co.uk/news/uk/this-britain/children-say-being-famous-is-best-thing-in-world-429000.html [Accessed February 17, 2014].

The Latest (2011). 'How big media's reporting of the "riots" was biased'. Available at: http://www.the-latest.com/how-big-medias-reporting-riots-was-biased [Accessed February 3, 2014].

The Mirror (2011a). 'UK riots: Why did the riots happen? Who are the rioters? What can we do to end this madness?'. Available at: http://www.mirror.co.uk/news/uk-news/uk-riots-why-did-the-riots-happen-who-147237 [Accessed February 4, 2014].

The Mirror (2011b). 'Unborn baby gets an asbo and the top 10 other bizarre anti-social behaviour orders'. Available at: http://www.mirror.co.uk/news/uk-news/unborn-baby-gets-an-asbo-and-the-top-178104 [Accessed February 15, 2014].

The Progressive (2001). 'George Carlin interview'. Available at: http://progressive.org/mag_intv0701 [Accessed February 15, 2014].

The Roper Center for Public Opinion Research (1996). 'The public perspective'. Available at: http://www.ropercenter.uconn.edu/public-perspective/ppscan/74/74050.pdf [Accessed February 10, 2014].

The Telegraph (2012a). 'Businesses pay £4000 for yob culture'. Available at: http://www.telegraph.co.uk/news/uknews/crime/9084070/Businesses-pay-4000-for-yob-culture.html [Accessed February 2, 2014].

The Telegraph (2012b). 'The 2011 English summer riots revisited'. Available at: http://www.telegraph.co.uk/news/uknews/law-and-order/9453633/The-2011-English-summer-riots-revisited.html [Accessed February 3, 2014].

The Telegraph (2013a). 'One surveillance camera for every 11 people in Britain, says CCTV survey'. Available at: http://www.telegraph.co.uk/technology/10172298/One-surveillance-camera-for-every-11-people-in-Britain-says-CCTV-survey.html [Accessed February 11, 2014].

The Telegraph (2013b). 'Cash for questions: scandal that should have changed face of British politics'. Available at: http://www.telegraph.co.uk/news/politics/conservative/10092681/Cash-for-questions-scandal-that-should-have-changed-face-of-British-politics.html [Accessed February 12, 2014].

The Washington Times (2014). 'MAGNUS: Upgrade of U.S. sea power has economic ripple effects'. Available at: http://www.washingtontimes.com/news/2014/jan/23/magnus-sea-power-means-economic-growth/?page=all [Accessed February 19, 2014].

Thoreau, H.D. (1863). 'Life without principle. Atlantic Monthly'. Originally sourced from Fromm, E. (2008). *The Sane Society.* Available at: http://thoreau.eserver.org/lifewout.html.

Wells, H.G., supposedly said in 1934. As quoted in: *December Magazine*, 33/34(1–2) (1990). Also in: *Across the Board,* 16, Conference Board (1979). Available at: http://izquotes.com/quote/195742.

3   Remembrance and the working class soldier hero in austerity Britain

Maggie Andrews

During the student riots, which erupted in Britain in December 2010, Charlie Gilmour, the son of the Pink Floyd guitarist David Gilmour, was photographed swinging from a flag on the cenotaph in London. In the months that followed there was lengthy legal and media debate about both the motivations that lay behind Charlie's actions on December 9, which had included throwing a dustbin at the Prince of Wales' car, kicking a window of Top Shop in Oxford Street and setting fire to a pile of newspapers, and about whether Charlie's subsequent jail sentence of sixteen months was appropriate. The motivations discussed focused on personal issues rather than the politics of the original demonstration that had spilled over into a riot. There were many elements to this media story and the furore that followed it, including celebrity, wealth, issues of paternity and fatherhood. The original motivation for the student protest (i.e. the new university fees regime, introduced as part of the UK's Coalition government's austerity measures) was deftly sidelined by the outrage over Charlie's disrespectful approach to the cenotaph. Similarly student outrage that the Liberal-Democrat party that had garnered votes from youth by an election pledge to abolish student fees instead supported the introduction of fees of £9,000 a year for undergraduates was airbrushed out of the news coverage.

Charlie Gilmour's actions at the cenotaph were not the legal crime for which he was imprisoned, but they were the focus of most of the media attention and were considered to be a social, even a moral, crime, which was unanimously acknowledged to be horrendous. As a history graduate at Cambridge, his statement that he did not recognize the cenotaph would have seemed incredulous had he not consumed an unfortunate mixture of 'LSD, whisky and valium' (*The Sun*, 2011). Charlie was quick to apologize for this element of his antics, announcing: 'Those who are commemorated by the cenotaph died to protect the very freedoms that allow the people of Britain the right to protest and I feel deeply ashamed to have, although unintentionally and unknowingly, insulted the memory of them' (*The Telegraph*, 2010).

Significantly the 'Charlie Gilmour event' brought together the inter-relationship between an economic climate of austerity, the cultural obsession with First and Second World Wars and remembrance, which is the focus of this chapter. I will argue that there is something metaphorical about the contemporary preoccupation with the war and the consequences of war in an era of austerity and economic crisis. For in both wartime and austerity, ordinary people's lives, experiences, dreams and fantasies are disrupted or destroyed by external and national factors, forces that are out of their control. This chapter traces a number of themes at times interrelated or overlapping which explore why so many of the British public have 'bought into' the idea of remembrance in a time of austerity. For the Coalition government of 2010–15, the First World War centenary may have seemed an ideal opportunity to tap into cultural memories of a British victory and nationalistic sentiments. To some the centenary seemed a natural follow-on to the success of the Olympics in 2012. But remembrance is never merely a top-down affair (Bagot-Jewitt, 2012); it speaks to people's attempt to make sense of their lives. The circumstances of austerity and the need for many to give up what has been the post-war expectation that standards of living will continually improve (Sinfield, 2011) have led to disaffection uncertainty and a search for identity.

Since the formation of the charity Help for Heroes in 2007, the current economic crisis and call for austerity has given rise to a new popular hero, the British Tommy, who has taken the place in popular culture once occupied by the 'miner' in twentieth century British popular culture. Like the miner, the Tommy is presented as something of a tragic hero, bravely making his 'own history' but in circumstances which are not of his own choosing (Marx, 1852). The 2014 response to the World War I centenary gave discourses of Tommy new resonances, building upon already existing obsessions with 'war industries'. However, as this chapter will argue, the Tommy, remembrance and the 'histories' of both wars are all somewhat *polysemic*. Their meanings are not merely multiple but unstable; these are stretchable discourses and emotional perceptions which are complex, contradictory and contested – never fixed, always in flux.

Remembrance and the war industries

The 'war industries', as Dorothy Sheridan refers to them (2010), have grown at a tremendous pace in recent years. For in the realm of public history, the past is consumed as one of many leisure activities via small or large screens, through museums, exhibitions and heritage trails and on Remembrance Sunday. Both the First and Second World Wars have provided scope for multiple commercial opportunities, not merely in the world of publishing but also for products as varied as bags, iPod covers and mugs with the ubiquitous 'Keep Calm and Carry On' slogan, 'Dig for Victory Cookbooks', and musical releases such as *We'll Meet Again: Classic Wartime Songs That Kept Us Smiling Through* (2011). Events such as 'Wartime in the Cotswolds' staged by the Gloucestershire and Warwickshire Railway television series such as *The Village* (2013) and films such as *Testament of Youth* (2015) all appeal to large audiences. Such artefacts, texts and activities have, alongside a range of remembrance activities, made World Wars I and II increasingly central to British culture in recent years. In the four years that mark the centenary of the First World War, there is little danger this trend will be abated.

Individuals and nations look for useable pasts – technological narratives of World War I emphasize the significance of the introduction of tanks for the Allies' victory, linking this innovation to British Industrial dominance in the nineteenth century rather than the country's industrial and economic decline in the twentieth century. Alternatively war-heritage may be put to good use, serving as a distraction and providing a space in which complex and difficult family relationships can be negotiated. The multigenerational museum visits in summer holidays or heritage drama viewings at Christmas are examples of this. There are now multiple competing, overlapping but inevitably selective narratives of twentieth-century wars and conflict endlessly stretched, subjected to slippage and reworking. For the 'war industries', the past, or, to put it more accurately, a range of pasts, always offers uses and gratifications to the consumer and there are multiple possibilities of how this may work; narratives of the First and Second World Wars, for example, enable consumers to affirm elements of their national identity. Britain's world significance during World War I can be endorsed by the dissemination of recent popular histories that draw attention to the contribution to the war effort made by the then British Empire, including for example Indian and Irish soldiers. Such narratives can be seen as offering a sense of shared past to numerous identity groups in contemporary multicultural Britain. They do however contain danger points – they can unwrap into uncomfortable versions of the past, including narratives of racial and class tensions, of the use of Chinese slave labour behind the Western Front, for example.

The constructions of war narratives are not the prerogative of the historian, the media or the heritage industries but rather products of the ebb and flow of private, personal, community, group, official and unofficial narratives of the past. They cannot be fixed by those in power, however much they may strive to do this; for as Raphael Samuel (1996) has pointed out, history is now made by a thousand hands, voices and images. It comes from family photographs, papers kept in the loft and the stories handed down or told by grandparents.

What constitutes a 'usable' past to the media and heritage industries relates to the need to appeal to consumers and institutional imperatives to raise finance and legitimate many organizations' roles in society. Such needs have been accentuated as heritage industries have experienced government austerity measures. Libraries, archives and museum services are now at the forefront of public sector spending cuts at a local level. In the current political maelstrom, such organizations face cuts in opening hours, services and staff alongside pressures to increase revenue. One way of counteracting this is the treadmill of Heritage Lottery Fund, and sometimes Art Council grant applications; preferably ones that contain an element of jeopardy which is time-specific – that is, there is a need for the funding to be granted at a particular time, this year rather than later. Anniversaries in relation to war and conflict are ideal for this and World War I commemoration has produced a plethora of applications. Anniversaries of conflict also tap into the late twentieth and early twenty-first centuries cultural preoccupation with remembrance and commemoration – evidenced for example by the nearly 400,000 people who visited the National Memorial Arboretum in Staffordshire in 2012, the growing visibility of remembrance on television and in other media, the way that the poppy and the cenotaph, as Charlie Gilmour discovered, have become almost sacred (Durkheim, 1912).

Cultural preoccupation with remembrance

Jay Winter and others have persuasively argued that many traditions of remembrance and commemoration were established in Britain before World War I (Winter, 1995; Atherton and Morgan, 2012; Grant, 2012). Nevertheless the 1914–18 conflict arguably continues to frame and shape the performance of contemporary national military remembrance – in terms of dates, for example, with the iconic use of the red poppy and spatially in relation to the cenotaph and war memorials. Although some have seen the rituals and practices of remembrance which developed after the First World War as 'legitimating the state's right to call on citizens to die' (Winter, 1995: 94) or 'affirming the state's authority undermined by the mass causalities of the first mechanized war'

(Helias, 1977), the preoccupation with remembrance in Britain rests upon a range of complex factors. One is that, like sport, remembrance allows men to publically articulate emotions, such as loss and grief. Significantly as people encounter death less directly in their everyday lives, both the fear and fascination with death grows. Shared grief, mourning and remembrance are not reserved for the victims of war and conflict – rather the 'myth' of a spontaneous shared outpouring of emotion in response, for example, to Princess Diana's death in a car accident in 1997 awarded cultural legitimacy. The myth of the 'Diana moment' has not been undermined by the work of the late James Thomas (2012: 74) who, drawing upon mass observation research, pointed out: 'the nation were very far from "united in grief" and indicated that and on the contrary, opinions were both divided and polarised across a range of themes, composed of complex, contradictory and ambivalent responses'. Some, such as Mica Nava (2007), suggested the response to Princess Diana's death indicated the emergence of cosmopolitan sensibilities that acknowledged the precariousness of life across national boundaries. The twin towers disaster on 9/11, the 7/7 London bombings, and the consequent 'war on terror' undermined this, and in the years since tensions have grown between the West and the Middle East and between Russia and Europe (see Andrews, 2014b).

In the twenty-first century, remembrance, like sport, has also become an acceptable space for the British to give vent to expressions of national identity. This is because so ubiquitous are the narratives of the First and Second World Wars that they constitute for the British what Landsberg (2003: 148) described as 'prosthetic memories', whereby it is possible 'to have an intimate relationship with memories of events through which one did not live'. Her concept of prosthetic memories rests upon assertions that such memories are not 'authentic', rather they are 'sensuous memories', 'worn on the body', a consequence of trauma, and interchangeable rather than fixed (Ibid.: 149). Although some have critiqued Landsberg's metaphor suggesting that she overstates the case by using the term 'prosthetic', thus implying people are disabled if they lack access to these memories, on the contrary, this aspect is the important crux of her argument. However unstable, liable to slip and slide and be stretched or reworked they may be, memories of the First and Second World Wars have become intrinsic to British national identity, reference points for cultural inclusion in Britishness, even cultural capital (Bourdieu, 1984).

The First and Second World Wars are linked to a perception of Britain as wielding power and influence on the world stage rather than being a small island off Europe. In an era of economic decline and austerity, these conflicts suggest a time when the US did not have economic and political hegemony. More worryingly, for some, these wars are inaccurately associated with a pre-immigration 'authentic' Englishness. For example, the English Defence League (EDL), in many ways a symptom of disaffection experienced by working class masculinity in a time of recession, has made its presence felt at some remembrance activities. In 2011, over 170 of its members were as the police explained, 'arrested outside the Red Lion public house in Parliament Street, SW1, in order to prevent a breach of peace' (*Huffington Post*, 2011). The EDL activities are a reminder that, like history, remembrance and remembering are not the prerogative of the historian, or government or even established organizations. Try as they might, even The Royal British Legion (RBL) – the self-acclaimed 'guardians of remembrance' – cannot control the competing meanings, interpretations and uses to which remembrance activities in Britain are put; as Winter (2006: 152) points out: 'the multiple voices of remembrance are rarely harmonious and never identical'.

A part of the appeal of Remembrance Sunday and Armistice Day for organizations such as the EDL lies in the media attention that these events have received in the last one hundred years. Indeed in the inter-war period, broadcast media enabled the two minutes of silence on Remembrance Day to become a national event, shared through the airwaves, which ensured some uniformity and accuracy of when the silence would begin across the country. In the following week, many watched recordings of Remembrance Day ceremonies shown in cinemas where McKernan (2009: 1) explains the Remembrance Day service was 'the most hallowed day in the newsreel calendar ... the story often occupying an entire newsreel'. Watching newsreel footage of remembrance ceremonies in cinemas mirrors to some degree the public ceremonies themselves – albeit with a time lag. The audience is still in a public space, in the main surrounded by strangers with little control or input into events; alternatively, broadcast media consumed within private domestic spaces makes remembrance part of everyday life.

In the late twenty-first century there has been an expediential growth in the broadcast programming that accompanies Remembrance Day, facilitated by the economic framework of the contemporary multichannel television landscape and the scope to re-screen programmes in another year, on another channel and/ or in another country. Broadcasting gives remembrance a domestic focus in both programme content and style, and the medium necessitates a more informal, intimate mode of address. In recent years the feminized mediums of television and radio particularly articulates the increasingly familiar discourses of remembrance centred on *soldiers as victims* and, even more, *families as victims* of war that can be seen in contemporary news coverage of armed conflict which are consistent with Winter's (2006: 6) suggestion that women are increasingly at the heart of remembrance as 'war has moved out of the battlefield into every corner of civilian life'. This cultural emphasis on families as victims of war and conflict can be identified in the recent introduction of the Elizabeth Cross awarded to the next of kin of members of the British Armed Forces killed in action or as a result of a terrorist attack after the Second World War (Andrews, 2012).

Furthermore, the media coverage of war and conflict has been shaped by the proliferation of television hours facilitated by the popularization of digital and satellite technology since the 1990s, which has brought about an expansion of cheap programming with a high level of audience or 'ordinary person' input – chat shows, reality and lifestyle programming have multiplied beyond daytime television. First-person narratives (i.e. people's stories) are now a core element in articulating the experience of war along-side domestic even 'feminized' emotions in the confessional and therapeutic culture evidenced in the world of *The Jeremy Kyle Show*, Twitter and other social media. In this cultural context, it becomes possible to understand the phenomenal success of the Military Wives choir. Their first single came to fame via the docu-soap *The Choir* and a performance at the televised Royal British Legion Remembrance Service from the Albert Hall and dislodged the 2011 winner of the television talent show *X Factor* from their expected Christmas number-one slot. The continued popularity of the Military Wives choir keeps the personal domestic consequences of war and armed conflict in the public domain. In August 2014, on the eve of the centenary of the outbreak of World War I, the BBC Proms featured a Proms Military Wives choir conducted by Gareth Malone alongside the life-sized puppets from the National Theatre's production of Michael Morpurgo's *War Horse* (1982); through popular culture, women and animals have earned their place in contemporary remembrance.

Broadcast media and World War I

Personalizing the experience of war has enabled remembrance and commemoration to offer media industries a winning combination of audience numbers and cultural legitimacy. Hence, un-surprisingly, the BBC, still smarting from a range of scandals involving sexual misconduct and overpaid executive payoffs, has seen the remembrance and commemoration of the First World War very appealing, producing programmes and accompanying web materials, which schools and colleges will use, enables this public service broadcaster to fulfil its educational remit and enhances the corporation's credibility. The BBC is all too aware that the corporation's monopoly over the licence fee and the public service status may be a target in the next batch of austerity measures, which will potentially follow the 2015 election. For all broadcasters in the commemoration of the First World War, there have been two particular areas of attention: the Home Front and the British Tommy. For example, the BBC produced two multi-episode new Radio 4 series to mark the centenary; *Home Front's* 600 episodes dramatized the multitude of ways in which war impacted on everyday lives of ordinary people. *Tommies* is structured into six afternoon dramas each year over the four years of commemoration, looking at those on or behind the battlefront and based on historical diaries.

A range of factors have shaped the media commemoration of World War I; programmes are the products of a particular cultural moment. They articulate the anxieties, preoccupations and something of 'the structure of feeling' (Williams, 1966) of the era of austerity in which they are broadcast. Historical texts must appear authentic, something which, as Noakes (1998: 12) points out, for the audience, is primarily established in relation to other representations of the past on television or in films. A lexicon of popular images of the conflict already existed, created in part by popular Sunday evening dramas. Series 2 of *Downton Abbey* (ITV, 2012), which gained an audience of 11.7 million, and *The Village* (BBC, 2013–14) explored how World War I was experienced in homes and workplaces (Andrews, 2014a) but were shaped by the era of austerity in which they were produced. The Home Front may be seen as presenting a softer, more palatable, nostalgic version of the war suitable for a mass domestic audience; however, as Wendy Wheeler (1994: 57) has argued, 'nostalgia isn't nasty' rather it is rejection of the status quo. It could be argued that the Home Front be seen as depoliticized narrative, able to avoid problematic questions of the whys and wherefores of the causes and decisions about war; but it is not that simple.

There is something metaphorical about the contemporary preoccupation with the Home Front, which is not reserved for television drama but can also be identified in art and museum exhibitions and in popular historical publishing. The early twentieth-century Home Front's preoccupation with family lives and personal relationship can be seen as both a distancing and a rejection of the primarily masculine world of politics and military armed conflict. This enables it to sit well with the broadcasting domestic viewing and focus; most importantly, the consequences of both war and economic crisis are austerity. In wartime, women's experiences, lives, dreams and fantasies are disrupted and destroyed by external and national factors, forces out of their control. Widows and wives of those in the forces – military wives – are the socially acceptable version of single motherhood (Andrews, 2014b).

Housewives in war and austerity are required to make sacrifices, to limit spending, to save and put up with problems created by national decisions which affect their mundane domestic lives; little wonder dramas focusing on wartime home fronts have a resonance for those in an age of austerity. Conditions on the World War I Home Front made savings in food consumption, particularly of bread, an individual and a national day-to-day concern for all classes. A 1916 poster warned women with the following message: 'To dress extravagantly in war time is worse than bad form it is unpatriotic' (IWM ART IWM PPST 10122). This was directed at the spending of those able to indulge in conspicuous consumption rather than the everyday necessities. Histories of the Home Front in Britain portray it as a 'period of enforced austerity for the greater good' giving it a contemporary cultural reference. Dramas' focus on the personal and domestic consequences of war, the economic and emotional hardship and deprivation of traumatized friends, families and relations of those involved in conflicts may raise political issues. It leaves space to question the decisions, risks and mistakes of politicians that have led to consequences for others. In heritage dramas, the soldiers, as well as their families, are victims; in *Downton Abbey* attention is drawn to the poor welfare provision for wounded soldiers when Mrs Crawley's servants felt compelled to set up a soup kitchen for impoverished veterans. The young footman William Mason who volunteered for war is portrayed as naïve and misguided in both his understanding of war and his fiancé – Daisy Robinson's – feelings for him. William returns home injured to die at Downton where the cook's nephew, similar to the son at the centre of narrative in *The Village*, are the ultimate victims – shot at dawn.

The Tommy as victim

In the first few months of the First World War centenary commemorations, there were echoes of *Downton's Abbey's* portrayal of British Tommies as victims. In the popular imagination, the young men who participated in the First World War, so often symbolized by names on war memorials and Commonwealth War Grave Cemeteries, are innocent victims. There is an assumption that the majority of soldiers, like Baldric in the sitcom *Blackadder* (Season 4 Episode 6 aired 11/2/89) spent the war in trenches before meeting an untimely death on the Western Front. Arguably they are portrayed as victims, not so much of the opposing forces, but of incompetent generals and politicians motivated by self-interest who sent them over the top to their death. Approximately one in nine First World War soldiers did not return home at the end of the conflict, yet pathos surrounds the myth of a lost generation. There is purity in focusing only on those who have died, in presenting them as innocent victims of propaganda, naivety and patriotism.

This version of the British Tommy denies them any complicity or responsibility for their actions during war or in the period that followed, denies them agency, or any part in making their own histories. An entry on the *Guardian* blog in 2013 conveys this version of the past:

> My uncle and many of my relatives died in that war and they weren't officers or NCOs; they were simple Tommies. They were like the hundreds of thousands of other boys who were sent to their slaughter by a government that didn't care to represent their citizens if they were working poor and under-educated. My family members took the king's shilling because they had little choice, whereas many others from similar economic backgrounds were strong-armed into enlisting by war propaganda or press-ganged into military service by their employers.

This quote, which is representative of many others and familiar cultural tropes and prosthetic memories of the First World War, also demonstrates the role of war narratives in giving voice to a language of class exploitation and antagonism; arguably this could be used to belittle contemporary class frictions. However, given the slippage in popular consciousness between the Tommy of the First World War and contemporary conflicts, it may be more complex. Histories of World War I are one of the few spaces within the neo-liberal agenda of contemporary culture in which language of class may be articulated. This perhaps goes some way to explaining the enduring appeal of World War I in contemporary culture, which may provide narratives through which people make sense of their lives. Perhaps most significantly they are a reminder of the vulnerability of ordinary people in austerity Britain.

The World War I trope that most strongly articulates class oppression involves the 306 members of the British armed forces who were *shot at dawn* as part of the processes of military discipline. Alan Bleasdale's radical drama *The Monocled Mutineer* (1986) was one of the first popular portrayals of the practice and one of the few to convey the victim as someone with a middle-class background. The subsequent public campaign led to the soldiers being granted a pardon in 2007. The Shot at Dawn Memorial erected at the National Memorial Arboretum in 2000 and media representations have laid emphasis on many of the victims' youth and their working class status. A present-centred approach to these men sees them as victims of a modern phenomenon of post-traumatic stress (McCartney, 2014: 310) rather than World War I–specific shell shock or indeed the harsh disciplinary systems and approaches to criminality in the era. Helen McCartney's (2014: 314) argument highlights this phenomenon suggesting that this campaign and

> the growth of the family history industry, the public interest in psychological reactions to war, and the recent experience of British involvement in the Iraq and Afghanistan conflicts have all helped to reinforce the dominant image of the victimized soldier of the First World War.

However, even this version of soldier as a victim is a selective memory; World War I veterans, whose emotional and physical injuries rendered them susceptible to the appeal of alcohol and who subjected their families to physical violence, have all too often been airbrushed from history. Calder (2012: 4) suggests that the construction and reconstruction and perpetration of myth involve purifying narratives, simplifying and in time the imposition of a cohesion that may be unrecognizable to historians. An interesting challenge to this has been the BBC drama series *Peaky Blinders* (2013–), which has portrayed World War I veterans as frequently violent and users of drink and drugs.

McCartney (2014: 313) points out that 'the current widespread acceptance, indeed expectation, that soldiers will be psychologically damaged by war experience has pervaded the debate, shaping both its character and, in the process, the broader image of the soldier'. With the public discomfort and criticism of wars in Afghanistan and Iraq, there has been a merging in the popular consciousness between these current conflicts and WWI; both arguably seen as situations where ordinary soldiers' lives are lost as a result of questionable political decisions. It is now a 'common sense' perception that all past and present soldiers are victims of emotional trauma and in need of support. When BBC *West Midlands* covered the installation of ice statues for each man who died in the conflict on the steps of Chamberlain Square in Birmingham, they began with a Birmingham captain in the Worcestershires with shell shock who took his own life in 1922. The 'voice of God' narrator explained it thus: 'a monument to the common man no less a hero' (BBC, July 30, 2014). In a similar vein, television programmes such as *Extreme Makeover* have chosen veterans as the working class heroes deserving community and charities' support, and a number of house builders, such as Barratt and Taylor Wimpey, give discounts to the armed forces purchasing new homes.

All soldiers in World War I and since are now seen as deserving recipients of both charity and welfare. For the first time, in May 2011, a government document titled 'Today and Tomorrow' articulated in writing a national commitment to those serving in the armed forces (Ministry of Defence). The following year, Chancellor George Osborne donated £35 million from fines levied on banks that had manipulated the LIBOR rate to the MOD to support this; it was a popular political move. In the present climate of austerity, mental health services have been experiencing government spending cuts, and many patients have suffered as a result of inadequate care. Yet the charity Help for Heroes received £2.7 million to support their £7.5 million–pound 'Hidden Wounds' programme for 'veterans and their families suffering from the early symptoms of potentially more serious mental injuries'. The Tommy who survives now has the victim status of those soldiers who lie in Commonwealth War Graves First World War Cemeteries and whose names are inscribed on war memorials.

All Tommies are heroes

In the complex interweaving of past and present that constitutes the construction of historical narratives in the centenary of the First World War combatants, particularly Tommies, of that war and more contemporary conflicts are also seen not merely as victims but, as Woodward *et al.*, (2009: 214) suggests, as 'vulnerable heroes'. The *hero-fication* of military personnel would not, however, have been possible without the Northern Ireland Good Friday Agreement (1998), and it still remains a geographically specific phenomenon. The Bloody Sunday inquiry conducted by Lord Saville (2013) did little to assuage the antagonism of many in Northern Ireland towards British troops, but there are no longer images of British troops in action on British soil being seen on the evening news. Furthermore, for many the personalization and domestication of remembrance culture that developed at the turn of the millennium has enabled people to distance their support for military personnel from support for the government decision to send troops to participate in unpopular conflicts, including the Iraq War.

This shift in perceptions of the military can be attributed to being both part of a particular cultural milieu and a consequence of deliberate interventions by government, charities, the media and the military themselves. Kelly (2013: 728; BBC, 2007) notes the following: 'In September 2007 the British army chief, General Dannatt, called for greater public support of "the troops"'. Soon after, a multi-agency campaign of the newly created 'support the troops' initiatives emerged. Official events included homecoming parades and an annual Armed Forces Day (Kelly 2013: Ibid.). The British Legion was responsible for what has been described as the 'Wotton Bassett phenomenon' which both 'opened spaces for critical reflection on UK foreign policy' and was 'part of a trend of the rehabilitation of the military' (Jenkins *et al.*, 2012: 358).

The most important intervention in changing public perception was perhaps the formation in October 2007 of the charity Help for Heroes, the brainchild of the media-savvy cartoonist and ex-member of the Royal Green Jackets Brynn Parry and his wife, Emma Parry. Its stated aim is 'to support veterans and serving personnel, wounded or injured by war'. It restricts itself to providing support and rehabilitation facilities for British servicemen and women who have been wounded since September 11, 2001. Strong celebrity endorsement, high-profile fundraising events and widespread support from the media, including *The Sun* newspaper, have enabled this organization's support to grow, particularly amongst the young who enthusiastically purchased the *X Factor 2008* and *2010* release, a 'song for heroes', which also raised funds for the charity. Alternatively beleaguered Labour leader Ed Miliband's reticence to support the *The Sun's* Help for Heroes campaign provided an excuse for further vilification (*The Guardian*, 2014).

Kelly (2013: 728) points out that Chomsky has drawn attention to the power of slogans like 'support our troops' and 'help our heroes' in that by camouflaging the ideological premises upon which they rest they are difficult to oppose. Indeed the process of both simultaneously being strongly political in supporting military solutions to diplomatic disputes and denying this political significance in this approach is best exemplified by the supposedly non-political members of the Royal Family supporting and of course serving in the military. Prince Charles, for instance, gave an extended BBC primetime interview on the 'tough and testing duties' of serving UK soldiers (BBC1, 2008) and the Queen's 2009 Christmas message focused on supporting the military (Kelly, 2013: 728). Prince Harry's subsequent role in *Walking with the Wounded* to the South Pole (2013) and organizing the Invictus Games that took place for the first time in September 2014 further contributed to aligning public consciousness to the icon of 'the soldier hero'.

The Invictus Games, international Paralympic-style multi-sporting event for wounded soldiers, alongside the language and imagery used by Help for Heroes, unsettles and dislodges the centrality of discourses of soldiers as victims and contributes to shifting the status of all military so that they are now all seen as heroes. Indeed Kelly (2013: 730) has pointed to the role played by a number of sports in the *hero-fication* of the military. For example English and Scottish Premier League football clubs were 'asked to display a specially embroidered Earl Haig poppy on club shirts' over the remembrance weekend in 2008, 2009 and 2010, and in December 2011 'The Heroes Rugby Challenge' at Twickenham raised funds for Help for Heroes. Many argue that these cultural shifts are part of 'processes that present militarism as necessary and natural extensions of nation-states' civil society' (Ibid.: 732). Arguably this ignores the complexity of the phenomenon and the way in which some sectors of society have actively taken up such discourses and others have rejected them. As Kelly points out, Celtic football fans were less than enamoured by the militarist iconography and discourse.

The coupling of sport and remembrance sits comfortably with the role both now play in providing a space that at times couple nationalism with a traditional possibly redundant version of masculinity. Both sport and the military masculinity reinforce a version of masculinity premised upon physical prowess. The most popular British sporting events and teams in football, cricket and rugby involve men only, despite the success of British women rowers, cyclists, boxers and football players in the Olympics of 2012 who extended gendered associations of sport. Front-line combatant soldiering role – the archetypal Tommy – has remained the prerogative of men in Britain, something that has been reviewed recently and is planned to change. It is no coincidence then that on the back of this cultural preoccupation with commemoration and remembrance, the British Tommy has simultaneously gained almost iconic status and, as stated above, taken over from the miner as the working class hero. Mining has been since 1842 restricted by law to men, the job being linked to physical strength, danger and bravery. In the twentieth century, the miners were in the forefront of economic crisis. In the General Strike in 1926 and inter-war depression of the 1920s and 1930s and the mass unemployment of the Thatcherite era, miners were seen by many as an emblem of working class struggle against capitalism. In the twenty-first century in Britain the mining industry lies decimated. The Tommy, like the miner, can be seen to stoically do the nation's dirty work – a traditional, physical and honest version of masculinity. They can be juxtapositioned against the bankers and hedge fund managers and the London elite, who are often perceived as responsible for and untouched by the current austerity measures.

Unlike the miner, the Tommy appeals across social classes, operating as a unifying icon rather than a socially divisive symbol with specific regional or class associations.

The Tommy has had an increasingly glamorized and heroic place in popular television programmes; the actor Ross Kemp's character, Grant Mitchell, was a Falkland's veteran who suffered from post-traumatic stress in *East Enders* (BBC, 1990–99). Kemp followed up his starring role, in what was once the country's most popular soap opera, with his series of documentaries *Ross Kemp in Afghanistan* (2008). More recently, the Channel 4 documentary series *Royal Marines Commandos School* (2014) focussed on the tough regime of the commandoes training school and affirmed a discursive slippage, which now seems to define all soldiers as heroes. It is no longer individual acts that are seen as heroic but the very act of joining the military and getting through the training. This shift both negates the heroism of everyday life, of fire fighters, policeman and individuals in unexpected circumstances and also suggests the actions of the military are beyond criticism. This valorising and heroic representation of those in the armed forces has shaped the commemoration of the World War I centenary. The BBC series *Our World War* (2014) portrayed the heroic exploits of Tommies in the Manchester Pals and tank regiment, as well as members of the British Expeditionary force who faced heavy casualties during the first days of the war.

Media texts play a constitutive role in the Tommy being seen as heroic, but they do not work in isolation; they are part of wider cultural shifts around class and of stretching and shifting values. The idea of the heroic Tommy is not merely the construction of dominant groups in society, but operating in the overlap between the values of different social groups, it becomes malleable. In working practices and discursive construction, the heroic fireman or the miner is far more difficult for the twenty-first century dominance groups to incorporate, to stretch for their own political ends. Thus, the government's participation in World War I commemoration has involved the funding of children from every secondary school to visit the Western Front battlefields and encouraging the allocation of funding to World War I engagement. Another initiative is the laying of commemorative paving stones in the birthplaces of World War I Victoria Cross recipients across the UK. The contemporary slippage between participation in the armed forces and being a hero is also retrospectively applied. All World War I soldiers have been reframed to be heroes, thus the *Daily Express's* (2014) headline 'Revealed: Unusual and fascinating mementoes treasured by families of WW1 heroes' explained that the 'Diary of First World War hero to be blogged 100 years after each day's entry was written'. His heroic status rested upon his inclusion in voluntary enlistment and participation in the conflict alone as it was explained:

> Private Arthur Linfoot volunteered for the Royal Army Medical Corps when he was 25 in 1915 and kept a diary of his experiences in the trenches of France. Before enlisting in the war he worked as a clerk at a paperworks in Hendon from 1914 and returned to work in the capital after the war finished.

In volunteering for the Royal Army Medical Corps, Linfoot was a model hero for the contemporary culture: brave, facing danger but saving lives rather than killing. Arguably all icons are, like the Tommy, polysemic, but the Tommy is particularly problematic being at the same time a military person and the domesticated everyday boy-next-door hero who through naïvety, idealism, ignorance, financial hardship and a romanticized view of the heroic Tommy becomes a soldier. Popular soap operas reinforce this trope by often portraying the young men who join the army, for example Gary in *Coronation Street* (2010–12) and Shaun in *Emmerdale* (2011–14), as having limited job opportunities in an age of austerity.

Structuring absences and the Christmas Truce

The twin overlapping discourses of Tommy as victim and Tommy as hero could be seen to 'strip the military's "work" of its realities, which include substantial civilian deaths' (Kelly, 2013: 734). Those who join the armed forces are trained to kill and actively do so, something that could compromise their victim status, especially if they have volunteered instead of having been conscripted to fight. In the introduction to her book, Joanna Bourke (2014) points out:

> During the commemorations around the centenary of the First World War, history books, television and radio programmes, newspapers and museums showcased grandfathers, great uncles and other 'ordinary people' who were physically or psychologically wounded during that war. We heard a great deal about suffering, but what about those British and American soldiers, airmen and sailors who bayoneted, bombed and torpedoed other women's sons? Were they not our grandfathers or great-uncles too?

Support for the Tommy, the wounded hero or the bereaved family rests upon a sense of distance being created between the soldiers and the actual business of war. Indeed an audience watching the popular *Sun* Military Awards could surmise that the military were not merely worthy recipients of charitable giving but rather charitable and humanitarian workers first and foremost. Subtitled *A Night of Heroes*, the event garners support from a range of celebrities including David Beckham, Simon Cowell, Rod Stewart, Cheryl Fernandez-Versini and Katherine Jenkins in 2014 and in the introduction described as a night 'dedicated to the thousands of men and women who devote their lives to serving our country' and in the montage of images that the event begun with, merged action in contemporary conflicts with the images of the First World War, Commonwealth War Graveyards, the army's role in assisting the victims of the floods in Britain, and the Navy undertaking humanitarian missions.

Distancing support from the Tommies from their role in combat is necessary, indicated perhaps by the Royal British Legion (RBL) panicking at the popularity of the Help for Heroes charity adoption of the slogan 'Standing Shoulder to Shoulder with those in the armed forces' which caused friction with some supporters. They had misjudged the popular mood and perhaps forgotten that: 'it was rare for memorials to show British soldiers in aggressive poses, clearly eager and ready to slaughter their foe' (Bourke, 2004: 280). When war veteran Harry Leslie Smith, along with a number of people, announced he would not wear a poppy again in 2013, objecting to his remembrance of those he had served with and seen killed, being co-opted, 'to justify our folly in Iraq, our morally dubious war against terror' (*The Guardian*, 2013), RBL then abandoned the slogan in 2014 and in December captured the mood of the moment much more accurately as it aligned with the supermarket Sainsbury's feature advert on the Christmas Truce of 1914.

The Christmas Truce is a popular narrative trope of the First World War; the idea that British and German soldiers laid down their arms, sung Christmas carols, exchanged gifts and played football has featured strongly in 2014 World War I commemorations, including BBC's *World War One at Home* road show, websites, a number of carol services, the Queen's Christmas message and a range of materials produced by the Football Association and used in schools: the idea of the Christmas Truce struck a chord. The narrative suggests the ordinary British Tommy does not really want to kill, that he was not aggressive and was involved in warfare only as a result of the actions of politicians and generals. It is a perspective that I have heard articulated by speakers at Western Front Association events, alongside the idea that British snipers were unpopular with their own side as well as the enemy.

For Sainsbury's, who is steadily losing its market share to cut-price stores owned by European companies, such as Aldi and Lidl, the three-minute long expensive advert was a desperate attempt to jump on the World War I bandwagon and associate its stores with quality, heritage and Britishness. It portrayed young British and German soldiers climbing out of their trenches to exchange gifts and play football on Christmas Day. The public response was varied: some saw it as blatant commercialization, cynical appropriation of a war which has an almost sacred status in British culture. There were 240 complaints to the Advertising Industry watchdog within two days. Although the heritage chocolate bars featured in the advert sold well, it commercially proved an unsuccessful gamble as Sainsbury's market share continued to drop, 3 per cent in the six weeks up to Christmas.

Conclusion

The public obsession with remembrance is not a consequence of the current age of austerity; as has been argued, it has an established place in British culture that has accelerated in the multichannel media–saturated world of the latter twentieth century. The obsession with war and remembrance also rests upon other complex factors, including the space they create for acceptable expressions of national identity, masculine emotions and class frictions in contemporary culture. But practices and meanings of remembrance and the cultural memories of war are contested, slipping and sliding so that people trying to make sense of their lives can use them. Austerity has however exaggerated an already existing trend towards the iconic centrality of the Tommy in British culture, the victim and the hero who can appeal across previously identifiable political and social boundaries whilst valorising physical masculinity at a time when it is increasingly sidelined in the workplace. Perhaps most significantly, the Tommy and war are reminders of the limited control that ordinary people have over their lives and their vulnerability in austerity Britain.

Bibliography

Andrews, M. (2012). 'Mediating Remembrance: personalization and celebrity in television remembrance'. *Journal of War and Culture Studies*, 4(3): 357–70.

Andrews, M. (2014a). 'Contemporary images and ideas of the Home Front'. In: M. Andrews and J. Lomas, eds., *The Home Front: Images, Myths and Forgotten Experiences*. Basingstoke: Palgrave Macmillan.

Andrews, M. (2014b). 'Potential Cosmopolitan Sensibilities in Feminised and Mediated Remembrance'. In: Y. Aybige, T. Ruxandra and M. Aris, eds., *Media and Cosmopolitanism*. New York: Peter Lang, 51–70.

Atheron, I. and Morgan, P. (2012). 'The battlefield War Memorial: Commemoration and the battlefield site from the Middle Ages to the Modern Era'. *Journal of War and Culture Studies*, 4(3): 289–304.

Bagot-Jewitt, C. (2012). 'Unpicking Some Threads of Remembrance'. In: M. Andrews, N. Hunt and C. Bagot-Jewitt, eds., *Lest We Forget? Cultures of Remembrance*. Stroud: The History Press.

Bourdieu, P. (1984). *Distinction: a social critique of the judgement of taste*. New York: Harvard University Press.

Bourke, J. (2004). 'Introduction to Special Issue Collective Memory: "Remembering War"'. *Journal of Contemporary History*, 39(4): 473–85.

Bourke, J. (2014). 'Introduction' to *Wounding the World: How Military Violence and War-Play Invade Our Lives*. London: Virago. Available at: http://www.virago.co.uk/read-introduction-wounding-world-joanna-bourke/.

Calder, A. (2012). *The myth of the blitz*. London: Random House.

Daily Express (2014). 'Diary of First World War hero to be blogged 100 years after each day's entry was written'. Available at: http://www.express.co.uk/news/world-war-I/452952/Diary-of-First-World-War-hero-to-be-blogged-every-day-100-years-after-entries-were-written.

Durkheim, E. (1912, reprinted 2008). *The elementary forms*. Oxford: Oxford Paperbacks.

Grant, S. (2012). 'Constructing a Commemorative Culture: American veterans and the memorialization from Valley Forget to Vietnam'. *Journal of War and Culture Studies*, 4(3): 305–22.

Helias, Y. (1977). *Les Monuments aux Morts*. Rennes: Mémoire pour la diplôme d'etudes approfondies d'etudes politiques.

Help for Heroes. 'Hidden Wounds'. Available at: http://www.helpforheroes.org.uk/get-support/hidden-wounds/.

Help for Heroes. Homepage. Available at: http://www.helpforheroes.org.uk/how-we-help/about-us/faqs/.

Huffington Post (2011). 'More than 170 "English Defence League" Supporters Arrested on Remembrance Day'. Available at: http://www.huffingtonpost.co.uk/2011/11/11/english-defence-league-whitehall_n_1088155.html.

Jenkins, K.N., Megoran, N., Woodward, R. and Bos, D. (2012). 'Wootton Bassett and the political spaces of remembrance and mourning'. *Area*, September 2012, 44(3): 356–63.

Kelly, J. (2013). 'Popular culture, sport and the "hero-fication" of British militarism'. *Sociology*, 47(4): 722–38.

Landsberg, A. (2003). 'Prosthetic memory: The ethics and politics of memory in an age of mass culture'. In: P. Grainge, ed., *Memory and Popular Film*. Manchester: Manchester University Press, 144–61.

Marx, M. (1852). 'The eighteenth Brumaire of Louis Bonaparte'. *Die Revolution Magazine*.

McCartney, H.B. (2014). 'The First World War soldier and his contemporary image in Britain'. *International Affairs*, 90(2): 299–315.

McKernan, L. (2009). Topical film company (BFIwebsite). Available at: http://www.scree-nonline.org.uk/filmlid/669796lindex.html [Accessed July 20, 2011].

Ministry of Defence (2011). 'The armed forces covenant: today and tomorrow'. Available at: https://www.gov.uk/government/uploads/system/uploads/attachment_data/file/49470/the_armed_forces_covenant_today_and_tomorrow.pdf.

Nava, M. (2007). *Visceral cosmopolitanism: gender, culture and the normalisation of difference*. London: Bloomsbury.

Noakes, L. (1998). *War and the British: gender, memory and national identity*, London: I.B. Taurus.

Samuel, R. (1996). *Theatres of memory: past and present in contemporary culture*. Cambridge: Verso.

Sheridan, D. (2010). 'The Second World War Industry: Wartime Mass Observation and how we understand it today'. WHN Women, War and Remembrance Conference at the National Memorial Arboretum, 13 March 2010.

Sinfield, A. (2011). *Literature, politics and culture in postwar Britain*. London: Continuum.

The Guardian (2013). 'This year, I will wear a poppy for the last time'. Available at: https://www.theguardian.com/commentisfree/2013/nov/08/poppy-last-time-remembrance-harry-leslie-smith.

The Guardian (2014). 'Sun mocks Miliband for turning down Help for Heroes photo op'. Available at: http://www.theguardian.com/politics/2014/sep/25/sun-ed-miliband-help-for-heroes.

The Sun (2011). 'Pink Floyd Gilmour's LSD-crazed son Charlie is given 16 months'. Available at: https://www.thesun.co.uk/archives/news/667635/pink-floyd-gilmours-lsd-crazed-son-charlie-is-given-16-months/.

The Telegraph (2010). 'Tuition fees riots: Pink Floyd's star's son could be prosecuted over attack on Cenotaph'. Available at: http://www.telegraph.co.uk/education/educationnews/8195146/Tuition-fees-riots-Pink-Floyd-stars-son-could-be-prosecuted-over-attack-on-Cenotaph.html.

Thomas, J. introduced by Sheridan, D. (2010). 'Beneath the mourning veil: mass observation & the death of Diana'. In *Of Remembrance*. Stroud: The History Press.

Wheeler, W. (1994). 'Nostalgia Isn't Nasty: the Postmodernising of Parliamentary Democracy'. In: M. Perryman, ed., *Altered States: Postmodern Politics and Culture*. London: Lawrence Wishart.

Williams, R. (1966). *The long revolution*. Harmondsworth: Pelican Books.

Winter, J. (1995). *Sites of memory, sites of mourning: the Great War in European cultural history*. Cambridge: Cambridge University Press.

Winter, J. (2006). *Remembering war*. New Haven and London: Yale University Press.

Woodward, R., Winter, T. and Jenkins, K.N. (2009). 'Heroic anxieties: the figure of the British soldier in contemporary print media'. *Journal of War and Culture Studies*, 2(2): 211–23.

4 'We have to keep going, whatever happens'

The austerity narratives of *Girls*, *Breaking Bad* and *Downton Abbey*

Sallie McNamara

'We have to keep going, whatever happens. We have to help each other keep going'. (2:4). The earl of Grantham makes this statement in *Downton Abbey* to those on the Home Front during World War I. Grantham's rallying cry, uttered at a time of crisis, carries a notion of stoic resilience presumably deemed necessary to deal with the specific conditions being experienced. It is also a statement that seems equally appropriate when considering the fallout of the economic crisis of 2008, a comment to be addressed to or possibly uttered by those who lost their jobs, their homes, and their livelihoods. While it might not always be welcomed when trying to deal with and find a way through changing and difficult circumstances, how different individuals cope with adversity is one issue shared by the three television drama series that are the focus of this chapter: *Girls* (2012–), *Breaking Bad* (2008–13) and *Downton Abbey* (2010–15). They were broadcast in the period from 2008 to the present, thus coinciding with the crash and its aftermath, and were – indeed still are – extremely popular award-winning programmes, striking a chord with audiences and critics alike. In terms of prizes, *Downton Abbey*'s include Primetime Emmy, Golden Globe, BAFTA, and Screen Actors Guild awards for the series, the cast and production team (both individual and collective). Awards for *Girls* include Writers Guild of America, Golden Globe, Primetime Emmy award, BAFTA, Directors Guild of America, while *Breaking Bad*'s include Golden Globe, Emmy, and Primetime Emmy Best Actor awards for Bryan Cranston as the antihero, Walter White. Their success is such that at the time of writing, a sixth series of *Girls* is being filmed, *Breaking Bad* is still available to view online, while *Downton Abbey* concluded its stately progress through the early twentieth century with six series. Through discussions on social media, fan sites, and via the Twitter hashtag, they also continue to have a 'life' outside of broadcast television.

This chapter will examine these three popular television serial dramas to consider how they disseminate ideas relating to the financial crisis, to suggest they can be seen as 'austerity narratives', and that they all raise issues concerning economic insecurity. First, though, the differences between them are important to note. *Downton Abbey* is a period drama set in Britain in the early twentieth century, while both *Breaking Bad* and *Girls* are contemporary set in the US, the former in Albuquerque, New Mexico, and the latter in New York City, New York. However, popular culture has the ability to engage audiences in different ways, sometimes by commenting directly on their experiences, sometimes in providing escape (and the notion of 'escape' itself is a political commentary on the prevailing situation), but crucially by always linking to the contemporary *zeitgeist*: in this respect, and as Glen Creeber (2004: 15) comments, the television serial 'may actually better reflect, engage with and respond to the subtle nuances, political preoccupations and social realities of the contemporary age'. This engagement is evident in the three drama series as they articulate concerns relating to economic circumstances as well as issues of identity, gender and sexuality. Further, as Stuart Hall (1981: 233) argues, popular culture is a sort of battlefield, the ground on which transformations are worked (Ibid.: 228). It is, Hall argued, a site of contestation, people are not cultural dupes, and the cultural industries do not work on us as if we were blank screens, rather,

> there is a continuous and necessarily uneven and unequal struggle, by the dominant culture, constantly to disorganise and reorganise popular culture; to enclose and confine its definitions and forms within a more inclusive range of dominant forms. There are points of resistance, there are also moments of supersession (Ibid.: 233).

In this sense then, these different narratives can offer both conformity and challenge to the status quo, and their popularity is testament to their ability to engage with audiences in different ways and on many levels. This chapter will offer readings that show links to contemporary concerns, set in the context of a financial collapse which Ben Bernanke, Chairman of the US Federal Reserve (and former Princeton professor), has described as 'worse than the Great Depression' (Worstall, 2014).

The discussion of *Downton Abbey* will look to find the present in the past and the past in the present and will focus on the first three series (2010–12) to consider issues of power, suggesting it presents a view of a society where, through the creation of a power-sharing coalition, any real political dissent is reincorporated and hegemony maintained. Both *Breaking Bad* and *Girls* address contemporary issues, such as the cost of healthcare, employment and unemployment, concerns clearly relevant to a global audience. This chapter will examine Series 1 and 2 of *Girls* (2012–13), and focusing on its New York City setting, it will be argued that *Girls* unpacks the 'success myth' that characterized series such as *Sex and the City* to show young women struggling to conform to the expectations of late modernity – that is, to be successful. Ideas of success also inform *Breaking Bad*; here, the focus is on the family and the masculine identity of the father figure. It will be suggested that the series shows a shift from a marginal to hegemonic masculinity as the way to achieve material success but crucially in the alternative, not mainstream, economy. Reference will be made to the entire series (2008–13).

Girls: I'm scared all the time

> Hannah Horvath: 'All I want is $1,100 a month for the next two years [to finish my book]'.

Written by and starring Lena Dunham, also executive producer and director, *Girls* was first broadcast in the US in April 2012. To date, there have been five series, with a sixth having been commissioned. It focuses on four white middle-class young women living and working in New York City: Hannah Horvath, Marnie Michaels, Jessa Johansson and Shoshanna Shapiro. Male characters include aspiring actor/artist Adam Sackler (Hannah's on/off boyfriend), Ray Ploshansky who runs Grumpy's coffee shop and dates Shoshanna, and computer app designer Charlie Dattolo, Marnie's on/off boyfriend. HBO describes it as 'a comic look at the assorted humiliations and rare triumphs of a group of girls in their mid-20s'.[1] While it is hard to deny the humour, painful as it sometimes is, it also has pathos and a sense of struggle as these young women deal with relationships, employment, depression, financial problems, addiction, and life in twenty-first-century urban America. In terms of themes, and, of course, setting, it can invoke some comparison with two other very popular and recent series which also feature this age group: *Friends* (NBC, September 1994–May 2004) and *Sex and the City* (*SATC*) (HBO, 1998–2004). The exterior shot of Adam Sackler's apartment block is one obvious link as it is reminiscent of Monica's apartment in *Friends*. References to *SATC* are made explicit in the first episode, as Shoshanna's apartment has a poster from the first *SATC* film (2008). She discusses the *SATC* characters with Jessa and thinks she's 'Carrie at heart, but

Samantha comes out' and she's 'Miranda at work' (1:1), although Shoshanna, a virgin at this time, is some distance from the sexually experienced and successful *SATC* women. Clearly concerns regarding identity, gender and sexuality are also indicated here.

The contrasts between the series are important to note and speak of the changing context for employment and economic issues. Both *Friends* and *SATC* are closer to the genre of romantic sitcom but raised similar concerns to those of *Girls*: employment, relationships and finances, for example, as well as serious illness (Samantha's breast cancer in *SATC*). However, whatever hardships are experienced, overall there is a sense of optimism and lightness in the earlier two series shown by the different aesthetic styles and the storylines, indicative of the different context of production. *SATC* has a glossy and expensive 'filmic' *mise en scène* together with an air of affluence (Creeber, 2004: 145), while the bright sets and the comedy of *Friends* sets it apart. These aspects are not apparent in the much darker *Girls* with its more indie realist aesthetic. The characters share shabby apartments; their clothes are functional rather than designer. Hannah's financial problems are not resolved by another character donating her Tiffany engagement ring in the way Charlotte York helps Carrie Bradshaw (*SATC* 'Ring a Ding Ding', 4:16). When Marnie and Hannah argue, it transpires Marnie has been supporting Hannah by paying the rent on their shared apartment, similar to Chandler Bing's support for Joey Tribbiani in *Friends*. However, Marnie's largess does not continue as they argue and she leaves, Hannah thus becoming responsible for the rent, and her own finances (1:10). Hannah is a struggling writer and, like Carrie Bradshaw, works in her apartment on her Apple laptop. The similarities end here, though, as Hannah's apartment is untidy, she is not well groomed, her clothes and underwear are not stylish or designer, and in Series 2 she suffers a breakdown and has writer's block.

Employment and/or unemployment are clearly crucial at any time, but this comes more into focus in a time of austerity. This is a key theme *Girls* explores when a link between graduate employment and contemporary economic problems is made explicit in the opening scene of the first episode. It starts by referring to the status of the intern, and the discussion is perhaps one familiar to many young people as the unpaid intern is now an established fact of working life for many undergraduates and graduates. Undergraduates undertake not only the long-term graduate internship but also in the UK what is sometimes euphemistically called 'work experience'. This work, which lasts one or two weeks, is generally in the culture industries, primarily journalism, along with politics and law, is encouraged by universities and sought by thousands of students hoping to get into these occupations.[2] Effectively, however, it provides many employers with free workers and, when undertaken by undergraduates, is the unpaid internship broken down into fifty-two weeks. In *Girls* Hannah has been an unpaid intern with a publisher for over a year but receives financial support from her parents. They have decided to withdraw their assistance because they want to enjoy their money and Hannah to find paid employment, commenting: 'You have an internship you say is going to turn into a job'. Hannah: 'I don't know when' (1:1), and, 'Do you know how crazy the economy is at the moment? All my friends get help from their parents' (1:1). Hannah's parents may be, as they put it, 'only college professors' (1:1), but clearly this unpaid internship and financial support is something only available to the more privileged. What the episode also hints at are the numbers seeking work as Hannah's employer refers to the economy and indicates he will have no problems finding another graduate intern as he receives 'fifty applications per day' (1:1). The high cost of education is also emphasized as Roy Ploshansky says he went to college and left $50,000 in debt with student loans (1:1).

Anita Harris (2004: 7) comments on the standing of young women in the new class/gender structure of late modernity, particularly for the middle classes: 'Whereas once a comfortable middle-class position was attained or sustained through marriage, today this process is much less assured'. These young women have to become successful, to earn their own income, which means doing well academically and professionally (Ibid.). Both Hannah and Marnie have degrees, English and art history respectively; however, employment is not assured, and both receive financial support from parents (Marnie's pay for half of her Blackberry [1:4]). Adam Sackler also receives help, though he says, somewhat ironically, he 'wouldn't take shit' from his parents, 'But my grandmother gives me $800 a month. It gives me the freedom not to be anyone's slave. You should never be anyone's fucking slave' (1:1).

For all the unreality of actually being able to live in New York City while working as an intern (Hannah), low-paid gallery assistant (Marnie), or nanny (Jessa), the setting is, of course, connotative of glamour and excitement and for many a destination for consumer spending. Steven Miles (2010: 7) argues the post-industrial city is defined by consumption; it is 'no longer simply an expression of who or what we are, but no more or less than a venue for consumption experiences; experiences that tie us to the capitalist priorities that underpin our social norms'. These comments are appropriate when looking at the women in *SATC* who are defined by their conspicuous consumption (see '*Flânerie, Sex and the City* and Touring around Manhattan', a list of the locations under 'Restaurants, Bars and Nightclubs and Stores, Shopping and Around Town' includes upmarket galleries and designer shops [Akass and McCabe, 2004: 219–27]). However, this is not the case in *Girls*.

While the characters visit bars and cafes and go to parties and gallery viewings, the overall experience is more negative, one of urban alienation, not the pleasures associated with consumption; the city as a consumer destination is not apparent. For example, although Hannah has friends, she remains isolated in her apartment during her breakdown when she does not answer her phone; her friends cannot help her with her anxiety. She says: 'I'm scared all the time' (2:1). This is not a confident young woman, but one with a sense of self-loathing, as she comments: 'No one could hate me as much as I hate myself' (1:9). When she meets the much older Joshua, spending a brief time in his luxurious townhouse with its modern interiors, it suggests an escape from her daily life and momentarily turns into a female romance fantasy. However, she cries to him: 'I wanna be happy', 'something's broken inside of me' and realized she was 'lonely in such a deep, deep way' (2:5). Later to Adam she says, 'I feel like I'm unravelling, Adam, and I'm really, really scared' (2:10). The clever use of Daniel Johnston's 'Life in Vain' as the soundtrack in the closing credits (2:9) contributes to this overall sense of contemporary urban alienation, and this alienation and emptiness are not solely confined to the female characters. An interesting view of Manhattan is shown from Ray's perspective while on a trip to Staten Island to return a dog taken by Adam. He looks across at the New York City skyline at dusk, shown without the lights that add to its mystery and glamour. He says sadly to the dog: 'You think I'm a kike? I'm not even that. I'm nothing' (2:6). The unlit city looks grey and perhaps reflects his sense of self as well as the experiences of these young people.

The realist aesthetic of *Girls* thus does not dwell on the spectacle of the modern city but creates, rather, a sense of anonymity. One of the most popular features of *SATC* was its fashion, and the styling of the four women, particularly Carrie Bradshaw. It was frequently a feature in the fashion press and magazines, inspired fashion shoots, and linked fashion journalism and popular culture (König, 2004). The popularity and spectacular nature of the fashion in the series was such that Stella Bruzzi and Pamela Church Gibson examine its impact to refer to it as the fifth character (2004). The women themselves are spectacular and 'own' the city streets; they are easily the focus. This is certainly not the case in *Girls* where the costume and styling create an idea of character but do not make them stand out. It is, to use the term coined by K-Hole, a New York trend-forecasting group, in October 2013, 'normcore'. Normcore is a combination of the words 'normal' and 'hard-core' and, as taken up by the fashion press, has been described as 'a bland anti-style' and is the idea of dressing in a conventional, unremarkable way (Farrell, 2014).[3] It is unbranded and anonymous: 'fashion insiders are rejecting the razzmatazz that has become a fashion norm and, instead, they're blending into the crowd' (Cochrane, 2014). While the comment suggests adopting 'normcore' is a choice, clearly in the economic climate inhabited by *Girls*, it is necessity. In the second decade of the new millennium, and in a time of austerity, there is none of the optimism or the bling associated with the first (Carrie Bradshaw's obsession with Manolo Blahnik shoes would cost easily upwards of £300 at today's prices). Normcore adds to anonymity and 'ordinariness', something emphasized at the end of the first episode as Hannah walks on the New York City streets, her normcore styling assisting this merging into the throng: she becomes part of the mass.

It is easy to criticise the programme for its self-obsessed characters, their perhaps unrealistic expectations, and wonder why Hannah does not find paid employment instead of relying on freelance writing or pleading with her parents for assistance. Interestingly, Hannah is also criticised by her friends for her self-absorption, but it is no less than that of the much-admired Carrie Bradshaw, with her sometimes simpering approach to the men in her life. The series does, however, capture a particular moment and shows the struggle to conform to the myth of success, noted by Harris above, and demythologises the idea that this is easily achieved. The 'success myth' is common and all-encompassing – witness the yearly UK media obsession with A Level and GCSE exam results where the message is clear: it is essential to do well. *SATC* was one series that perhaps helped feed this myth; the women *are* successful with well-established careers and incomes. Carrie Bradshaw turns her reflections and relationship ups and downs into paid features for the fictional *New York Star* while Charlotte York is a gallery director, a career followed by volunteer work when married with children. Both Hannah and Marnie in *Girls* share similar dreams of being a writer and art curator, respectively, but in this changed, more austere environment, success is not easily achieved. When trying to write about her sexual exploits, Hannah, as noted, suffers writer's block, a breakdown and the return of her obsessive-compulsive disorder. Marnie is fired from her low-paid gallery job, an action euphemistically described by her boss as being 'downsized' and by her mother as 're-transitioning' (2:1). She comments that there are 'no curatorial openings in the city' (2:3) and instead works as a PA for an artist, who sexually exploits her. In an interesting reflection on the contemporary job market, Shoshanna suggests that she capitalise on her attractiveness by commenting 'You could get a pretty person job ... like a hostess' (2:2), advice Marnie follows up. At the end of Series 2, Marnie decides that she loves her former boyfriend, Charlie, and it is interesting to speculate as to whether this coincides with his new-found financial success, owning his own media linked app-design company in stylish, trendy offices, which has just hit 20,000 MAUs (monthly average users) and is doing a 'lip-dub thing for YouTube' (2:8 and 2:9).

Anthony Giddens (1991: 81) argues that a preoccupation with the self is a characteristic of late modernity and that lifestyle choices are a crucial part of this. He states:

> Each of the small decisions a person makes every day – what to wear, what to eat, how to conduct himself [*sic*] at work, whom to meet with later in the evening – contributes to such routines. All such choices (as well as larger and more consequential ones) are decisions not only about how to act but how to be. The more post-traditional the settings in which an individual moves, the more lifestyle concerns the very core of self-identity, its making and remaking.

The linking of lifestyle and self-identity is important, and an interesting one to consider when looking at *Girls* and the context of a more austere environment. Glen Creeber's (2004: 122) discussion of the series *This Life* (1996–97) argues that this reveals young people dealing with a proliferation of choice where social taboos of the past, such as drugs, casual sex and relationship instability, have become an accepted part of everyday life. These are similarly featured in *Girls*, which includes Hannah's experimentation with cocaine as well as the characters' different sexual relationships (again with a very different focus to that in *SATC* with its discussion of female pleasure and fetishization of the slim, honed and fragmented body). They are also concerned with issues of self-identity and life in contemporary urban America. However, the question is whether the notion of 'choice' of lifestyle is appropriate in the second decade of the millennium, or is it expediency that drives them? At the end of Series 2, Hannah is incapable of doing anything and has a breakdown, while Adam (a man she has been rejecting) is a denim-wearing contemporary knight who races to her rescue; Marnie becomes engaged to Charlie; Jessa has disappeared (in Series 3 it transpires that she has been in rehab to deal with the return of her drug addiction); and Shoshanna dumps Ray because of his 'negativity' and lack of ambition for someone who presumably fulfils her criteria. Are these decisions reactions to circumstances, the result of necessity, rather than proactive choices? Zygmunt Bauman's argument, where he, as Angela McRobbie (2009: 18) puts it, 'bewails the sheer unviability of naked individualisation as the resources of sociality (and welfare) are stripped away, leaving the individual to self-blame when success eludes him or her' are perhaps applicable here.

Breaking Bad: I did it for me

> Skyler White: 'Where did that come from, and why was it so damn good?'
> Walter White: 'Because it was illegal' (1:7).

This conversation follows a bout of energetic sex in the back of Walt's car while parked in the grounds of the high school where he works, sex that follows Walt unobtrusively sexually stimulating his wife while they are in a PTA meeting listening to visitors from the DEA (Drug Enforcement Administration). One of the (disturbing?) pleasures of this series is watching the formerly law-abiding high-school chemistry teacher become the millionaire drug baron and charting the transformation of this unassuming man, who works part-time in a carwash to supplement his income, appearing passive when on the receiving end of mildly mocking comments from his alpha-male brother-in-law.

The serial-drama *Breaking Bad* was first broadcast in January 2008 on AMC for five seasons and ended in January 2013. It was never officially shown on British television but is included in the *Guinness World Records*, 2014 edition, as the 'highest rated TV series' (Janela, 2013). It follows an 'ordinary' white-collar worker living in Albuquerque, New Mexico, the American southwest, and covers his shift from hardworking teacher to drug manufacturer of blue crystal meth, becoming a multimillionaire *en route*. Walter (Walt) White is the impecunious chemistry teacher at J. P. Wynne High School who gets involved with former student Jesse Pinkman in the production of crystal meth, activities initially unknown to his wife, Skyler, pregnant with their second child, his seventeen-year-old son, Walt Jr. (also known as Flynn), and Skyler's sister and brother-in-law, Marie and Hank Schrader. Some of the tension in the series comes from Walt's relationship with Hank who works for the DEA and is actively involved in the hunt for Walt, a.k.a. 'Heisenberg', and Jesse who adopted the name from Werner Heisenberg, the German theoretical physicist, one of the creators of quantum mechanics. Walt's adoption of the name 'Heisenberg' is a joke known only to him and the viewers. The relationship and duel between Walt and Hank and their different caring but combative masculinities is crucial to this discussion of contemporary American society.

Its broadcast in 2008 was prior to Barack Obama's presidential campaign, and his inauguration in January 2009 as the first African American and forty-fourth president. Alongside other issues, Obama placed healthcare on his policy platform in 2008 and the subsequent Affordable Care Act (Obamacare) is an attempt to open up private medical insurance to those who were previously excluded (Taverner, 2014). As political writer Louise Taverner points out, the Republican 'authoritarian' model of citizenship ('pull yourself up by the bootstraps') discursively positions healthcare as a *privilege* to those who can afford it, thus not a human right (Ibid.; (my emphasis)). This issue is one that had been prevalent in American politics for some years, and Obama's solution is ironically a Republican idea that Mitt Romney implemented when governor of Massachusetts in 2006.

While *Breaking Bad* explores various themes, healthcare is central from the beginning. Walt is diagnosed with Stage IIIA lung cancer, the prognosis is not optimistic, and his treatment and problems with medical insurance, specifically the implications when it is unavailable, are made apparent. Its broadcast also prefaced the financial crash of 2008, and as this follows the business ventures of Walt and Jesse in the world of drug manufacture and dealing, money and power are clearly related themes. *Breaking Bad* placed the drug economy, which has always been the alternative economy for the disenfranchised (particularly the urban ethnic poor), as an entrepreneurial route to American prosperity (Taverner, 2014). As Brett Martin (2013: 272) comments, the series

> anticipated a national mood soon to be intensified by current events – in this case the great economic unsettlement of the late aughts, [*sic*][4] which would leave many previously secure middle-class Americans suddenly feeling like desperate outlaws in their own suburbs.

Continuing with the theme of healthcare, this is clearly linked both to the family's income and also to Walt's sense of his own masculinity, shown through his different relationships – with his family, with Jesse Pinkman, and with those involved in the drugs trade. Walt's is a traditional masculinity that sees it as important that *he* provides for his family. When they are informed of his cancer news, Hank states, 'Whatever happens, I'll always take care of your family' (1:4). This is not an option for Walt, and as he continues manufacturing drugs there are many instances of him calculating not only the cost of his medical care but also the amount needed to look after his family after his death. The estimate for his treatment is $90,000 with each course of chemotherapy costing

$1,900, a sum clearly out of reach of the average person, particularly someone with poor medical insurance. The family's lack of finance is clear and is discussed by them all as Marie and Hank are party to the discussions. Skyler, who is in control of the family finances, comments: 'Money has always been an issue' (1:5), perhaps something Walt would prefer *not* to broadcast to his sister- and brother-in-law.

In order to supplement his income, Walt works part-time in a carwash, primarily on the checkout, but much to his anger, the owner insists he also wash cars. His anger increases when two students he previously disciplined for necking in class see him and pass on the information concerning his job, work presumably categorized as demeaning. Although Walt and Skyler live in what looks to be a reasonably affluent middle-class neighbourhood, and with a small swimming pool, the interior of their home is decidedly down-at-heel; old, hand-knitted and crocheted (not expensive designer) throws on the furniture and the sludgy brown palette suggest dinginess. These are possessions the family has owned and used for many years. The kitchen and bathroom are basic and old. This is to be compared to the light, spacious and slightly more modern interiors of Marie and Hank's house, which, unlike the suburb inhabited by the White family, is a property overlooking the mountains and desert.

R. W. Connell's (2005: 80) examination of masculinities draws attention to the complexities of gender and the interplay with structures such as class and race. In many respects, Walter White's status as a high school chemistry teacher, a highly qualified post-graduate who had worked on research that won a Nobel Prize, places him in the position of privileged white professional, part of the hegemonic masculinity of the dominant group. His privilege is clear when set in the context of class and race in the United States. Hugo Archulcta, the kind Native American janitor at J. P. Wynne High School, is automatically blamed for thefts from the chemistry laboratory (objects Walt took for his own enterprise), and when a search of Hugo's home reveals a small amount of marijuana, he loses his job. However, as Connell comments, '"hegemonic masculinity" and "marginalized masculinities" are not fixed character types but configurations of practice generated in particular situations in a changing structure of relationships' (Ibid.: 81). Walter White is initially marginalized within the context and structure of his own immediate relationships. His former partners in Gray Matter Technologies (the company he helped form), Gretchen and Elliott Schwartz, are wealthy and successful. Walt and Skyler's difference in terms of class, wealth and taste is shown when they attend Elliott's birthday party as their light and spacious house displays their 'superior' taste, with a large swimming pool, library and oak panelling. Walt and Skyler, wearing a double-breasted blazer and 1980s-style blue prom dress, respectively, are out of place in the sea of beige American designer casualwear. In this instance, taste and class boundaries are reaffirmed (Bourdieu, 1979).[5] Walt's status as high school teacher rather than university professor also diminishes him in the eyes of other guests (1:5). In addition, and at a more personal level, the sex scenes in the early episodes show Walt slow to respond to his wife's advances, but following his early successful involvement in drug manufacture and contact with drug dealers, he is the instigator of sex, penetrates her from behind, in the dark, with Skyler responding, possibly with both awe and incredulity: 'Walt … is that you?' (1:2). The scene referred to in the opening of this section is also indicative of this change in Walt's sense of self-identity and his assertion of masculinity.

Walt's public performance of 'self' varies depending on context. Given his involvement in illegal activities, while with his family, and particularly with his brother-in law, Hank, he maintains his more self-effacing manner. On other occasions, with Jesse and other dealers, he is tough, assertive and threatening. The relationship between Walt and Hank is extremely important. Hank's job with the DEA, taking part in drug raids and carrying weapons (with possible similarities to the cowboy in the New Mexico desert landscape), shows him as active, loud, and even though he is somewhat 'laddish', a respected team leader: his presentation of self at work and with Walt Jr. is of a tough and fearless man. This is to be compared to Walt's quieter and more sedentary occupation and ostensibly more passive demeanour. Walt is subtly, but consistently, undermined and suggested as lacking by both Hank and Walt Jr. with comments such as: Hank: 'Nothing personal, but you wouldn't know a criminal. …' When playing poker, Hank says: 'You gonna man up, you gonna puss out?' (1:6). When hearing of Walt supposedly smoking pot, Hank laughs: 'I didn't think he had it in him!' (1:5). Discussing Walt's initial decision not to have treatment for his cancer, his son's response is: 'You're a pussy. You're like ready to give up' (1:5), and '… why don't you just fucking die already? Give up and die' (1:4). Walt Jr. idolises his uncle Hank, is fascinated by the weaponry, and is keen to hear of his exploits with the DEA, about the drug raids, and particularly about Hank's shootout with drug dealer Tuco (2:2). Walt Jr. is not, of course, privy to his father's involvement in some of these events, and for him Walt is the unglamorous high school chemistry teacher. Interestingly, when Walt loses his hair following chemotherapy and shaves his head, Walt Jr. expresses his admiration for this signifier of a tough masculinity by referring to his 'badass dad' (1:6). It is via Walt Jr. that he retaliates and asserts control when at a party he pushes his son to drink too much tequila until he is sick (the tequila drinking being a rite of passage for Walt Jr.), and this becomes a battle for supremacy between Walt and Hank's more moderate and conciliatory approach. Overall Walt's change is such that by Season 4 he says: 'I am not *in* danger, Skyler. I *am* the danger' (4:6), a point where private meets public self.

Caring for his family is something Walt sees as his individual responsibility, not something to be shared or passed on to others, thus it is up to him to 'pull himself up by the bootstraps'. What *Breaking Bad* suggested is the difficulty of achieving this in mainstream society, the failure of the American Dream. Walt is intelligent, well-educated and hardworking. However, opportunity according to ability or achievement is not easily won, nor does it bring sufficient reward necessary to support ones' health and family within an unequal society. It is the alternative economy that welcomes his enterprise and skills; it is here the meritocracy works, and as the story develops Walt's and Jesse's enterprise is shown as paralleling mainstream business practices. Albuquerque and New Mexico are divided into drug-selling territories, but Walt's aim is to expand to take over the entire territory, and he creates a hierarchy with himself at the helm. A division of labour is evident from the outset, and although Jesse helps Walt 'cook', he is initially responsible for what happens on the street, selling to the network of dealers; Jesse does not have the expertise to manufacture to the standard Walt has set. When developing the business, Walt uses the rhetoric of contemporary business practices, saying: 'We lack initiative. You [Jesse] need to employ more dealers', and refers to 'exponential growth' (2:7), language Jesse repeats when meeting his dealers: 'I'll be king … we need more dealers. Working for you, you working for me. Layered, like nachos. Exponential growth, that's success' (2:7). The RV they use as the meth lab has 'work stations', the product is carefully monitored and weighed with projected sales figures discussed: 42 pounds equals $42,000, minus distribution, $672,000 each (2:9). Walt initiates the colonization of a new sales region, threatening anyone who attempts to move in: 'Stay out of *my* territory' (2:10). This parallel with the mainstream continues when Walt and Jesse work for fast-food businessman and regional boss for a Mexican cartel, Gustavo (Gus) Fring, in his purpose-built laboratory, going to work each day and donning the appropriate hazmat protection; these are jobs, and they share contemporary preoccupations with health and safety.

Breaking Bad's complex plot explores relationships, the interfamilial as well as those created through the business enterprise, showing both the workings and the effects of a market, albeit the alternative market, economy. This is global capitalism; Walt is an entrepreneur creating demand at home and overseas, and in the process, there are battles to control production and supply. Walt's popular clean crystal meth cannot, of course, be patented; thus there are power struggles over ownership of his recipe, and as with any new formula in either the mainstream or alternative economy, this knowledge not only brings power but also crucially brings huge financial rewards. Walt asserts: 'This is *mine, my* formula. This is *my* product' (3:4; my emphases). Potential rivals and anybody who poses a threat are eliminated – that is killed (some by Walt or Jesse) – including members of the cartel, Gus, Mike Ehrmantraut (the lawyer, Saul Goodman's, and Gus's 'enforcer'), Gale Boetticher (a chemist hired to assist Walt), while Walt allows Jesse's girlfriend, Jane Margolis, who poses a threat to his enterprise, to die. The market and competition is ruthless and corrupt, it is survival at the expense of others, and clearly there will be consequences to all these actions both for his immediate family and for society in general. Walt's initially happy family life is destroyed, he is alienated from his wife and son, his house is burnt and destroyed, and Hank is killed. Several episodes also indicate the effects of both drug taking and the drug trade; the child of addicted parents Jesse finds living in squalid surroundings and fending for himself is one example (2:6).

The effects of the 2008 crash were (and still are) widespread, causing bankruptcies, unemployment, and loss of homes. While its more punitive aspects might be experienced by the very poor, those who have the least reserves, as Brett Martin's comment above notes, it also impacts the more comfortable middle class. The drugs trade similarly has no boundaries in terms of class, evidenced in *Breaking Bad* by Jane Margolis's addiction. Following the destruction of Gus's laboratory, Walt's enterprise moves to the heart of middle-class suburban America as manufacturing takes place in homes vacated while they are being fumigated. Interestingly, this aspect of the alternative economy remains unnoticed, as unobtrusive and as taken for granted as businesses which are part of the mainstream and seen on the High Street or Main Street, thus becoming part of the every day. What makes Walt's business different from those that caused the crash and the bankers with their high bonuses? Matt Taibbi (2010: 6) quotes the vast sums made by one investment bank and states Goldman Sachs paid '$4.7 billion in bonuses and compensation in the first three months of this year, an 18 per cent increase over the first quarter of 2008'. Andrew Ross Sorkin (2009: 67) refers to one former partner at Goldman Sachs being worth more than $100 million, and the issue of bankers' bonuses is one that continues to rumble through the media.

Walt distances himself from dealers and the effects of drugs by saying that he is only the manufacturer. He also adopts a discourse no doubt employed by millions: he is doing this for his family, to provide for them after his death, including college funds for his children. This is reiterated by Gus Fring who says, 'A man provides for his family' (3:5); Mike Ehrmentraut is similarly concerned to leave funds for his granddaughter. Walt continually asserts that he earned the money and that it is his (3:3). Its seductive power is evident as Skyler overcomes her initial anger and distaste at Walt's 'job' to help with money laundering (seduced by the under-floor heating in her lover's, Ted Beneke's, house), and the sums are so vast that she eventually hires a storage facility showing Walt the money loaded on a pallet (5:9). It is worth repeating Taibbi's reference to Goldman Sachs: 'The world's most powerful investment bank is a great vampire squid wrapped around the face of humanity, relentlessly jamming its blood funnel into anything that smells like money' and speculating, or trying to visualise, how much storage space $100 million or $4.7 billion would take.

When first discussing Walt's cancer and treatment with his doctor/oncologist, Skyler insists: 'it's not about the money ...' (1:4). Obviously health is of greater importance, but given the context, this somewhat utopian and naïve comment, while being evidence of her love and concern, does not acknowledge the financial implications and the realities of their economic situation. Walt's is perhaps a more realist/pragmatic approach as it clearly *is* about the money and it is impossible to avoid this aspect of US, or indeed any, society. His intelligence and skill is largely unrecognized within his own milieu but offers rewards within the alternative economy. However, Walt's rationalization that he did it for his family finds no favours with Hank, who maybe showing more awareness of the competitive aspects of their relationship, of contemporary masculinity and of Walt's need to assert power and control, comments towards the end: 'Like you give a shit about family!' (5:9). As Walt says, 'I did it for me. I liked it. I was *good* at it and ... I was *alive*' (5:16).

Downton Abbey: We're all in this together

> The Earl of Grantham: 'We have to keep going whatever happens. We have to help each other keep going' (2:4).

Series 1 of *Downton Abbey* was first broadcast in September 2010 and followed the victory of the Conservative Party in the British election in May of that year. Interestingly, it also coincided with a rise in popularity of the UK's most famous aristocratic family, the

Windsors, and this was reinforced by two events. First, the engagement of Prince William and Catherine Middleton was announced, with its accompanying romance narrative, and their marriage in 2011; this also provided the media with opportunities to discuss Diana, Princess of Wales, the 'people's princess', and the royal family's intention to 'learn from the mistakes of the past'. Second, in 2012 there were celebrations for the diamond jubilee of Queen Elizabeth II and her accession to the throne, which continued into 2013 when the actual coronation in June 1953 was commemorated. All of these celebrations took place amidst concerns at the economic downturn with some comments in the press on the cost; one report estimated these as more than £1.3 billion, the majority of this due to the economic effects of an extra day's holiday 'during a time of financial uncertainty' (McAviney, Flyn and Oliver, 2012). Some dissenting views commented on the cost, with an estimate of £3 billion, 'while poorest families starve' (Peytors, 2012).

Downton Abbey can be placed in this context of 'financial uncertainty', and one theme the series explores is a change in economic circumstances along with the possible impact on an aristocratic family and their dependents – by dependents, I am referring to the people who work for them. It looks at the fortunes of the earl and countess of Grantham (the birthplace of Margaret Thatcher does not seem to be coincidental), their daughters, Lady Mary, Lady Edith and Lady Sybil, Grantham's heir, Matthew Crawley, as well as the 'below stairs' cast who work to maintain their leisured lifestyle. The story initially revolves around the entail that stipulates the Grantham title and money, aside from their dowries, cannot pass to the daughters (a ruling not dissimilar to that in effect until recently with the royal family). One of the main storylines in the first three series is the effort to incorporate the new heir and the love affair between him and the eldest daughter, Lady Mary, and the hope the family will retain their land, wealth and privilege.

First, there are debates about the status of heritage film/costume drama. Andrew Higson (1993: 110) argues that these texts offer a seductive escape from the contradictions of the present past:

> By turning their backs on the industrialized, chaotic present, they nostalgically reconstruct an imperialist and upper-class Britain. ... The films thus offer apparently more settled and visually splendid manifestations of an essentially pastoral national identity and authentic culture: 'Englishness' as an ancient and natural inheritance, *Great* Britain, the *United* Kingdom.

However, texts are polysemic and offer contradictory pleasures. Clare Monk (2002) looks at their complexity and lifts them from those arguments which critique the texts for their seeming nostalgia and implicitly place audiences as passive and cultural dupes. Maggie Andrews' (2014: 255) discussion of heritage films, for example, where she looks at *The Duchess*, *The Other Boleyn Girl*, and *Young Victoria*, argues that they present 'popular and pleasurable women's history in films which have both fragments of feminism and spaces in which audiences are encouraged to challenge and question gendered power relations and scripts'. Broadcast in the UK on a Sunday evening, *Downton Abbey* was the perfect antidote to reflections on the start of the working week, and watching the early series, my viewing dwelt on its many pleasures, including the costume, storylines such as Lady Mary's 'will she, won't she' marry Matthew, the death of Mr Pamuk, the Turkish diplomat, while in her bedroom (absolute delight), Lady Sybil's interest in women's rights and Irish politics, and Lady Edith's expressed wish not to be an invisible woman (3:5). At the same time, however, this pleasure was tempered by increasing irritation at the way critique of the family and the structures it represents and rebellion against authoritarianism were absorbed and reincorporated, and a particular way forward was suggested under the bland paternalism of the earl of Grantham. While acknowledging that there *are* spaces for critique, and fans will create many alternative narratives, equally other readings can also be made, and the three series can be seen as presenting a hegemonic view as dissent is reincorporated and the status quo maintained. It shows power being challenged by contesting groups, but through negotiation consensus is achieved and Grantham's power re-established and maintained. Reflecting on Gramsci, Dominic Strinati (2003: 165) comments:

> Dominant groups in society, including fundamentally but not exclusively the ruling class, maintain their dominance by securing the 'spontaneous consent' of subordinate groups, including the working class, through the negotiated construction of a political and ideological consensus which incorporates both dominant and dominated groups.

Hegemony in the Gramscian sense is maintained through the spontaneous consent to the dominant order, the workings of 'common sense'; there is a cultural universe where the future of all groups is shown as linked or united. R. W. Connell (2005: 77) comments: 'It is the successful claim to authority, more than direct violence, that is the mark of hegemony (though violence often underpins or supports authority)', and it is this successful claim that characterizes Grantham's power.

The programme is set in a period favoured by film and television programme producers as it precedes the life-changing events caused by World War I, and the period afterwards, enabling discussion of the many cultural, social, political and economic changes that took place as the century progressed. It starts in 1912, shows a family and society on the cusp of change, and is a representation of Britishness/Englishness at a particular moment. Historians have commented on the shifting terrain occupied by the ruling classes in the early part of the twentieth century (Cannadine, 1994, 1998; McKibbin, 1998). Class boundaries were transforming, and many landed elites were having problems maintaining wealth and ownership of property. Marrying outside money, from the US or elsewhere, was one way of adapting to economic pressures. The experiences of the Granthams and concerns about the retention of wealth and property are drawn from those of many aristocrats in the late nineteenth/early twentieth centuries: in this series, the earl of Grantham married an American heiress for her money, although there are assurances that he did fall in love with her (1:1). While they have disagreements and differences, overall there is a sense of a united parental couple at the helm, both of whom care for each other and for their dependants and take their responsibilities seriously. The economic problems faced by the family are also introduced (though these do not dent their privileged lifestyle) and the consequences if the eldest daughter does not marry the new heir, Matthew Crawley.

The series starts with news of the sinking of the *SS Titanic* being relayed to the earl. The enclosed world of Downton Abbey is suggested as it is transmitted via telegraph through the village post office, the postman, the downstairs servants, and finally to Grantham himself. He is the last of a long line of people to be informed, but the involvement of the entire household, and the extended 'family'/community in the village, is assured. At the same time Grantham's more liberal conservatism is shown as comments are made on the disaster. Carson the butler says, 'I understand most of the ladies were taken off in time', while Grantham replies, 'You mean the ladies in first class? God help the poor devils below decks, on their way to a better life' (1:1). His concern for others is emphasized with the arrival of the new valet, Bates, his former batman when he served in the Boer War (1880–81 and 1899–1902). Bates's leg injury makes it difficult for him to carry out some household tasks, and while it seems necessity forced Grantham to agree initially to his dismissal (with one month's wages) his conscience would not allow this: 'It wasn't right, Carson. I just didn't think it was right'. The concern of the family (and *some* of the servants) is shown when Bates is convicted of the murder of his first wife and they express support for his innocence. For the wedding night of Bates and head housemaid Anna, Lady Mary has one of the bedrooms transformed to create a romantic setting. Lady Sybil, the youngest daughter, who is committed to women's rights, helps a maid desirous of 'bettering herself' to get another job as a secretary. The mutual concern shown by all parties (i.e. the servants and the family) for each other's welfare is important to note. Representing the servants, Carson refers to Downton being his 'family/our family', for example: 'It's certainly a great day for Downton to welcome a duke under *our* roof' (1:1; my emphasis). The servants are shown as having a vested interest in the continuing success of the family and the estate.

As the series progressed, and we learn that Grantham's heir, and suitor for Lady Mary, died on the *Titanic*, the servants are equally as interested in the fate of the family. This shared concern for the fortunes of the Granthams finds echoes in the opening of the 2010 Conservative Party manifesto, particularly the oft-repeated phrase 'we're all in this together'. David Cameron's opening remarks state: 'But these problems can be overcome if we pull together and work together. If we remember that we are all in this together' (Manifesto, 2010). The manifesto also includes this slogan superimposed on a map of the UK and clearly talks to ideas of identity and nationhood to the 'imagined community' (Anderson, 1991). Tim Edensor (2002: 20) refers to national identity and everyday life and, taking Raymond Williams' arguments regarding 'structure of feeling', argues that there are 'national structures of feeling' that the national 'is constituted and reproduced, contested and reaffirmed in everyday life'. It is hard to escape the reaffirmation of ideas of a particular notion of tradition that imbue the series. Each episode begins with a view of Downton Abbey (filmed at Highclere Castle in Berkshire), the earl walking with a golden Labrador, a symbol of Englishness/Britishness, within a pastoral setting showing the house and its grandeur. This is followed by glimpses of the interior; the British stately home. It invokes the ideological power of the landscape, with rural England 'as supreme marker of national identity', and the celebration of the country house as marked by the National Trust (Ibid.: 40–41).

Grantham's position within the community, his own history and narrative of the past place him in this traditional economic and social structure. He states: 'Downton is in my blood and in my bones' (1:2), 'It's my third parent and my fourth child' (1:1), together with his personal manifesto, 'I am a custodian … not an owner. I must strive to be worthy of the task I've been set' (1:4), rhetoric worthy of any politician. His is thus a narrative of belonging, and these comments, interestingly, distance him from his ownership of property and his wealth. It creates a biological link and becomes duty, paternalism, suggesting an inalienable right to his position, and, to use Benedict Anderson's (1991: 4) term 'emotional legitimacy'. Grantham has to take tough decisions, as noted when he initially sacks Bates (1:1). His rousing political style rhetoric, again reminiscent of the 'we're all in this together' theme, is evidenced during the upheaval on the Home Front caused by the First World War and when the house is turned into a hospital for officers: 'We have to keep going whatever happens. We have to help each other keep going' (2:4).

Although the series suggests the shared interests of family and servants, it is a television drama, and there is, of course, dissension. The first footman, Thomas (Barrow), and Lady Grantham's personal maid, (Sarah) O'Brien, are often antagonistic towards the servants but present a mask of subservience to the family. O'Brien's anger at her employer as she imagines she is being replaced leads to a particularly callous act, one which culminates in the pregnant countess losing her child, a son who would have ensured the succession – i.e. title, property and money – remained within the immediate family. Thomas is displeased when he is not promoted to become valet to Lord Grantham, and he and O'Brien actively work against Bates to try to ensure his removal. Their machinations continue in the later series. In some ways, Thomas represents an alternative voice, as he comments on the injury suffered by second footman William Mason while fighting on the Somme (Thomas dislikes and usually ridicules Mason), saying they are both working class lads: 'I'm fed up with seeing how our lot always get shafted' (2:4).

Thomas's and O'Brien's dissatisfaction and scheming is not, however, motivated by politics and a desire to change the existing order but by self-interest. They do not, for example, join forces with the overtly political Irish chauffeur, Tom Branson. While more sympathy is shown towards Thomas and O'Brien in later series (see 3), and they do not always remain allies, they are both initially *othered* in specific ways. They are both smokers and frequently shown in discussion either outside the servants' hall or outside the building (although this can have the attraction of the 'outcast', witness the contemporary outdoors smoker). O'Brien is sharp-tongued, aloof and unfriendly. Thomas is gay and in this respect a sympathetic character, and although understanding is shown towards him in some quarters, in the context of his other actions, his scheming, blackmail, involvement in black market goods post World War I, injuring himself in order to avoid fighting and to get out of the trenches, his is a less powerful and more marginal masculinity.

Generally, however, consent is given to the moral universe of Downton Abbey, and dissent is neutralized and incorporated within the family as their interests are crucially linked with those of the servants. As the head of his community, Grantham is presented as tough but fair, a benevolent employer, one who will care for his family and servants. Examples of this include Mrs Patmore (the cook) and her operation for cataracts as she is sent, in these pre-National Health Service days, from Yorkshire to Moorfields Eye Hospital for private treatment. The housekeeper, Mrs Hughes, is promised a cottage on the estate if the lump in her breast turns out to be cancer, and thus will not become homeless; Lady Grantham also tells her, 'If you are ill, you are welcome here for as long as you want to stay. Lady Sybil will help us to find a suitable nurse. We will look after you' (3:3). Violet, dowager countess of Grantham (the earl's mother) a character who represents tradition and does not welcome change, intervenes to get William Mason, injured on the Somme, moved from Leeds to the officers-only hospital at Downton Abbey. Grantham is reluctant to dismiss people, evidenced by his concern for Bates, 'I owe him my loyalty', and, thinking they had become friends, 'I thought we had crossed the great divide' (1:1). They are motivated by notions of duty and concern for those who work on the estate, comments that are reiterated at different points in the series. As Grantham states when he learns of the extent of his financial problems: 'I have a duty beyond saving my own skin. The estate must be a major employer and support the house, otherwise there's no point to it' (3:1). The implication is that everyone will be cared for.

One of the most interesting relationships is the initial distrust of the Irish chauffeur, Tom Branson, and particularly his socialism (tolerated) and his Irish Republican politics. His politics are made apparent when in conversation with Lady Sybil he talks about '… social injustice. It's the conditions of the workers and the gap between the aristocracy and the poor'. He goes on to say that while he does not approve of Grantham as 'the representative of an oppressive class […] he's a good man and a decent employer' (1:6). The give-and-take, the negotiation that takes place, is important to note. Lady Sybil and Tom Branson elope, are brought back by her sisters, but, much to Grantham's dismay, eventually marry. They initially live in Dublin where Tom works as a journalist and continues with his Republican politics but return for political reasons as Tom is wanted in connection with the destruction of the castle of a Lord and Lady Drumgoole (an event also presented with some humour as the dowager approves on aesthetic grounds, describing the castle as 'hideous' [3:4]). Tom, however, is placed under some obligation towards Grantham when he demonstrates the extent of his power and beneficence by pulling strings to see the Home

Secretary, the result being that Tom is no longer wanted but can never return to Ireland where he would be imprisoned (3:4).

Series 3 dwells on the necessity of change, with challenges to the all-encompassing hegemony represented by Lord Grantham. The challenge is developed through the unity of the new guard, Matthew Crawley (whose suited suavity is worthy of any contemporary politician), now married to Lady Mary, and Tom Branson, having to negotiate with Grantham, who represents an older, conservative order, one whose code is paternalism, benevolence and duty. While these qualities are shared by Crawley and Branson, it is clear that the old order has mismanaged investments and the family could possibly lose their inheritance and their home and move to the much smaller and less grand Downton Place, though the difficulty needs to be set in context as it is 'one of his lordship's houses', Grantham still owning 'most of the village' (3:3). Matthew and Tom are brought together initially by their 'outsider' status, and Tom's inclusion is helped by his being best man at Matthew's wedding to Lady Mary, 'we're brothers-in-law with high-minded wives. We'd better stick together!' (3:1). With the help of money left to him by Lavinia Swire, Matthew's former fiancée, and her father, Matthew sees there is a role for him, invests his inheritance in the estate, Grantham stating they will be joint masters: 'It will be yours as much as mine' (3:3), thus a power-sharing coalition is introduced which later also includes Tom. Following the death of Lady Sibyl in childbirth, Tom's inclusion is in the balance as he plans to move to Liverpool with his daughter. Further negotiations take place when Grantham has to concede, reluctantly, to his granddaughter, Sibyl, being christened in the catholic faith, while Tom decides to stay at Downton as he is incorporated into the household/community by being offered the role of agent for the estate. There is, therefore, little scope for his politics and, crucially, the dowager countess refers to him 'watering down his socialism' (3:7).

There is also a clash between what is said to be financial efficiency represented by the newcomer/incomer Matthew Crawley and Lord Grantham's unwise investments, and the rhetoric bears an interesting resemblance to contemporary discussions of financial management. Grantham states: 'We have worked with the farmers as *partners*' (3:7; my emphasis), a statement which neatly avoids his actual power and ownership. Crawley says, 'We have to change our ways', Downton must be self-supporting if it's to have a chance of survival, and he refers to the importance of increasing productivity and reducing waste (3:7). Even though there has been previous financial mismanagement, and like new economic theories, the new ideas offered by Crawley are untried, the series suggests trust should be placed in the new men as they have the answers. Like Grantham, whose family expressed concern at what might happen to all the servants should they have to move to the smaller property, Crawley is similarly concerned for their dependents as it is suggested that no one will be hurt financially by these changes as the estate can offer compensation to the tenants, crucially, *'while the money's there'* (3:7; my emphasis).

Crawley and Branson are the new order bringing in ideas to help keep the estate (and parts of the old traditional order), thus they all work to maintain Downton Abbey as the status quo. There will be change, but these are 'reasonable' men. It is made clear that things have to transform, and while new ideas are assimilated, including those of the Irish Republican, Tom Branson, Grantham recognizes the need to concede in order to remain Downton Abbey's titular master; his role is assured and overall control maintained.

Conclusion

Girls, Breaking Bad and *Downton Abbey*, three popular serial dramas, all produced within the context of financial insecurity, engage with contemporary concerns and articulate different aspects of austerity living. It would be inappropriate to suggest that *Downton Abbey* shows an in-depth analysis of the many ways power operates as this is a complex concept (Lukes, 1986), but it does give an indication of some of the processes, the negotiations, the formal and informal structures that help to perpetuate the system. An interesting aspect is that while the series shows the maintenance of hegemonic power, at the same time it draws attention to the ways in which this is created and sustained. It shows challenges to an established position and the subsequent redrawing of allegiance and alliance. Through Lady Mary's relationship with tabloid newspaper magnate, Sir Richard Carlisle and the suppression of scandalous material, it also suggests the power of the press and the ability of the powerful to conceal stories of inappropriate behaviour, certainly relevant when considering exposés of the past few years. The creation of the coalition government in the UK is crucial as is the notion that 'we're all in this together', suggesting that even the wealthiest, those like the earl and countess of Grantham, will not renege on their responsibilities towards their dependents.

Even though the main protagonists in *Girls* and *Breaking Bad* face financial hardship, the 'we're all in this together' slogan is, however, not apparent. The operations of neo-liberal capitalism are all too evident and in this post-feminist more austere environment, the emphasis is placed upon these atomized individuals to take responsibility for their own futures. Walter White and his family have no National Health Service to fall back on (their plight hopefully inspiring British audiences to fight for its continuance); Walt is angry in a society that does not recognise nor reward his talents, a society that marginalizes his masculinity. For all its concerns over healthcare, *Breaking Bad* offers neo-liberal capitalism, albeit via the alternative economy, as a way out of hardship, with Walt becoming the hegemonic male who adopts the discourse of 'doing it for the family'. It is an inverted view of the American Dream. The young women in *Girls* have friends, but these are not the all-encompassing groups seen in *Friends* and *Sex and the City*. Marnie comments: 'a friendship between two college girls is greater and more dramatic than any romance ...' (2:10). This may be the case, and while they do care for each other, these are changed times, and living in the city is tough; thus, the women appear to be more self-obsessed, focusing more on themselves rather than on continually working to maintain friendship groups. Rewards do not simply fall into their laps; success is not easily achieved.

Finally, what further unites these three different drama series is their representation of individuals, working within shifting circumstances, trying to achieve and/or maintain a position, a particular identity, within society. As with most television dramas, the focus is on the individual and not the structures which create them. However, what Creeber (2004: 13) refers to as the 'soap opera-isation' of long-form television drama offers 'an arguably more contemporary articulation of present social experience', and in this sense they are austerity narratives.

Notes

1 http://www.hbo.com/girls#/girls/about/index.html.
2 One survey reports approximately 21,000 people working as unpaid interns in the UK at any one time, a six-month unpaid placement in London after graduating costing around £5,500, not including transport (Molloy, 2014).
3 K-Hole has subsequently stated that normcore has nothing to do with clothes but more to do with personalities. It is the notion that an individual adapts to the situation they are in 'and embraces the normalcy of where they are and who they're with' (Gorton, 2014).
4 Nickname for the decade 2000–10.
5 Bourdieu argues that aesthetic stances adopted in matters like cosmetics, clothing or home decoration are opportunities to experience or assert one's position in social space.

Bibliography

Primary Sources

Breaking Bad, 2008–13. [TV] AMCTV.
Downton Abbey, 2010–12. [TV] ITV.
Girls, 2012–13. [TV] HBO.

Secondary Sources

Akass, K. and McCabe, J. (eds) (2004). *Reading Sex and the City*. London: I.B. Tauris.

Anderson, B. (1991). *Imagined communities: reflections on the origins and spread of nationalism*. London: Verso.

Andrews, M. (2014). 'Fantasies, factions and unlikely feminist heroines in contemporary heritage films'. In: M. Andrews and S. McNamara, eds., *Women and the Media: Feminism and Femininity in Britain, 1900 to the Present*. London: Routledge, 244–57.

Bauman, Z. (2000). *The individualized society*. Cambridge: Polity Press.

Bourdieu, P. (1979). *Distinction: a social critique of taste*. London: Routledge.

Bruzzi, S. and Church Gibson, P. (2004). '"Fashion is the fifth character": fashion, costume and character in *Sex and the City*'. In: K. Akass and J. McCabe, eds., *Reading Sex and the City*. London: I.B. Tauris, 115–29.

Cannadine, D. (1994). *Aspects of aristocracy*. London: Penguin.

Cannadine, D. (1998). *Class in Britain*. London: Penguin.

Cochrane, L. 'Normcore: the next big fashion movement?' Available at: http://www.theguardian.com/fashion/fashion-blog/2014/feb/27/normcore-the-next-big-thing [Accessed July 3, 2014].

Connell, R. W. (2005). *Masculinities*, Second edition. Cambridge: Polity.

Creeber, G. (2004). *Serial television: big drama on the small screen*. London: BFI Publishing.

Dunleavy, T. (2009). *Television drama: form, agency, innovation*, Basingstoke: Palgrave Macmillan.

Edensor, T. (2002). *National identity, popular culture and everyday life*. Oxford: Berg.

Farrell. A. 'Meet Norma Normcore'. Available at: http://www.vogue.co.uk/topic/k-hole [Accessed July 3, 2014].

Giddens, A. (1999). *Modernity and self-identity: self and society in the late modern age*. London: Routledge.

Guffey, Ensley F. and Koontz, K. Dale (2014). *Wanna cook? The complete, unofficial companion to Breaking Bad*. Newcastle upon Tyne: Myrmidon.

Hall, S. (1981). 'Notes on deconstructing the popular'. In: R. Samuel, ed., *People's History and Socialist Theory*. London: Routledge and Kegan Paul, 227–40.

Harris, A. (2004). *Future girl: young women in the twenty-first century*. London: Routledge.

Janela, M. (2013). '*Breaking Bad* cooks up record-breaking formula for Guinness World Records 2014 edition'. Available at: http://www.guinnessworldrecords.com/news/2013/9/breaking-bad-cooks-up-record-breaking-formula-for-guinness-world-records-2014-edition-51000/. [Accessed August 1, 2014].

König, A. (2004). '*Sex and the City*: a fashion editor's dream?'. In: K. Akass and J. McCabe, eds., *Reading Sex and the City*. London: I.B. Tauris, 130–43.

Lukes, S. (1986). *Power: a radical view*, Second edition. Cambridge: Blackwell.

Martin, B. (2013). *Difficult men: behind the scenes of a creative revolution*. London: Faber & Faber.

McAviney, V., Flyn, C. and Oliver, M. 'Queen's Diamond Jubilee: cost of the celebrations'. Available at: http://www.telegraph.co.uk/news/interactive-graphics/9197527/Queens-Diamond-Jubilee-cost-of-the-celebrations.html [Accessed August 1, 2014].

McKibbin, R. (1998). *Classes and cultures: England 1918–1951*. Oxford: Oxford University Press.

McNamara, S. (2014). 'Lady Eleanor Smith: the society column, 1927–1930'. In: M. Andrews and S. McNamara, eds., *Women and the Media: Feminism and Femininity in Britain, 1900 to the Present*. London: Routledge, 46–61.

McRobbie, A. (2009). *The aftermath of feminism: gender, culture and social change*. London: Sage.

Miles, S. (2010). *Spaces for consumption*. London: Sage.

Molloy, A. 'Unpaid internships cost graduates "£926 a month"'. Available at: http://www.independent.co.uk/news/business/news/unpaid-internships-cost-.graduates-£926a-month-9856552 [Accessed November 13, 2014].

Morton, A. D. (2007). *Unravelling Gramsci: hegemony and passive revolution in the global economy*. London: Pluto Press.

Peytors, R. 'Queen's Jubilee costs £3 billion while poorest families starve'. Available at: http://www.theopinionsite.org/queens-jubilee-costs-3-billion-while-poorest-families-starve/ [Accessed August 1, 2014].

Sorkin, A. R. (2009). *Too big to fail: inside the battle to save Wall Street*. London: Penguin.

Stiglitz, J. E. (2012). *The price of inequality*. London: Penguin.

Strinati, D. (2003). *An introduction to theories of popular culture*. London: Routledge.

Taibbi, M. 'The Great American bubble machine'. Available at: http://www.rollingstone.com/politics/news/the-great-american-bubble-machine-20100405 [Accessed December 5, 2014].

Taverner, L. August 23, 2014. Private email.

Wagner, E. 'The capitalist nightmare at the heart of *Breaking Bad*'. Available at: http://www.newstatesman.com/culture/2014/12/capitalist-nightmare-heart-breaking-bad [Accessed December 23, 2014].

Weedon, C. (2004). *Identity and culture: narratives of difference and belonging*. Maidenhead: Open University Press.

Worstall, T. 'Ben Bernanke: The 2008 financial crisis was worse than The Great Depression'. Available at: http://www.forbes.com/sites/timworstall/2014/08/27/ben-bernanke-the-2008-financial-crisis-was-worse-than-the-great-depression/ [Accessed November 19, 2014].

5 Managing the social impacts of austerity Britain

The cultural politics of neo-liberal 'nudging'

Emma L. Briant and Steven Harkins

Neo-liberalism, policymaking and social interventionism

The global collapse of the financial sector in 2007–08 led to criticism of neo-liberal economic policy and calls for a return to Keynesianism (Wolf, 2008). Yet the political response to the most recent financial crisis has been an austerity drive, targeted at the welfare state; this approach can be understood as a continuation of the neo-liberal project to roll back the state. A similar period of crisis following the end of the 'golden age of capitalism' and the dissolution of the post-war compromise between capital and labour (Marglin and Schor, 1992; Dumeneil and Levy, 2004; Harvey, 2005: 22) ushered in the development of neo-liberalism in the 1970s.

Neo-liberalism emerged from the ideas of a 'thought collective', the Mont Pelerin Society, who hosted an intellectual movement that attempted to counter the Keynesian collectivist policies that had emerged from the post-war settlement, and had subsequently led to the creation of the welfare state (Cockett, 1995; Harvey, 2005; Mirowski and Plehwe, 2009). Economists associated with the society, particularly classical Liberals like Ludwig von Mises and Friedrich von Hayek, constructed the state as a tyrannical and oppressive force, which interferes with the liberty of free individuals (Hall, 2012: 11).

This radical individualism remained on the fringes of political discourse until the collapse of economic growth in the 1970s which left Britain indebted to the International Monetary Fund (IMF) and committed to a requirement for deep public spending cuts (Burk, 1992). This crisis undermined Keynesianism as an economic model, and neo-liberal ideas came to dominate the policies of Margaret Thatcher's government (1979–90). Critics of neo-liberalism have described it as a reaction by the 'upper classes' who 'felt threatened' by the collapse of growth and moved to secure their interests (Harvey, 2005: 16). Neo-liberalism in Britain princi-pally aimed, over three decades, to cut back the 'social-democratic welfare state' which was seen as the 'arch enemy of freedom' because it interfered with the 'natural' mechanisms of the market (Hall, 2012: 9–11). The first phase of this project, implemented be-tween 1979 and 1986, involved deep cuts and restrictions in public spending, culminating in the deregulation of the City of London (Hills, 1998: 2; Scott-Samuel *et al.*, 2014: 54).

These reforms have led to increased economic inequality, which has been linked to a range of social problems (Thomas, Dorling and Smith, 2010; Wilkinson and Pickett, 2010). A sharp rise in unemployment throughout this period was linked to rising crime (Davies, 1997: 240). Benefit cuts led to an increase in homelessness, especially amongst teenagers (Scott-Samuel *et al.*, 2014: 55), which was worsened by the subsequent reduction of social housing stock through privatization. The development of these social problems led to a paradox in neo-liberal thinking and realization among the political and intellectual elite that 'less government' led to a need to 'mask and contain the deleterious social consequences' of rolling back the state (Wacquant, 1999: 323). The savings that were supposed to be made in public expenditure failed to materi-alize as the number of pensioners, lone parent families and unem-ployed people increased (Hills, 1998: 4). A 'socially interventionist' agenda developed which involved targeting a series of reforms aimed to ensure that 'As many costs as possible should be shifted from the state and back onto individuals, and markets, particularly labour markets, [which] should be as flexible as possible' (Gamble, 2001: 131–132). Peck and Tickell (2002) called this response an 'aggressive re-regulation, disciplining, and containment of those marginalised or dispossessed' (Ibid.: 389).

Criticism from the government was directed at 'people who make themselves homeless by moving from their home area' (Franklin, 1999: 111). Thatcher criticized the attitude of homeless people, arguing that their attitude was, 'I am homeless, the Government must house me!' and

> they are casting their problems on society and who is society?
> There is no such thing! There are individual men and women
> and there are families and no government can do anything ex-
> cept through people and people look to themselves first (1987).

This blaming of individuals for policy failings continued with John Major's 'back to basics' campaign following his election in 1992. During this time, the emerging 'underclass' theory was embraced by leading Conservative Party figures including Michael Portillo, John Redwood and Peter Lilley who argued that single mothers were an economic burden on society (Lund, 2008: 46). Local authorities enforced cohabitation rules for single mothers that meant sometimes they were forced to live with violent ex-partners and did not provide the infrastructure needed for their independence (Campbell, 1984: 28). Political and media rhetoric constructed them as both burden and threat to society because of their 'likely to be criminal' children (Silva, 1996: 178). Electoral support for the Conservatives dropped sharply after 1993, and some commentators blamed these policies for creating an image of the 'nasty party' that brought electoral defeat (Hasan, 2010).

The 1997 election ended eighteen years of Conservative governance, but 'New Labour' had embraced neo-liberal welfare reform policies that similarly emphasized individual responsibility. Prime Minister Tony Blair argued that the welfare state inherited from the Conservatives was still 'weighted heavily towards rewarding and supporting people who were not actively seeking to improve their situation, whether by looking for work or by taking part in training' (Marston, 2008: 363).

Between 2004–05 Blair sought to bring in cuts to the number of incapacity benefit claimants in what was a long-term issue dating back to the social impact of privatization and the lasting effects of the 'roll back' of the state in the 1980s (Beatty and Fothergill, 2010). Rising numbers of unemployed people had also been encouraged onto incapacity benefit in an effort to reduce the unemployment figures (Ibid.). Labour's binary discourse separated deserving taxpayers from undeserving benefit recipients and invoked 'the idea that ordinary taxpayers have a lot to fear from a large-group of "welfare dependent" spongers' (Marston, 2008: 364). They brought in a number of corresponding policy adjustments including reductions in welfare spending in the early years of New Labour's administration (Hills, 1998: 23); however this period also brought the creation of the minimum wage, the New Deal, and a package of redistributive tax policies like Working Tax Credit. This welfare spending was targeted at 'deserving' groups like children, those in work and pensioners; meanwhile cuts were targeted in other areas like unemployment and disability (Brewer *et al.*, 2002). These early initiatives were followed by a second phase of welfare reform focused on a 'gradual escalation in the requirements asked of benefit recipients' specifically targeted at 'lone parents, and the sick and disabled' (Brewer, 2007: 26).

Despite New Labour's tough stance on welfare, in 2010, Coalition Work and Pensions secretary Iain Duncan Smith again argued that his government had inherited a 'broken system' from Labour where people were 'parked' on benefits (Press Association, 2010). This focus on welfare cuts in Britain was echoed on a global scale following the economic crisis. The OECD's (2009) solution to the crisis recommended a reduction of what was described as the 'burgeoning welfare burden' and issued advice to countries, for instance, to 'activate existing disability benefit recipients' who were argued to be an obstacle to raising labour force participation rates and a major contributor to public expenditure (Ibid.: 5–9). Britain's coalition government made welfare reform a central aim and sought to impose new financial regimes based firmly in long-established precepts of neo-liberal economics.

Despite unprecedented transfer to the wealthiest citizens and bonuses to the banks (Bennett, 2014), austerity policies were targeted at benefit recipients, by definition the poorest members of society, and it is they who were claimed to be impeding global recovery. Paul Krugman (2009: 14) argues that opposition to capitalism lost its impetus after the collapse of socialism as an ideology, which has led to a tacit acceptance of inequality, unemployment and injustice as 'unpleasant aspects' of the system which are 'accepted as facts of life'. His words depressingly echoed Margaret Thatcher's famous maxim that 'there is no alternative'. The lack of political dissent at this narrative highlights how 'after forty years of a concerted neo-liberal ideological assault, this new version of common sense is fast becoming the dominant one' if indeed we can describe it as 'new' (Hall and O'Shea, 2013: 4).

In the next section, we will highlight some actions that constructed and supported this ideology after the crisis. We revisit Gramsci's concept of hegemony which can help in understanding why and how the 'common-sense' ideology of personal rather than state responsibility was supported in media coverage. The mainstream media coverage complemented the UK Government's ideological and policy apparatus in endorsing claims that benefit recipients were impeding global recovery and justifying massive reforms and a new wave of social interventionism.

Cultural hegemony, social interventionism and 'nudging'

Hegemony, for Gramsci (1971), emerges through various competing ideologies, some of which are theories created by 'traditional' intellectuals – academics or political activists – others are more 'organic', emerging within people's lived experience and articulated through religion, education, family, and the media. At this popular level 'common sense' and 'good sense' are developed as a form of practical philosophy (Ibid.: 328). But different groups and their ideologies develop in a way that resolves tensions between dominant and subordinate groups. Essentially for Gramsci this tension was necessary for the coordination of 'the dominant group' with 'the general interests of the subordinate groups' so that the state could modify any 'unstable equilibria' of interests (Ibid.: 182). Contemporary austerity has been supported by state interventionism which attempts to build personal responsibility and deflect the responsibility away from government and the failures of capitalism. But ideological adjustments are necessary to build acceptance from groups whose interests may conflict, structuring and presenting policy in such a way that it appears to meet the needs of all. Gramsci saw some scope for resistance and 'will' in what he called 'organic intellectuals' (Ibid.: 129), but this exists alongside their tendency to shape perceptions of institutions and wider society according to the dominant culture. Attention placed on the financial system or state responsibility through 'organic' discourses in the media needed to be managed by offering minimal adjustments whilst ensuring the overall continuation of the hegemonic system. One such system for these minimal adjustments was BIT, discussed below.[1] For Gramsci, this underpinned the appearance that dominant interests were the same as those of wider society and that government was 'based on the consent of the majority' as expressed through the media (Ibid.: 80). Gramsci articulated a theory of how the dominant group is able to manufacture consent and consensus in society, whilst allowing conflicts to be resolved or absorbed. Much of his theory is helpful in considering the way that democracies work today and how the dominance of neo-liberal ideology is maintained, both within the state and in its relation to civil society and the British public.

For Gramsci, the traditional intellectuals and 'party' reproduced most closely the dominant order. During the recent 'crisis' of capitalism, a team was established within government to build ideological change through modifying behaviour. The BIT would initiate 'interventions' across government by structuring behaviour modification into British policymaking in service of the government's wider policies to reduce the state and refocus on 'personal responsibility'. The unit was set up by its director, David Halpern, following the 2010 election around the principles of behavioural economics and the psychology of behaviour change.

It is instructive to examine the 'Mindspace' report – an early vision commissioned by Gus O'Donnell, the cabinet secretary under New Labour, which became central to BIT planning.[2] Mindspace states that behavioural approaches offer new 'potentially powerful' tools that are 'especially relevant in a period of fiscal restraint' (Dolan *et al.*, 2010: 7). Far from *transforming* the neo-liberal capitalist ideology identified above, behavioural economics was harnessed for 'shaping individual behaviour' around these goals instead of using 'legal and regulatory systems' (Ibid.: 13). The Mindspace report anticipates that 'fiscal challenges may sharpen interest in behaviour change further, as policymakers and public service professionals wrestle with the challenge of how to achieve "more with less"' (Ibid.: 12–13). It is unsurprising then that while the ideas were brewing under Labour, they were really seized upon by the Conservative-led coalition as a way to facilitate cuts while moderating social impact in a way that shifted the burden away from the state. BIT really took off after the financial crisis, which

> created the conditions under which people ... suddenly be-came much more interested in it ... because a lot of the be-havioural suggestions were ones that could be incorporated in a period when basically you're trying to run the public sector with no new money (O'Donnell 2014).[3]

The interventions 'tended to be cheap ... so in a world when you haven't got any more money ... suddenly behavioural ideas are very attractive' to government policymakers (Ibid.). In planning for BIT, O'Donnell was motivated by his experience with the 'IMF and its response to the Asian financial crisis'; he felt that 'the kinds of suggestions being put forward were very much taken from an economic textbook and they didn't really account for the political economy and the way people would feel ... and how they'd re-spond' (Ibid.). Traditional economic models assume citizens can analyse information to decide what is in their interest before act-ing, according to rational economic self-interest.

Behavioural economics originated in 1970s United States, partly *in response* to neo-liberalism. Psychologists such as Herbert Simon (1945; 1957) noted that the supposed 'rationality' of human be-haviour that these theories assumed was 'bounded' by effective intuition. For Simon, behaviour was far more complex than eco-nomic reductionism could admit and we should therefore study 'real people' in real-world contexts. This 'old behavioural econom-ics' was developed into its contemporary form by psychologists Daniel Kahneman and Amos Tversky (1974) and later, Richard Thaler. O'Donnell had been interested in these ideas since he was a student at Nuffield College, Oxford, when he recalled 'work-ing with ... Ian Little and Jim Mirrlees who were very interested in ways of handling situations where markets didn't work well, where prices were distorted and how in such cases you might come up with better decisions' (O'Donnell, 2014). But O'Donnell saw the focus of media discourse on behavioural economics as misleading due to BIT's social and public policy focus:

> it's very deliberately called behavioural insights team … because the whole point is that in a sense this is a failing in economics and the people who have done … very useful work on decision making are psychologists … social scientists … and now neuroscientists (Ibid.).

The Mindspace model draws on the notion that people's behaviour is frequently shaped by 'automatic' or unconscious 'contextual' factors and proposes utilizing psychology to influence these; to cause a desired behaviour without awareness or conscious decision being necessary (Dolan *et al.*, 2010: 14). Mindspace states that 'not all government communications focus on simple information provision; often they draw on more sophisticated techniques of persuasion' (Ibid.: 15). An important component is the design of communications, but nudging goes beyond this, to modify the 'choice architecture'; the circumstances in which behaviours happen and decisions to act are made (Sunstein and Thaler, 2008). Mindspace says that once an individual has been encouraged to make a small adjustment to their behaviour 'the powerful desire to act consistently takes over' and this means 'subsequent changes in behaviour … may go largely unnoticed' (Dolan *et al.*, 2010: 28).

Mindspace states that its effects need to be combined with 'a nuanced understanding of the capabilities and motivations of the target audience' (Ibid.).[4] Theory at the heart of Mindspace is drawn from classic work in psychology which has formed the core of commercial marketing strategies, for example (Gilovich *et al.*, 2002). 'Required reading' for Conservative MPs in 2008, the book *Nudge* by Thaler and Sunstein (2008) and the propaganda book *Influence: The Psychology of Persuasion* by Robert Cialdini (2007) have been central to Mindspace and BIT (where US Professor Richard Thaler is an advisor). These theories form the core of a detailed propaganda strategy and approach to social policy that, propelled by austerity, is influencing policy planning nationally and, increasingly, internationally.

The New Economics Foundation (NEF) is a think tank pushing for, among other things, a move away from neo-classical economics, but it sees behavioural economics as an acceptable alternative (Shah and Dawney, 2005). This wider 'libertarian paternalist' approach which the Coalition government was 'embedding into its broader gestalt' by rolling out BIT in fact 'represents an important set of challenges to the hegemonic assumptions of neo-liberalism, which have held sway since the rise of Thatcherism' (Whitehead *et al.*, 2012: 302). There was indeed resistance from some people in government, 'who had grown up with a certain way of thinking about [economics and] had got the traditional economic model [in their heads. They] were ... saying "it's all about prices" ... there was a bit of an old guard around who found new ways of thinking difficult' (O'Donnell, 2014). Think tanks are slowly embracing behaviour change.[5] Among them, O'Donnell mentioned NEF and that 'interestingly the regulators' were taking it up: the 'Financial Conduct Authority ... now starting to put out publications on how they're using behavioural economics. It's a massively growing area' (O'Donnell, 2014). The Institute of Fiscal Studies think tank also supports behavioural approaches, to inform and complement existing policy (see Leicester, Levell and Rasul, 2012). Behavioural economics is an effort to 'fix' the unpredictability and perceived 'errors' of human behaviour in relation to market expectations and as such is not actually to challenge neo-liberal policy.

While the idea of government 'interventions' runs counter to free market principles, in reality the latter never existed unmediated in the UK. This has led to a 'growing realisation that market-based forms of coordination have proved detrimental to long-term social, economic and ecological stability' (Whitehead *et al.*, 2012: 303). As detailed above, 'social interventionism' has been necessary to mediate the negative social impact of austerity. As Robert Gilpin (2000: 4) argues, in a capitalist system it is 'important that leadership ensure at least minimal safeguards for the inevitable losers from market forces and from the process of creative destruction; those who lose must at least believe that the system functions fairly'.

Cheap 'policy solutions', like BIT and individualist rhetoric, act as a pressure valve to prevent social impacts from becoming so severe that they threaten the stability of the state. This new behavioural economics views 'the human subject as a target of correctional re-rationalisation' (Whitehead *et al.*, 2012: 305). Other academic work, for example, Thrift (2007), points to other possible conclusions, that we should work with 'the vibrant unpredictability of life and human development' seeing this complexity as positive and essential to humanity, even though it may raise problems for government planning (Whitehead *et al.*, 2012: 305). Discussions around behavioural change are dominated by psychologists, neuroscientists, political scientists and economists, and the House of Lords Behaviour Change Inquiry in 2011 felt the emphasis was on efficacy and there was no opportunity to ask normative questions (Ibid.).

Mindspace rightly notes that 'government influences behaviour no matter what it does' (Dolan *et al.*, 2010; 16) and as such has a responsibility to consider the possible direct and indirect influences

its activities and communications might have in a real-world context to ensure this serves the public interest. The report explicitly
states that the practice of behaviour change might require 'careful
handling' and that 'the public need to give permission and help
shape how such tools are used' (Ibid.: 10). It considers 'issues
around gaining democratic permission for behaviour change policies' listing three key factors to consider: '*who* the policy affects;
what type of behaviour is intended; *how* the change will be ac-
complished' (Ibid.). Whose behaviour is to be modified is an important political issue and one which will be central to the analysis
hereon. It is important to examine the political contexts in which
these strategies are and are not applied.

As mentioned above, one social impact of neo-liberal policies
in the 1990s was a rise in crime. Initial foci detailed in the early
Mindspace report included 'safer communities', where interventions were designed to deal with this (largely poverty-related)
crime; 'the good society' (which includes encouraging individuals' pro-environmental behaviours and 'responsible parenting');
and creating 'healthy and prosperous lives'; prophetic at a time of
National Health Service (NHS) privatization (Ibid.: 29). BIT's support to the civil service includes initiatives for government bodies
such as Public Health England, a new agency charged with supporting public health after the shake-up of the NHS last year. It
has been criticized by medical organizations, including the British
Medical Association, for not being independent enough to con-
tradict changes to government policy (Campbell, 2014). But BIT
has been involved in interventions cross-government and 'are now
active in almost every area of domestic policy' (Service, 2013).
The recent 'priority areas' include 'giving of time and money',
'public service reform' and 'reducing regulation'. Due to initial resistance, BIT 'had to ... prove it was worth the money in setting
it up ... to win over the sceptics. What [Halpern] did first of all
was to implement some initiatives which showed [the] small unit
[had] come up with some ideas that saved vast multiples of what
you've spent' (O'Donnell, 2014). They claim to have saved £300
million between 2010 and 2012, twenty times BIT's cost. This was
largely through drawing forward income tax by appealing to the
conformist urges of already largely compliant late payers to pay
sooner (Benjamin, 2013).

The focus according to O'Donnell was on 'those who were making bad mistakes and that could range across the income span,
so people with rather a lot of money were making very stupid
decisions ... on terms of which [annuity] to buy for example'
(O'Donnell, 2014). But the Mindspace report states that 'someone
who has developed a dislike of government interventions may be

less likely to listen to messages that they perceived to come from "the government"' (Dolan *et al.*, 2010: 19), and regarding this it specifically emphasizes how 'those from the lower socioeconomic groups are more sensitive to the characteristics of the messenger' and this may make them resistant to targeting attempts at 'addressing inequalities' (Ibid.). The report states that 'we may irrationally discard advice given by someone we dislike' and 'the most effective strategy for changing behaviour may be to use third parties or downplay government involvement in a campaign or intervention' (Ibid.). This raises a conflict with the stated need to 'gain democratic permission' for the use of these behavioural methodologies. Thaler and Sunstein (2007: 244) also argue transparency and publicity are essential in nudging. Wilkinson (2012: 351) calls this an 'escape clause' to stop nudges being manipulative and ensure that they preserve an individual's liberty to choose, it means they can 'opt out' of nudges they dislike or that are designed poorly. On this, BIT's Deputy Director Owain Service said: 'We obviously work with Richard [Thaler] a lot and we know Cass [Sunstein] very well as well, and ... our starting position is ... what the best way of achieving a given objective is. So, we don't sort of ruthlessly apply that ... libertarian paternalistic approach.' He added, 'I don't think ... if you talk to Richard ... I don't think he would religiously apply that philosophy either' (Service, 2013).

The suffocation of differing agendas in propaganda and in the decision-making process are such that conflicts of interest remain unseen and is a way power can be exercised over a person 'by influencing, shaping and determining his very wants' (Lukes, 2005: 27). Behavioural propaganda in particular often aims to produce 'consent' (Gramsci, 1971) by engineering the situation whereby people will produce the 'right' behaviour without their rational awareness that they are being influenced. Lukes (2005: 22–23) observes how non-decision making is a crucial element of power analysis.

Mindspace further states that campaigns designed to *provide information* and allow for choice may be effective among the privileged but less effective among those disadvantaged in society. It argues that relying on the latter group making what are thought of as the 'rational' decisions about their interests is problematic and would lead to a behaviour change gap: 'the better educated, higher income, more advantaged minds are the first and easiest minds to change, inequalities in health and wellbeing may be widened by information campaigns' (Dolan *et al.*, 2010: 15).

Instead Mindspace proposes an 'Automatic System' that influences the 'context' in which *all* people act. By this rationale the public is there to enact behaviour, enacting paternalistic decisions and must be, often unconsciously, 'nudged' to comply. Far from libertarian, the removal of choice could be said to demonstrate a government fear of 'majoritarian democracy' (Williams, 1958: 298); non-compliance is perceived as an error in the system that must be corrected through communications or 'nudging'. Williams observed that communication requires 'not only transmission' but 'it is also reception and response. ... The failure is due to an arrogant preoccupation with transmission, which rests on the assumption that the common answers have been found and need only to be applied' (Ibid: 314).

The report justifies this, saying 'changing the context, rather than people's minds, might be more cost-effective' (Dolan *et al.*, 2010: 16). Certainly a change to the 'context' of someone living in one of Britain's most deprived communities, such as allocating funds to alleviate poverty, boost education, local job creation and re-allocation of resources to create incentives for investment in that region, might be more likely to result in improvements in their lives and decision making, but *systemic* change is not what is meant.

Many of those working in the field of 'behavioural science' have asserted that its incorporation into government has been too slow. Nigel Oakes, the CEO of contractor Strategic Communication Laboratories and founder of the Behavioural Dynamics Institute (their research arm) said: 'introducing ... influence and behavioural change into ... government organisations' was a slow process 'because up till now they've only ever understood ... attitudinal change and basically *PR* ... that's what we're up against. And, of course, hugely powerful people in government who specialise in' PR (Oakes, 2013). This was echoed by O'Donnell: 'Comms people ... were quite resistant ... kind of old-fashioned [believing] "what we need to do is to make an advert to tell people to put seatbelts on"' (O'Donnell, 2014). And politicians' views of this were traditional: '[pollsters] and focus groups'. This meant O'Donnell and Halpern were 'a little bit nervous about this being seen as just another form of marketing' (Ibid.).

O'Donnell chaired BIT's quarterly boards which set the team's strategic priorities until he retired and 'Jeremy Heywood took over', but Owain Service (2013), the deputy director of BIT, said that it had now became more 'institutionalized' (Ibid.). Though it is a small team, O'Donnell (2014) noted that their function is to set things in motion and mentioned how DWP and HMRC 'have been very good at picking up many of the ideas and taking forward themselves' (Ibid.). Their 'interventions' were designed to seek savings and efficiency and reduce government welfare spending. O'Donnell argued that 'the whole point of behaviour change is to improve people's wellbeing and the big society was an example of ... using the fact that volunteering and giving are really positive for people's wellbeing ... leaving aside the advantage to those who are the recipients of it' (Ibid.). While many 'nudges' can be and *are* positive, in encouraging people to eat more healthily for example, or give up smoking, when they want do so, the 'libertarian paternalism' of behavioural economics has been rolled out at a time when British welfare is being cut and the NHS privatized, and it exists as a way to facilitate these deepening cuts to services and greater deregulation.

Owain Service (2013) said that the unit is misunderstood: 'People think that ... you're trying to nudge people, actually what we're really interested in is how people behave, the process and how we can help them to change their behaviour so that it's more in line with what government objectives are' (Ibid.). The assertion from its director Dr David Halpern was more in line with its accompanying spin; that the government unit was to 'help people to make better choices for themselves' (Benjamin, 2013); for whom they are making the choices is crucial. BIT priorities reflect the policy concerns of Prime Minister David Cameron and his deputy Nick Clegg. They shifted after the initial focus and flurry of media coverage on health, 'well-being' and encouraging charity to an enhanced focus on economic growth and generating revenue by reducing regulation and public spending. BIT effectively performed two key functions:

- As PR – presenting the government as an innovator in public health, social policy and welfare, austerity as necessary and 'nudging' as the only 'realistic' solution within the (silent and largely unchallenged) constraints of capitalism;
- Within wider social policies supporting government cuts, by enabling government to refocus policy solutions away from the state, the financial sector and corporate tax avoidance.

Service (2013) said that 'a couple of days ago we had a steering board and [Jeremy Heywood] said I want you to work on employment and growth as your two priorities' (Ibid.). Such interventions have included a job centre in Loughton, Essex. Owain Service described how they utilize user-centred design:

> where you don't assume you can dream up your policy from sitting behind a desk in Whitehall, you spend time observing; working with those people who are actually experiencing the service themselves. So you go to the users of a service or the administrators of a service (Ibid.).

They chose to go to the administrators of the service:

> A lot of that initial part of that particular programme was sitting in with job advisors when they themselves are going through the process of working with somebody who is looking for work. And the reason we emphasize this is, quite a lot of the time, if you are a policymaker in any country ... and you're doing a ... programme around job centres you might go and visit a couple of job centres, but you might not actually. But what you won't do is spend a considerable period of time inside those job centres to really find out what it is truly like to be an administrator in a job centre. Or to be somebody who is looking for work (Ibid.).[6]

The intervention was designed to encourage advisors to give their clients a 'sense of progress', giving them a forward-looking focus on their plan rather than dwelling on the difficult realities of finding a job in the contemporary employment market. According to the *Guardian*, this formula is used in Starbucks reward schemes, marketing that gives customers 'a 12-stamp card, instead of a 10-stamp one, but when you buy your first coffee they give you two stamps straight off' which means customers will feel a greater sense of 'progress' and buy more coffee (Benjamin, 2013). These marketing strategies are being applied to those in the lower strata of the British economy to ensure those individuals give more readily into the economy. Loughton is an area with high unemployment, hard hit by the recession (*Epping Forest Guardian*, 2008). In its suburb of Debden, this is compounded by mental health problems which are more prevalent than elsewhere in the country. A food bank which opened in 2012 was inundated in its first month, leading to strained resources (Hardy, 2012).

BIT's blog states proudly that they are 'Designing interventions in partnership with the people who are going to deliver them' but in doing this they leave out recipients of the intervention. Any intervention that is designed to respond to the needs and work in the interests of jobseekers needs to engage with jobseekers themselves, their individual requirements and their experiences of the systems that have been targeted for change. This, therefore, wasn't a strategy designed around those who need most support, such as the long-term unemployed and those who have come off incapacity benefit. BIT stated that they 'don't have data on whether the customers had any disabilities' (Cabinet Office, 2012a). The experiences of the jobseekers, their diverse situations and needs are irrelevant in the planning which was designed to reduce costs and paperwork at the Department of Work and Pensions (DWP;

Cabinet Office, 2012b). The BIT boasted a small increase of 15 to 20 per cent more people off benefits after thirteen weeks, possibly due to less of the jobseekers' time being wasted on bureaucracy. While it is positive to reduce form-filling, if someone doesn't have a job after eight weeks it is likely part of a broader problem such as a lack of suitable employment, a problem 'expressive writing' will not solve. The onus is of course on the jobseeker to become more 'resilient', not for the government to commit to ensuring secure employment is available (Cabinet Office, 2012a).

A recent report by the Resolution Foundation think tank indicated recently that during the last six years, only London has seen a marked rise in employee jobs, and many of the increases seen nationally in those leaving welfare can be explained by a rise in often precarious self-employment (up to 15 per cent of all employment) with many becoming lone traders (D'Arcy and Gardiner, 2014). Other research by Manchester University shows that post-crisis growth and job creation has been focused in the southeast (Chakrabortty, 2013). A significant proportion of the employee jobs that have been created have, however, been on insecure 'zero-hours' contracts where there is no minimum guarantee of working hours.

Structured into some of the Mindspace framework is a focus on the poor for interventions. For example, it states that 'the value of something depends on where we see it from'; in other words, poor people need a smaller investment as an incentive to alter their behaviour. The poorer people are, the easier it is to motivate them with a lower financial incentive. The document describes how little was required to bring about a behaviour change in Malawi (Dolan *et al.*, 2010: 20). By the same rationale, with wealthy individuals, a financial incentive or cost is viewed according to the degree of change from that reference point. Recent research also indicates that the richer people get, the less empathy they have for those with less money and the more they defend their entitlement to that wealth. However, it has *also* been demonstrated that it is possible to 'nudge' such empathy with effects on wealth distribution. Psychologists (Piff, 2013a; 2013b) indicate that accumulating wealth decreases altruism and increases unethical behaviour, which drives up economic inequality. Yet Piff states that it is relatively easy to 'nudge' giving among the wealthy so that this decreases and 'cause[s] wealthier individuals to be just as egalitarian as poor people' (2013b). The majority of BIT changes, however, follow neo-liberal policies in predominantly focussing on 'nudging' ordinary individuals to pay more taxes etc., rather than nudging corporations or wealthy individuals to do so.[7] Some research indicates that policymakers themselves and organizations may be subject to 'behavioural biases'.[8] Armstrong and Huck (2010) argue that these biases can potentially intervene in and modify corporate profit-maximising behaviours.

In taxation, recent data by the Equality Trust advocacy group shows that the poorest 10 per cent of households already 'pay eight percentage points more of their income in all taxes than the richest', but the public perception is that the rich pay more (Allen, 2014). In 2011, the advocacy group Tax Justice Network estimated tax avoidance costs the UK economy £69.9 billion a year (2011) and point out that this represents '56% of the country's total healthcare spend' (Jenner, 2011). The HMRC (2012) declares proudly that it has 'more than 300 staff focused on' affluent tax evaders (Ibid.). This compares with 2,876 staff in 2012 at the DWP investigating social security fraud (Syal, 2012). BIT has also focused on tax, where Service (2013) said the techniques were 'wildly successful' (Ibid.). Again, instead of focussing on the far more costly *deliberate* tax avoidance BIT focuses, for HMRC, on encouraging those who might be slow to pay more quickly. They state that they 'brought forward an additional £210M of revenue'. It was 'brought forward', although 'HMRC normally get the money at some point … [the taxpayers] pay you sooner so you don't have to take them to court' (Ibid.). This strategy works by appealing to people's honesty and is likely to affect only those individuals who submit their own taxes. Research has indicated that almost a third of managers polled recently said they work in an unethical way putting this down to necessity for 'career progression' (Chartered Management Institute, 2013: 4).

A competitor, Nigel Oakes argued that BIT's methods were crude: 'I think they're looking at the economics of it and they're then … guessing at the solutions', and 'picking up … Robert Cialdini's book *Persuasion* which covers "50 most useful techniques" and they found one called social proof and so … said to people in the street, everyone else has paid their gas bill so you should pay yours'. Oakes said: 'it's like an ad agency … coming up with a lucky ad campaign that sort of really, really works and they go, see?' but not really understanding how and why they did it. One example he gave was their work on increasing gas bill payment saying, this 'wasn't bad … because when you're dealing with … hundreds of thousands of people … pretty much whatever you do is going to … achieve a positive result'.

However, Oakes argued that BIT was still better at 'behaviour change' than conventional PR. Increasingly, this is seen as an area of expertise Britain can capitalize on and the BIT helped establish a similar unit in Obama's White House. O'Donnell (2014) said: 'I suspect where the new version of the nudge unit will be most successful is in its work internationally with other governments' (Ibid.). The British Government has crafted an international image and reputation for being good at persuasion. In the US Government in particular, Britain is viewed as having particular skill in the area of persuasion, largely due to assistance in a security context (Briant, 2015). In *Assistant Head, Defence Media and Communications Operations Plans* MoD Col. Ralph Arundell, for example, said: 'the Americans like to think we're very good at this sort of activity. Because we have a long historical background with it' (Ibid.: 216). In 2012 the New South Wales (NSW) Premier Barry O'Farrell set up a similar 'nudge' unit with BIT's guidance. The plan was similar 'looking at ways documents issued by the Office of State Revenue – which collects state taxes and traffic fines – can be reworded to deliver better results' (Wade, 2013) and 'debt recovery, fraud prevention and preventable health issues' (Hollingworth, 2012). Chris Eccles, director general of the NSW Department for Premier and Cabinet even echoed the same rhetoric used by Halpern: they were 'enabling people to make better choices for themselves' (Cabinet Office and Shapps, 2012).

BIT has now become a mutual, partnered with Nesta, and is seeking more commercial contracts.[9] British government departments will now pay consultancy fees for any advice provided. According to the *Financial Times* in 2013, 'the value of government contracts handed to the private sector' has 'doubled in four years to £20 [billion]' (Plimmer, 2013). The move was not anticipated from the beginning: 'I certainly hadn't imagined that it would become a joint venture' O'Donnell (2014) recalled, 'that happened after my time' (Ibid.). O'Donnell himself now works for Frontier Economics, a consultancy which lobbies government ministers on behalf of commercial clients.[10]

Media 'scapegoats' and individual responsibility

The cultural politics of neo-liberal 'nudging' – evidenced in discourse and persuasion tactics – can further be evidenced in the way scapegoats emerge from media discourse in relation to the liberal notion of 'individual responsibility' across the cultural landscape. While BIT's interventions fall far short of managing the impacts of austerity, some media have presented a selective or distorted history that deflects attention away from state responsibility.

Gramsci (1971: 462) saw the relationship between historical knowledge and praxis as crucial to ensuring philosophy and planning responds to the needs of the people and that 'consent' is a clear indication of how the establishment attempt to manage the cultural political field. Media coverage has also helped to manage

conflicts of interest and manufacture consent for austerity by de-
monizing the poor by creating moral panics, which are driven by
ideology.

As Cohen (2011: 9) argued, moral panics are produced when 'a
condition, episode, person or group of persons emerges to become
defined as a threat to societal values and interests'. Demonized
'folk devils' concerned 'deviant youth cultures', yet crucially key
features of Cohen's model in relation to the 'cycle of a moral panic'
(Ibid.: 24), and 'folk devils', can be seen in recent contexts facilitating policy changes. Examples include disability and incapacity
benefit claimants mentioned above.

Emphasizing 'individual responsibility' isn't particularly new, although in the age of austerity it clearly produces specific narratives
that affect cultural politics. For example, Golding and Middleton
(1982: 3) had argued in the eighties that emphasizing individual
responsibility led to a culture of 'indicting welfare and convicting
the poor' for that era's financial crisis through the creation of new
'folk devils' in the media like 'welfare scroungers', 'single mothers' and 'dole cheats' (Cohen, 2011). Further the moral panic of a
'campaign against scroungers' (Franklin, 1999: 2) led to the demonization of welfare recipients, ignored the structural issue of rising
unemployment (Campbell, 1984) and built intense pressure to cut
back welfare spending.

These historical details are replicated today when we consider
the 2010 Coalition government's welfare reforms which included a
reassessment of people claiming incapacity benefit.[11] Similar cuts
to the austerity measures in 2010–11 had been proposed for incapacity benefit by the previous Blair government in 2004–5. Research by Briant, Philo and Watson (2011) demonstrated a surge
in media coverage of disability following the financial crash as
government cuts were directed at reducing the welfare budget by
reclassifying disabled people as fit for work. This news coverage
focused on people who it said claimed disability benefits fraudulently and linked them with the crisis through welfare spending.

Although this type of news framing existed before the financial
crash, what is clear is the idea of 'austerity' – as ideology – helps to
construct a different narrative within the field of cultural politics.
For example, the phrase 'we're all in it together' is an ideological
construct that legitimizes government and often media actions to
apply policy and to forward a philosophy that argues for individuals taking responsibility for their actions.

Research indicates that mainstream reporting of the banking
crisis favoured city source perspectives and proposed solutions
which placed the burden on the public (Berry, 2012). As the cuts
were underway in 2010–11, most newspapers were supportive of

the government's policies (Briant, Watson and Philo, 2013: 6) to justify the austerity cuts to disability benefits in the wake of the financial crisis where the media debate became more *personalized* around individual responsibility and less focused on 'problems in the system'. Some articles even blamed the whole debt crisis on incapacity benefit claimants: 'Shirker's Paradise; Exclusive: IDS on Benefits Britain, Wagner's one of Million who Claim Incapacity, Work-shy are Largely to Blame for Deficit Crisis' (Ibid.: 8). Negative coverage blamed welfare claimants themselves for austerity to deflect blame from government and created scapegoats for the cuts (Briant, Watson and Philo, 2011).

The portrayal of the welfare claimants as fraudulent has been a central theme since the late 1970s and research showed that the use of this theme increased following the financial crash (Briant, Watson and Philo, 2013). Deacon (1978: 346) argued that in the 1970s media levels of hostility towards the poor contrasted with the existence of 'virtually no abuse' of the system. And similarly following the financial crash, an exaggerated prominence of fraud as a tabloid theme conflicted with the reality of low-recorded and estimated levels of fraud (for Disability Living Allowance estimated to be at 0.5 per cent and for Incapacity Benefit to be at 0.3 per cent by DWP 2012). It served to focus public perceptions on claimants rather than systemic problems of the labour market or government economic policies. Exaggeration and distortion provide one way folk devils are constructed and reinforced (Cohen, 2011: 31). Cohen describes how individual cases are taken within the media discourse 'as confirming a general theme' (Ibid.: 81) and then seen as part of a broad trend – in this case, it was benefit fraud. There is a strong public belief that benefit fraud is high; a recent poll indicates that 'on average people think that twenty seven per cent of the welfare budget' is fraudulently claimed – compared to the reality of just 0.7 per cent (TUC, 2013). In fact, benefit *underpayment* is far greater than total benefit fraud, and both are far surpassed by even the modest HMRC estimates of tax avoidance, at £30 billion per year (Ball, 2013).

The fraud theme was reflected in language: benefit claimants were described by the media using pejorative terms such as 'scrounger' and 'workshy', terms that were used before the financial crash but which increased following it (Briant, Watson and Philo, 2013: 8). Politicians and ministers contributed to this, for example George Osborne, the Chancellor of the Exchequer, who 'claimed living on incapacity benefit had become a "Lifestyle Choice"'; this phrase was 'recycled' in the media (Ibid.). Cohen (2011) claimed that political influence plays a role in determining the form the 'inventory' or process of media interpretation/response takes; he identified two interrelated factors that determine this: 'the institutionalised need to create news and [...] the selective and inferential structure of the news-making process' (Ibid.: 45). Cohen argues that 'the media adjudicate between competing definitions of a situation and these definitions are made in a hierarchical context – agents of social control are more likely to be believed' (Ibid.: 46). Newspapers were broadly in support of the coalitions' welfare cuts and continued, as Cohen argued, selecting stories to fit with their pre-existing themes (Ibid.: 47).

Following the financial crash, there was also a redrawing of the category of 'disabled' by the government, distinguishing the undeserving (many) and the deserving (few) with an emphasis on 'work' capabilities rather than 'health'. This allowed the vilification by government ministers and the mainstream media of 'folk devils' who had formerly been encouraged to claim. Those previously classified as disabled were now 'described in the popular media and in political discourse as people who have taken illegitimately from the taxpayer and cheated "genuine" claimants' (Briant, Watson and Philo, 2013: 14). It reduced claimants, whilst reassuring the public that support was provided for (those who continued to be classed as) disabled people, and press coverage often included, as a minor theme, small concessions for the 'genuine' disabled which served to add emphasis to the idea of large numbers of 'fraudulent claimants' (Ibid.: 10). The financial crisis thus facilitated the expansion of the neo-liberal conceptualization of poverty as caused by 'individual inadequacy' and demanding individual, not state, solutions to include people in receipt of disability and incapacity benefits. News discourses were used to question the citizenship and rights of welfare recipients in a way that reflected recent research into news discourses on asylum seekers.

Conclusion

We have shown here how BIT's 'nudging' is being used as a complement to an ideological system which, alongside media creation of 'folk devils', refocuses responsibility for the financial crisis and subsequent austerity measures on individuals. This exposes an inherent contradiction in the neo-liberal adherence to free-market fundamentalism. Instead of being interpreted as a crisis for neo-liberal ideology, the 2008 financial crash was rationalized through a discourse of austerity that focused on reforming the behaviour of those most affected by the crash, and this is how *cultural politics* proceeds in the age of austerity in the contexts discussed in this chapter.

In his seminal work 'The Sociological Imagination', C. Wright Mills (1959: 8) draws a distinction between 'private troubles' and 'public issues'; he illustrates this idea by arguing that the solution to complex social problems like mass unemployment cannot be found 'within the range of opportunities open to any one individual'. Mills stresses the importance of understanding the causal structural conditions that drive social problems. The individualist rationale that underpins the neo-liberal ideology represented in recent policy and media narratives inverts this logic to rationalize *public issues* as *private troubles* (Ibid.). Briant, Watson and Philo (2013: 15) concluded that 'The creation of widespread concern about fraud and misclaiming follows from deliberate political interventions'. Žižek describes how 'pseudo concrete' images are used to embody 'all the evils of society' and form part of an 'ideological edifice' to scapegoat individuals and groups. Žižek's example of the 'unemployed single mother' (2012) could just as easily be incapacity benefit claimants or other marginalized groups. Media representations have an impact on how the public understand poverty (Briant, Watson and Philo, 2011). Joseph Rowntree Foundation's latest research found that public attitudes towards poverty and welfare have hardened (Clery, Lee and Kunz, 2013). A fundamentalist free-market approach has dominated political decisions about social welfare in Britain since the late 1970s but is being further entrenched and justified with reference to the recent crisis. Social effects have been masked in an approach which blames individuals for social problems and ignores the structural causes, leading the media to call for sanctions against those individuals. In these political and media narratives, people are valued by their 'ability to produce wealth' (Katz, 1990: 7), justifying cuts and the resultant social exclusion of those who do not.

Notes

1 The 'Behavioural Insights Team' (BIT) is often articulated as a *rejection* of classical economics in favour of the more socially sustainable approach of behavioural economics. These strategies, originally developed by New Labour (Prime Minister's Strategy Unit 2004) were taken up within the coalition's austerity drive so that responsibility for social problems could be shifted onto individuals. Reducing the role of the state, they aim to use knowledge of natural psychological biases and errors to modify behaviour.

2 An economist, Gus O'Donnell had overseen implementation of many of the neo-liberal policies mentioned above that contributed to widening inequality in the UK. From 2002 to 2005, he was permanent secretary at HM Treasury then became cabinet secretary until 2011.

3 Gus O'Donnell had formerly been the United Kingdom's Executive Director to the International Monetary Fund and the World Bank (1997–98), then the Treasury Director of Macroeconomic Policy and

Prospects and Head of the Government Economics Service – with overall responsibility for professional government economists. From 1999 to 2002 as Managing Director of Macroeconomic Policy and International Finance, he was made responsible for the UK's fiscal policy, international development and EMU. As a lecturer at Glasgow University, one of his specialisms for teaching was 'welfare economics' (O'Donnell, June 25, 2014).

4 Therefore to be effective psychological profiling would be needed to successfully shape an intervention for a specific target, at a time when increasing government information gathering and privacy issues are of strong public concern.

5 Nigel Oakes, founder of behaviour change defence contractor Strategic Communication Laboratories and the Behavioural Dynamics Institute, said: 'the key people from the behavioural nudge unit all came to see us [at SCL/BDI] ... when it was in its infancy ... to see how they could ... shape it'. He described how they also 'worked with [BIT] in the past ... briefed them on a number of occasions' as they were growing (Oakes, 2013).

6 They did not, however, interview *anyone* looking for work.

7 Corporate nudges are quite possible: Service mentioned one in relation to mobile phone theft that would impact on the market to produce a solution that would reduce the burden on policing: 'the normal approach would be to say ... mobile phones get stolen all the time, how can we crack down on this particular problem? What powers can we give the police to solve this particular crime-type? And that might be a legitimate response, but ... it will cost money'. BIT instead created a Mobile Phone Theft Index: because, 'for example ... iPhones are about four times more likely to get stolen than the next most likely brand of phone, which are blackberries ... and there are peaks just before new model's about to be introduced, which is an ... indication of the nature of ... this problem [which] is ... an insurance issue'. So the index would 'gather the data on this and put it out so consumers can be more informed when they're making their decisions, but more importantly, it will put pressure on the manufacturers in a slightly different way' (Service, 2013). The motivation is not redistributive but to adjust markets and reduce need for regulation of business.

8 On this O'Donnell said behavioural biases in government 'absolutely' exist and 'a key point I've been making about politicians is that ... Secretaries of State ... spend a lot of time in the [House of Commons or Lords]' and so 'are automatically going to think that's where I'm going to find the solution for things, hence you have a very strong bias towards legislative solutions' (O'Donnell, 2014).

9 These must have a 'social purpose' – Service clarified that this meant that the intervention cannot be for purely commercial objectives such as increasing profits (Service, 2013). Beyond this, what kind of social purpose or who defines the social value of it is unclear.

10 Including Heathrow Airport which some have argued is a conflict of interest (Cohen, 2013).

11 The changes included tests for people who receive Employment Support Allowance (ESA) introduced by the previous administration and continued by the current one. A 'Universal Credit' benefit was introduced along with a change in indexation of uprating benefits from the higher retail price index (RPI) to the lower consumer price index (CPI), changes to entitlement to Disability Living Allowance (DLA) and a range of other service changes and welfare cuts impacting adversely on disabled people.

Bibliography

Allen, K. (2014). 'British public wrongly believe rich pay most in tax, new research shows'. *The Guardian*. Available at: http://www.theguardian.com/money/2014/jun/16/british-public-wrong-rich-poor-tax-research?CMP=fb_gu [Accessed on January 29, 2015].

Armstrong, M. and Huck, S. (2010). 'Behavioural economics as applied to firms: a primer, Office of Fair Trading'. Available at: http://economics.ouls.ox.ac.uk/15236/1/oft1213.pdf [Accessed January 29, 2015].

Ball, J. (2013). 'Welfare fraud is a drop in the ocean compared to tax avoidance'. *The Guardian*. Available at: http://www.theguardian.com/commentisfree/2013/feb/01/welfare-fraud-tax-avoidance [Accessed January 29, 2015].

Beatty, C. and Fothergill, S. (2010). 'Incapacity benefits in the UK: An issue of health or jobs?' Available at: http://www.social-policy.org.uk/lincoln/Beatty.pdf [Accessed January 29, 2015].

Benjamin, A. (2013). 'We try to avoid legislation and ordering'. *The Guardian*. Available at: http://www.theguardian.com/society/2013/feb/05/david-halpern-government-nudge-unit [Accessed February 5, 2013].

Bennett, A. (2014). 'Banks paid twice as much in bonuses as tax since 2008 crash', *Huffington Post*. Available at: http://www.huffingtonpost.co.uk/2014/02/11/bank-bonuses-tax-crash_n_4766066.html [Accessed January 29, 2015].

Berry, M. (2012). 'The *Today Programme* and the Banking Crisis'. *Journalism*, 14(2): 253–70.

Blinder, S. (2011). 'Migration to the UK: Asylum'. *Oxford Migration Observatory*. Available at: http://migrationobservatory.ox.ac.uk/briefings/migration-uk-asylum [Accessed January 29, 2015].

Brewer, M. (2007). 'Welfare Reform in the UK: 1997–2007'. *Fiscal Studies*, IFS Working Paper W07/20.

Brewer, M., Clark, T. and Wakefield, M. (2002). 'Social Security under New Labour: what did the Third Way mean for welfare reform?' *Fiscal Studies*, 23(4): 505–37.

Briant, E. L. (2015). *Propaganda and counterterrorism: strategies for global change*. Manchester: Manchester University Press.

Briant, E. L., Watson, N. and Philo, G. (2011). *Bad news for disabled people: how the newspapers are reporting disability*. Report for Inclusion London. Available at: http://www.gla.ac.uk/media/media_214917_en.pdf [Accessed January 29, 2015].

Briant, E. L., Watson, N. and Philo, G. (2013). 'Reporting Disability in the Age of Austerity: the changing face of media representation of disability and disabled people in the United Kingdom and the creation of new folk devils'. *Disability and Society*, 28(6).

Burk, K. (1992). *Good-bye, Great Britain: the 1976 IMF crisis*. London: Yale University Press.

Cabinet Office (2012a). 'New BIT trial results: helping people back into work'. Available at: http://www.behaviouralinsights.co.uk/blog/ [Accessed January 29, 2015].

Cabinet Office (2012b). 'Designing interventions in partnership with the people who are going to deliver them'. Available at: http://www.behaviouralinsights.co.uk/blog/ [Accessed January 29, 2015].

Cabinet Office and Shapps, G. (2012). 'Government's nudge unit goes global'. Available at: https://www.gov.uk/government/news/governments-nudge-unit-goes-global [Accessed January 29, 2015].

Campbell, B. (1984). *Wigan pier revisited: poverty and politics in the eighties*. London: Virago.

Campbell, D. (2014). 'Government health agency is not up to job, say MPs'. *The Guardian*. Available at: http://www.theguardian.com/society/2014/feb/26/government-health-agency-inadequate-mps [Accessed January 29, 2015].

Chakrabortty, A. (2013). 'London's economic boom leaves rest of Britain behind'. *The Guardian*. Available at: http://www.theguardian.com/business/2013/oct/23/london-south-east-economic-boom [Accessed January 29, 2015].

Chartered Management Institute (2013). *Managers and the moral maze*. Report Available at: http://forms.managers.org.uk/subpages/ethics/downloads/Managers_and_the_moral_maze_sept13.pdf [Accessed January 29, 2015].

Cialdini, R. (2007). *Influence: the psychology of persuasion*. London: Harper Business.

Clery, E., Lee, L. and Kunz, S. (2013). 'Public attitudes to poverty and welfare, 1983–2011'. Joseph Rowntree Foundation.

Cockett, R. (1995). *Thinking the unthinkable: think-tanks and the economic counter-revolution 1931–1983*. London: Harper Collins.

Cohen, S. (2011). *Folk devils and moral panics*. London: Routledge Classics.

Cohen, T. (2013). 'Next O'Donnell faces flak as he lands Heathrow role: Former Cabinet Secretary accused of "cashing in" by accepting job'. *Daily Mail*. Available at: http://www.dailymail.co.uk/news/article-2381655/Former-Cabinet-Secretary-Gus-ODonnell-accused-cashing-accepting-job.html [Accessed January 29, 2015].

D'Arcy, C. and Gardiner, L. (2014). 'Just the job or a working compromise'. Report by Resolution Foundation. Available at: http://www.resolutionfoundation.org/publications/just-job-or-working-compromise-changing-nature-sel/ [Accessed January 29, 2015].

Davies, N. (1997). *Dark heart*. London: Vintage.

Deacon, A. (1978). 'The Scrounging Controversy: Public Attitudes Towards the Unemployed in Contemporary Britain'. *Social Policy and Administration*, 12(2), 120–35.

Dolan, P., Halpern, D., King, D., Vlaev, I. and Hallsworth, M. (2010). 'Mindspace: Influencing Behaviour Through Public Policy'. Institute for Government and Cabinet Office. Available at: http://www.institute forgovernment.org.uk/our-work/better-policy-making/mindspace-behavioural-economics [Accessed January 9, 2015].

Dumeneil, G. and Levy, D. (2004). *Capital resurgent: roots of the Neo-liberal Revolution*. Cambridge: Harvard University Press.

DWP (2012). *Fraud and error in the benefit system: 2011/12 estimates*. Available at: https://www.gov.uk/government/collections/fraud-and-error-in-the-benefit-system [Accessed January 29, 2015].

Epping Forest Guardian (2008). 'LOUGHTON: Grim new year as unemployment bites'. *Epping Forest Guardian*. Available at: http://www.guardian-series.co.uk/news/4001520.print/ [Accessed January 29, 2015].

Franklin, B. (1999). *Social policy, the media and misrepresentation*. London: Routledge.

Gamble, A. (2001). *Neo-liberalism, capital and class*, 25(3): 127–34.

Gilovich, T. Griffin, D. and Kahneman, D. (2002). *Heuristics and biases: the psychology of intuitive judgment*. Cambridge: Cambridge University Press.

Gilpin, R. (2000). *The challenge of global capitalism*. Princeton: Princeton University Press.

Golding, P. and Middleton, S. (1982). *Images of welfare: press and public attitudes to poverty*. Oxford: M. Robertson.

Gramsci, A. (1971). *Selections from the Prison Notebooks*. London: International Publishers.

Hall, S. (2012). 'The neoliberal revolution'. In: J. Rutherford and S. Davison, eds., *The Neo-liberal Crisis*. London: Soundings.

Hall, S. and O'Shea, A. (2013). *Common sense neoliberalism*. London: Soundings.

Hardy, C. (2012). 'Debden: New Food Bank Feeding 40 a week'. *Epping Forest Guardian*. Available at: http://www.guardianseries.co.uk/news/9709283.DEBDEN__New_food_bank_feeding_40_a_week/?ref=rss [Accessed January 29, 2015].

Harvey, D. (2002). *A brief history of neoliberalism*. New York: Oxford University Press.

Hasan, M. (2010). 'The Tories are still the Nasty Party'. *New Statesman*.

Hills, J. (1998). 'Thatcherism, New Labour and the Welfare State, Case, Paper 13'. Available at: http://people.ds.cam.ac.uk/mb65/documents/hills-1998.pdf [Accessed January 29, 2015].

HMRC (2012). 'Closing in on Tax Evasion Report'. Available at: http://www.hmrc.gov.uk/budget-updates/march2012/tax-evasion-report.pdf [Accessed January 29, 2015].

Hollingworth, C. (2012). 'Nudged Down Under'. *Research-Live.com*. Available at: http://www.research-live.com/opinion/nudged-down-under/4008464.article [Accessed January 29, 2015].

Jenner, M. (2011). 'Tax avoidance costs UK economy £69.9 billion a year'. *New Statesman*. Available at http://www.newstatesman.com/blogs/the-staggers/2011/11/tax-avoidance-justice-network [Accessed January 29, 2015].

Kahneman, D. and Tversky, A. (1974). 'Judgement under uncertainty: heuristics and biases'. *Science*, 185: 1124–31.

Katz, M. B. (1990). *The undeserving poor: from the war on poverty to the war on welfare*. New York: Pantheon Books.

Krugman, P. (2009). *The return of depression economics and the crisis of 2008*. New York: W.W. Norton & Co.

Leicester, A., Levell, P. and Rasul, I. (2012). 'Tax and Benefit Policy: Insights from behavioural economics'. *Institute for Fiscal Studies*. Available at: http://www.ifs.org.uk/comms/comm125.pdf [Accessed January 29, 2012].

Lukes, S. (2005). *Power: a radical view*. London: Palgrave MacMillan.

Lund, B. (2008). 'Major, Blair and the Third Way in Social Policy'. *Social Policy and Administration*, 42(1): 43–58.

MacAskill, E. (1999). 'Labour Rebels go for Darling on Tax Cut'. *The Guardian*. Available at: http://www.theguardian.com/politics/1999/nov/04/welfarereform.politicalnews [Accessed January 29, 2015].

Marglin S. A. and Schor, J. B. (1992). *The golden age of capitalism: reinterpreting the postwar experience*. Oxford: Oxford University Press.

Marston, G. (2008). 'A war on the poor: Constructing welfare and work in the twenty-first century'. *Critical Discourse Studies*, 4(5): 359–70.

Mills, C. W. (1959). *The sociological imagination*. New York: Oxford University Press.

Mirowski, P. and Plehwe, D. (2009). *The road from Mont Pelerin: the making of the neoliberal thought collective*. Cambridge: Harvard University Press.

Oakes, N. (2013). Strategic Communication Laboratories – Interview, October 24, 2013.

O'Donnell, G. (2014). Former Labour Cabinet Secretary – Interview, June 25, 2014.

Peck, J. and Tickell, A. (2002). 'Neoliberalizing Space'. *Antipode*, 34(3): 38–404.

Philo, G., Briant, E. and Donald, P. (2013). *Bad news for refugees*. London: Pluto.

Piff, P. K. (2013a). 'Wealth and the inflated self: class, entitlement, and narcissism'. *Personality and Social Psychology Bulletin*, 40: 34–43.

Piff, P. K. (2013b). *Does money make you mean?* TED Talks. Available at: http://www.ted.com/talks/paul_piff_does_money_make_you_mean [Accessed January 29, 2015].

Plimmer, G. (2013). 'Outsourcing soars in public services'. *Financial Times*. Available at: http://www.ft.com/cms/s/0/13a4e68e-6610-11e2-bb67-00144feab49a.html [Accessed January 29, 2015].

Press Association (2010). 'Iain Duncan Smith vows to tackle "absurd" welfare dependency'. *The Guardian*, May 27.

Prime Minister's Strategy Unit (2004). *Personal responsibility and changing behaviour: the state of knowledge and its implications for public policy*. London: Cabinet Office.

Scott-Samuel, A., Bambra, C., Collins, C., Hunter, D. J., McCartney, G. and Smith, K. (2014). 'The impact of Thatcherism on health and well-being in Britain'. *International Journal of Health Services*, 44(1): 53–71.

Service, O. (2013). Behavioural Insights Team – Interview, September 18, 2013.

Shah, H. and Dawney, E. (2005). 'Behavioural Economics: Seven Principles for Policymakers'. New Economics Foundation. Available at: http://www.neweconomics.org/publications/entry/behavioural-economics [Accessed January 29, 2015].

Silva, E. B. (1996). *Good enough mothering? Feminist perspectives on lone motherhood*. London: Routledge.

Simon, H. (1945). *Administrative behaviour: a study of decision making processes in administrative organisation*. New York: The Free Press.

Simon, H. (1957). *Models of man: social and rational*. London: John Wiley & Sons.

Syal, R. (2012). 'Fewer DWP staff to investigate fraud claims against welfare contractors'. *The Guardian*. Available at: http://www.theguardian.com/politics/2012/mar/30/fewer-investigators-fraud-claims-welfare [Accessed January 29, 2015].

Tax Justice Network (2011). *Tackle Tax Havens* – Report. Available at: http://www.tackletaxhavens.com/Cost_of_Tax_Abuse_TJN%20Research_23rd_Nov_2011.pdf [Accessed January 29, 2015].

Thaler, R. H. and Sunstein, C. R. (2008). *NUDGE. Improving decisions about health, wealth, and happiness*. New Haven: Yale University Press.

Thatcher, M. (1987). 'Interview for Woman's Own'. *Margaret Thatcher Foundation*. Available at: http://www.margaretthatcher.org/document/106689 [Accessed January 29, 2015].

The Telegraph (2008). 'In full: the reading list issued to Tory MPs'. Available at: http://www.telegraph.co.uk/news/2493248/In-full-The-reading-list-issued-to-Tory-MPs.html [Accessed January 29, 2015].

Thomas, B., Dorling, D. and Smith, G. D. (2010). 'Inequalities in premature mortality in Britain: observational study from 1921 to 2007'. *British Medical Journal*, 341.

Thrift, N. (2007). *Non-representational theory: space, politics, affect*. Abingdon: Routledge.

TUC (2013). 'Support for benefit cuts dependent on ignorance, TUC-commissioned poll finds'. *TUC Online*. Available at: http://www.tuc.org.uk/social/tuc-21796-f0.cfm [Accessed January 29, 2015].

Wacquant, L. (1999). 'How penal common sense comes to Europeans'. *European Societies*, 1(3): 319–52.

Wade, M. (2013). 'What a difference a nudge in the right direction can make'. *The Sydney Morning Herald*. Available at: http://www.smh.com.au/comment/what-a-difference-a-nudge-in-the-right-direction-can-make-20130406-2hdab.html [Accessed January 29, 2015].

Whitehead, M., Jones, R., Pykett, J. and Jones, M. (2012). 'Commentary: geography, libertarian paternalism and neuro-politics in the UK'. *The Geographical Journal*, 178(4).

Wilkinson, R. and Pickett, K. (2010). *The spirit level*. New York: Bloomsbury Press.

Wilkinson, T. M. (2013). 'Nudging and manipulation'. *Political Studies*, 61(2): 341–55.

Williams, R. (1958). *Culture and society: 1780–1950*. London: Chatto and Windus.

Wolf, M. (2008). 'Keynes offers us the best way to think about the financial crisis'. *Financial Times*.

Žižek, S. (2012). *The perverts guide to ideology*. Channel 4 DVD.

6 Class and cultural colonization in the era of austerity

The dialectics of identity and de-subordination

Mark Hayes

Introduction

This chapter examines themes surrounding notions of class and culture in contemporary Britain. Class is a controversial category in sociological analysis, and the purpose of this intervention is to focus on developments that have been accentuated by 'austerity' imposed by governments after the financial collapse in 2008. As Milne (2012: viii) points out, 'the first decade of the twenty-first century shook the international order to its foundations, turning the received wisdom of the global elites on its head – and 2008 was its watershed'. The collapse of Lehman Brothers in the US was the catalyst that sparked the worst global economic crisis since 1929. Indeed the former governor of the Bank of England, Mervyn King, referred to the financial meltdown as the worst crisis in the history of capitalism (Ibid.: xv).

Overnight the underlying assumptions of neo-liberal orthodoxy were rendered obsolete as the apostles of free-market capitalism began anxiously re-reading the work of John Maynard Keynes. Capitalism was rescued by the largest government intervention in the history of economics in order to save the banks and the financial system (Leys, 2014). It was ironic that the agencies of the state – much maligned in conventional neo-liberal economic theory – were deployed in order to salvage the 'self-regulating' free market. Hence, the neo-liberal 'free enterprise' credo which had prevailed for a generation came to resemble the ancient catechism of a defunct religion. However, this systemic crisis has precipitated an era of austerity which sought to re-stabilize the economic system by cutting welfare budgets, ensuring that ordinary people would pay the price of saving capitalism from itself. In Britain the proposed scheme of 'Universal Credit' and 'work capability assessments', the scrapping of the Social Fund and Educational Maintenance Allowance, along with the imposition of the so-called 'bedroom tax' were all clearly indicative of a desire to focus economic retrenchment on those citizens at the bottom of the social ladder (Atkinson *et al.*, 2012). The result has been an increase in the number of people using foodbanks and payday loans (O'Hara, 2014). Clearly such reforms reflected a more general recalibration of social provision toward 'voluntary' and 'charitable' solutions, and 'austerity' has constituted one of the 'most radically regressive and distinctive economic experiments the UK has ever seen' (Ibid.: 1). In this broader context of 'austerity', some observations will be made about the complex connections between class and cultural politics in the contemporary era.

The reality of class and social stratification

Historically social stratification has occurred as a consequence of a range of factors, including slavery, caste and estate, but more prevalent in the capitalist era are distinctions made on the basis of social class. Class might be defined as a large-scale group of people who share a similar level of economic resources and consubstantial social experiences and is therefore a category used to denote differential locations within a hierarchical order of unequal groups. The concept of class, and what constitutes its precise essence, has preoccupied sociological theorists since Marx and Weber (Savage, 2000). In fact, Marx (2004: 124) said: 'in so far as millions of families live under economic conditions of existence that separate their mode of life, their interests and their culture from those of the other classes, and put them in hostile opposition to the latter, they form a class'. This seems to be a logical starting point, and clearly '"class" is about unequal resources and status, and the social hierarchies to which they give rise' (Bottero, 2009: 8). Features such as ownership and control of the economic means of production, the ability to accumulate capital, types of occupation, and differences in social status are key aspects in the categorization of the social entities known as 'classes'.

However, '"class" also means different things to different people, and its exact meaning, in both academic and everyday use, is notoriously slippery' (Ibid.). Not only is class an ambiguous, ill-defined and contested concept, it would also be true to say that under capitalism, class boundaries have become less clear-cut than under previous social systems, and there are few formal or legal restrictions on movement within and between classes. As a consequence there is a sense in which such social divisions are conceived as more rational, functional and meritocratic, and there is also an assumption that 'free' liberal democratic societies such as Britain are characterized by a level of fluid mobility in terms of class position (Crompton, 1998).

Many studies have been conducted in order to try to identify distinctions between (and within) the capitalist class system; for example, sophisticated surveys were designed to elucidate the difference between lower, middle and upper class, between clerical and manual workers, or skilled and unskilled workers, between homeowners and non-property owners and so on (see the classic work of John Goldthorpe and John Westergaard; Milner, 1999: 78, 97). These academic studies attempted to monitor the increasing complexity of social classes in modern nation states. Inevitably confusion occurred over the use of terminology; for example, debates took place about what constituted 'blue' and 'white' collar work, and some academics suggested that the changing pattern of work and, more importantly, the increasing affluence of people in employment, meant that the 'working class' had diminished in size and significance.

Sociologists coined the inelegant word 'embourgeoisement' to explain the thesis that significant sectors of the working class were being subsumed into the middle class (Savage, 2000). Hence, the summative assertion of prominent sociologist Anthony Giddens (2009: 471) that 'the working class is composed of those in blue-collar or manual occupations' indicated that those people contained in this category were a minority in Britain. It is certainly true that the traditional 'blue collar' working class has been fragmented and re-configured, and the proportion of 'manual' workers has indeed fallen from 75 to 38 per cent during the course of the twentieth century (Bottero, 2009: 8). However, despite the fact that some iconic working class occupations, such as mining and shipbuilding, have largely disappeared, the notion that the 'working class' has also dematerialized does not stand up to serious scrutiny. (As we shall see, this debate has had serious consequences in terms of social and political theory.)

Class remains relevant, as Erik Olin Wright (2000) explained, although contemporary capitalism is characterized by a much more intricate class system, 'class' retains its salience as a concept. Indeed Wright himself offered his own class-based categorization of capitalist society in terms of three dimensions of control over the economy: investments and resources, the means of production, and labour power. Capitalists, Wright argues, have control over all three, the worker over none (although there is ambiguity when it comes to the intermediate categories). According to Wright, 85 to 90 per cent of people had to sell their labour power and a majority of people (55 to 75 per cent) were identified as 'working class' (Ibid.: 261). It is an interesting fact that most people in Britain regard themselves as working class, and manual and clerical workers make up around two-thirds of the total workforce; indeed a

survey of social attitudes by the National Centre for Social Research revealed that 57 per cent of adults claimed to be working
class, a figure which the NCSR itself noted as 'remarkable' (BBC,
2007; see Milne 2012: 104). If nothing else class should be considered a matter of importance because people actually believe it
exists (Savage, 2000: 23). It is also worth remembering that the
existence of class is always an inherently comparative phenomenon in that *relative* position (inequality) with regard to separate
categories is a critical factor in assessing the relationship between
classes. So this is our starting point – that social stratification exists and classes, despite being less cohesive and homogenous than
was historically the case, remain a prominent feature of the social
landscape in Britain. Class remains a critical explanatory variable
which determines the pattern of social existence – it still has a
profound impact upon key sociological factors such as life expec-
tancy, educational attainment, risk of illness and quality of life
(Atkinson *et al.*, 2012).

Not only is class in Britain an enduring social phenomenon, the
inequality between the classes has increased dramatically in recent
years, with differences in income, wealth and status more pronounced. 'Thatcherism' reversed the gradual drift toward greater
social justice which had been the priority of successive governments after 1945. The post-war political settlement in Britain was
constructed upon social democratic ideas about 'positive freedom'
and social rights of citizenship, which led to the creation of a welfare state. However, when that consensus came under severe strain
in the 1970s, as a consequence of serious economic difficulties,
Thatcher emerged as the standard bearer of a 'New Right' credo
which prioritized the free market as the only sustainable route
to prosperity. Thatcher's political success resulted in increases of
inequality between the classes and an erosion of the foundations
upon which post-war social democracy was constructed (Hayes,
1994). The broad trajectory of Thatcherism was subsequently endorsed by the 'New' Labour Party which displayed a similar devo-
tion to the utility of free enterprise, a fact which was confirmed by
chief Labour strategist Peter Mandelson when he declared himself
to be 'intensely relaxed about people getting filthy rich' (Milne,
2012: 99). The gap between rich and poor widened under New
Labour, with the proportion of wealth held by the richest 10 per
cent of the population increasing from 47 to 54 per cent (Ibid.).
By 2011, in the grip of austerity, living standards for the average
British person were declining at the fastest rate since the 1920s,
and millions of children were living in poverty, yet boardroom
pay in the previous year had increased by 55 per cent; indeed, the
wealth of the richest 1,000 individuals in Britain doubled in the

five years up to 2014 (Jones, 2011: viii; Sayer, 2012; Duggan and Owen, 2014; *Sunday Times*, 2014).

Social division in Britain is not going to alter anytime soon; twenty-three out of twenty-nine members of David Cameron's first Cabinet were millionaires and most went to private school (as did nearly 50 per cent of top civil servants, 70 per cent of financial directors, over 50 per cent of the top journalists and nearly 70 per cent of barristers; Jones, 2012: 171). The Coalition government, imposing its austerity measures, has implemented policies which have cut back drastically on social and welfare provision yet has provided tax cuts worth £42,000 per year for those people earning an annual salary of over £1 million per year (Mulholland, 2012; O'Hara, 2014). Indeed Therborn (2009: 5) claims that 'the gap in income between those at the top and the average worker is now much wider than it was in pre-modern times'. (See also Equality Trust 2011 and Williams, 2013.) It does not require detailed knowledge of the Gini coefficient or an ability to understand the precise purpose of a Lorenz curve to grasp that in Britain there has been a persistent and prevailing pattern of class inequality which has been the consequence of the concentration of wealth in the hands of those at the apex of the social scale; class inequality is a brutal reality in austerity Britain, moreover as Milne (2012: 100) says,

> The evidence is clear that greater inequality fuels crime, corrodes democracy, divides our cities, prices people out of housing, skews the economy, is an engine of social apartheid, heightens ethnic tensions, is a barrier to opportunity and stifles social mobility.

Not only is the Coalition government's slogan 'we are all in it together' exposed as duplicitous drivel, but equally the assertion made by Tony Blair in 1997 (and repeated by prominent politicians ever since) that 'the Britain of the elite is over. The new Britain is a meritocracy' has been revealed as risible nonsense (Jones, 2012: 169). (See also Bragg, 2012.) The mantra of meritocracy and social mobility obscures the reality of life in austerity Britain – a neo-liberal plutocracy characterized by social division and divergent class interests (Sayer, 2012).

The social reproduction of cultural politics and the working class

Identifying the existence of social stratification and class precipitates the thorny question of its relationship to *culture/cultural politics* in relation to austerity. For our purposes, *culture* means a 'way of life' or 'way of doing things' rather than an identifiable aesthetic preference used by elites when imposing *culture* from high. Here, culture is bottom-up, is rooted in aspects of community and is a descriptive anthropological and sociological (rather than evaluative) category. This particular usage of the term 'culture', which can refer to the extent to which a society or the classes therein evolve distinctive patterns of life, is the sense in which the term will be deployed here – or to be more precise, *cultural politics* which is often the process of making culture at odds with higher class preferences of culture or subsuming and accepting such preferences.

Much of the available sociological evidence still shows 'class' to be a primary determinant of identity and in the process of cultural politics (Milner, 1999: 11–12). In short, classes tend to share the same interests, social experiences, traditions and value system; therefore, it is important to consider class differentiated experiences and patterns of action. Although they cannot simply be 'read off' in terms of class position, cultures exist in distinct relation to class and the interesting question to consider is the relationship between 'class' and 'austerity' in the making of culture from the processes of cultural politics. Wilkinson and Pickett (2010: 28) suggest,

> we should perhaps regard the scale of material inequalities in a society as providing the skeleton or framework, round which class and cultural differences are formed. Over time, crude differences in wealth gradually become overlaid by differences in clothing, aesthetic taste, education, sense of self and all the other markers of class identity.

This feature of society has been noted by many theorists, including Pierre Bourdieu, who developed the idea that culture was critically important when looking at class. Bourdieu identified notions of 'cultural', 'social' and 'symbolic' capital (in addition to economic capital), whereby class distinctions are powerfully reinforced by differences in culture and lifestyle. In this way 'habitus' and the capacity to operationalize certain norms and values can inscribe an image of the social world and a sense of place and worth within it (Atkinson *et al.*, 2012). As a result wealth becomes overlaid with cultural markers of social difference, and people are judged by accent, clothing, appreciation of art and music, type of leisure pursuits enjoyed, club memberships and so on. Indeed in some ways this is how social categories are maintained, and matters of 'taste' become transformed into prejudice (this is what Bourdieu calls 'symbolic violence'), which inevitably leads to hostility, resentment and shame as individuals internalize their perceived inadequacy. As Atkinson (2012: 13) says, the distribution of resources 'endows differential capacity to impose one's own tastes as *legitimate* – as what all should strive to be and do – through the fields of cultural and ideological production'. There is no single, straightforward axis or mode of economic exploitation and domination, since the cultural dimension creates a much more complex matrix of social subordination.

So we can legitimately talk of class culture and, moreover, a specifically working class culture and way of life, and if so how does austerity impact upon the processes of cultural politics associated with the working class? The British working class has developed an intricate web of traditions, norms, values, habits, practices and dialects which separate its inhabitants from those of other social classes. This distinct way of life emerged during the early nineteenth century as a consequence of industrialization and urbanization and was to persist, with some modifications, into the twentieth century. This working class culture, reinforced by common occupation, residence, and language (accent), had at its core a number of social features such as non-conformist churches, company bands and choirs, craft societies, public houses, libraries, association football, dance/music halls, cinema, betting shops, working men's clubs and so on. Indeed significant numbers were also involved in cooperative societies, the Workers' Educational Association, trade unions and the Labour Party, and the clear sense of difference between 'us' and 'them' was underpinned by an (albeit unformulated) moral code based on solidarity, mutual cooperation and fairness (Kirk, 1991: 203). In this way the working class, who were not the beneficiaries of more obvious 'cultural' attributes possessed by other classes, nevertheless fought to achieve a sense of pride and self-respect in onerous circumstances.

This working class culture has been the subject of some sustained academic attention. For example, Raymond Williams (1992: 115) identified a 'structure of feeling' that reflected the 'lived' experience of the community and which provided a framework through which members of the social group experienced the world, helping them to explain their existence. Working people were thus able to negotiate their own pathway through life with its own particular priorities and parameters. Similarly Richard Hoggart (1973: 325), through his own more personalized observations, identified a 'working class culture' in northern England that was rich and creative with a clear 'ethical rudder', which resisted the pressures imposed by economic hardship. E. P. Thompson (1981) documented a proletarian consciousness and culture emerging from the urban slums that was brutal in certain aspects, but which was also caring and compassionate – and no less distinctive than the culture which defined the middle classes or the upper echelons of the nobility. Thompson identified a culture that was not only impervious to the exogenous exhortations of 'social betters', but it could also be admirable in terms of its intelligence and moral passion – indeed Thompson concluded his seminal work by saying: 'we may thank them for these years of heroic culture' (Ibid.: 915). Although described as 'sentimental' in some quarters (Savage, 2000: 33) Williams, Hoggart and Thompson mapped the contours of a distinctive working class culture.

In fact it might be argued that this working class culture was central to the post-1945 political dispensation which created the social democratic consensus. The collectivist ethos, which was reflected most clearly in working class neighbourhoods, and in organizations like trade unions, the cooperative movement and the Labour Party, began to permeate society as a whole. Given impetus by the experiences of economic depression and world wars, this credo of solidarity and social justice gradually secured enough political leverage to change the nature of society. This process of qualitative social transformation reached its peak in the construction of corporatist policy making structures and the creation of the welfare state (particularly the NHS), which provided a symbolic institutional testimony to the ascendancy of working class disposition toward mutual assistance: 'from the cradle to the grave'. In the immediate post-war era, the working class became more prosperous and more self-confident, and its members began to make tangible inroads into politics and popular culture. Parliament, local government, theatre, film, television, popular music, art, fashion and soap operas reflected this process and in turn made the working class more worthy of attention (Bragg, 2012). As Selina Todd (2014: 1, 121) says, after the Second World War the working class became 'the people' and 'the backbone of the nation', whose 'interests became synonymous with those of the country'. Subordination continued, but it was a socio-political settlement which had been re-negotiated to the benefit of the mass of ordinary people, and to be 'working class' was not just fashionable, it was to be in possession of a certain set of socio-cultural attributes which were viewed positively and which possessed the inherent capacity for collective political agency. It was possible to be proud of being working class, and the immediate post-war period may indeed have been the high point in the 'forward march of labour', when ordinary people were in a position to secure tangible victories (Hobsbawm, 1978). However, all of this was to change dramatically in the 1970s.

Demonization of the working class and the assimilation of the dominant culture

After the collapse of the post-war social democratic consensus, the ascendant ideology of Thatcherism and the New Right in Britain reinvigorated a pre-war culture of competitive individualism and private enterprise, which critically undermined the working class ethos of collectivism and social solidarity. In effect the working class suffered a specific kind of 'institutional de-mobilisation' (Savage, 2012), as Jones (2012: 10) explained:

> Margaret Thatcher's assumption of power in 1979 marked the beginning of an all-out assault on the pillars of working class Britain. Its institutions, like trade unions and council housing, were dismantled; its industries, from manufacturing to mining, were trashed; its communities were, in some cases, shattered, never to recover; and its values, like solidarity and collective aspiration, were swept away in favour of rugged individualism.

The miners' strike in 1984 was a pivotal moment in the political and economic history of Britain, and represented the symbolic castration of the labour movement and the industrial power of the working class. In the new 'enterprise culture', the acquisition of wealth was to be glorified and entrepreneurs were idolized as never before, whilst the trickle-down theory dominated economic discourse. People were, in effect, encouraged to escape the working class.

However, this was not simply an attack on the working class in terms of resource allocation, because what ensued was a cultural offensive against those at the bottom of the social hierarchy which continued ever since. It has been argued that in recent years the working classes have been increasingly derided and demonized. Those who were once described as the 'salt of the earth' have been transformed, in the space of a generation, into the 'scum of the earth' (Collins, 2005).[1] The working class was increasingly portrayed as irredeemably vulgar, ignorant, immoral, lazy, drunken, violent and racist. Indeed the term 'Chav' became common currency and was used to denote people who embodied these traits. Comedic representations like 'Wayne and Waynetta Slob' and 'Vicky Pollard' reflected the extent to which such derogatory representations penetrated popular consciousness. As Smith (2013: 31) says, 'the humour behind such stereotypes is the kind that confirms prejudices' and 'provides a neat fit with the caricatures of poverty found in the tabloids'. Indeed British tabloids often referred to the 'underclass' as little more than social scum, a collection of feral teenagers, unrepentant criminals, and parasitic scroungers, and this image contributed to a 'moral panic' which reflected a deep, visceral loathing for the dispossessed (Ibid.: 30). The message was simple – do not feel sorry for them because they are grotesque, the feckless 'other', deserving of nothing but contempt (Sveinsson, 2009: 5 note 20; Jones, 2012). There is a cruel streak in contemporary society and a meanness in cultural values that has seldom been so explicit (Lawler, 2008: 122, 128; Smith, 2013: 30). This cultural condescension constitutes the construction of a coded hierarchy of identity. The middle and upper classes, triumphant in the security of their own wealth and status, no longer threatened by lower orders, feel able to simply point and laugh (Jones, 2012). As Jones concludes, 'the demonization of the working class is the ridiculing of the conquered by the conqueror' (Ibid.: 247, see also xiii).

Yet there is a more insidious dimension to this cultural offensive because poverty, once seen as a consequence of social processes and structural inequalities, is now seen as a purely cultural phenomenon, a question of individual choice and the failure to assimilate appropriate values. Indeed Bottero (2000: 7) maintains: 'to focus on the cultural differences of unequal groups is just a short step from arguing that the poor are disadvantaged *as a result of* their supposed cultural differences'. This ongoing process has been identified before and marks the most recent manifestation of the traditional distinction between 'deserving' and 'undeserving poor'. As Westergaard and Resler (1977: 22–23) said, some analysts argue that poverty is simply an issue of culture: 'the product of an accumulation of collective incompetence and lack of initiative by those at the bottom of the pile', thus the blame for inequality 'falls neatly on its victims'. Unemployment, homelessness and educational failure are therefore seen as a consequence of personal inability rather than a result of economic inequality and systemic failure. The new poor are thereby designated as unworthy of empathy; they are the 'flawed consumers' who are not only maligned and marginalized, they are dismissed as useless (Bauman, 2005). This process of cultural exclusion, unsystematic though it is, has been accentuated by austerity and has had the effect of sealing off some working class areas as untouchable Bantustans, where the new serfs on bleak council estates barely exist in a class system which is becoming as rigid as any caste structure.

However, the demonization of the working class is an integral part of a much broader cultural process which reflects the continuing hegemony of neo-liberal ideology. In contemporary capitalist societies, including 'austerity Britain', commercialism is the dominant cultural credo, and as Bauman (2011: 17) explains, 'the function of culture is not to satisfy existing needs but to create new ones'. In this culture, the social world is shown as a bewildering kaleidoscope of products and images, which effectively bribe consumers with a semblance of free, authentic self-expression and autonomous individuality. The interest of the *individual as consumer* takes priority over those of the community, and while goods are advertised to all, they are distributed on the basis of who can afford to pay. Hence, the culture of unfettered free enterprise creates a vortex of wants but lacks the capacity to meet most basic needs. Indeed as O'Kane (2002: 17) asserts:

> Culture's merged half-life spawns an aesthetics of choice which mimics the spectacle through a bewildering array of images. Its excessive presence reinforces the experience of choosing as freedom, but capitalism's effective mix of super-fluous triviality and reduction of real options blinds us to the social outside.

This is a culture which, in embodying the distorting prism of exchange value and the cash nexus at its core, not only facilitates the 'aesthetics of consumption' via the accumulation of capital, but it continuously emphasizes that we *are* what we own (Bauman, 2005). Thus, the possession of material goods confers a sense of worth, and in this way personal identity becomes inextricably connected to wealth; as Wilkinson and Pickett (2010: 30, 70) explain: 'put crudely, second-rate goods are assumed to reflect second-rate people. Possessions are markers of status everywhere'. Family life, relationships and quality of life invariably suffer in a culture which remains obsessed by the outward signs and symbols of success.

Moreover, the greatest con-trick perpetrated by the culture of free-market commercialism has been to equate the configuration of wealth with personal perspicacity or intelligence (rather than luck) and to make people believe not only that they are to blame for their social situation but that there is no adequate alternative (Lynch, 2014). This overall perception is reinforced by the constant, insidious insinuations of the entertainment industry and celebrity culture. Indeed 'the culture of capitalism, with its boundless choices and omniscient dreams of celebrity and fame, disassembles human wanting and need' (Rutherford, 2008: 15). In austerity Britain, it is easier for working class people to imagine themselves on the *Jeremy Kyle Show* than being active in a trade union, and it seems more plausible to secure an audition on *X Factor* than become an MP. Meanwhile people are shamed and silenced into individual, egotistical self-scrutiny and the constant search for new identities. Self-improvement, psychoanalysis and therapy are central to the zeitgeist. The widespread assimilation of this prevailing culture makes capitalism seem so natural, normal, eternal and impossible to challenge. This is the predominant culture in the 'age of austerity', and it helps explain how a catastrophe created by the greed and ineptitude of financial and political elites became so easily transformed into a crisis of public spending, to be paid for by ordinary people – the permanent revolution of capitalist culture and the anarchy of consumerism has a way of pointing people in the direction required by those social elites who possess economic resources and political power (Rutherford, 2008; Savage, 2012). Domination becomes internalized by the dominated (Sayer, 2012: 177).

The 'death of class' thesis and the dangerous dead end of multiculturalism and identity politics

The ascendancy of neo-liberal ideology and the culture of commercialism with the changing nature of the working class led many academics to deconstruct and downgrade the concept of class. In the pluralist, post-structuralist world there is no capitalist exploitation; there are only hybrid identities, disparate discourses and tropic displays of difference. Contemporary cyber-capitalism is far too complicated to be analysed by reference to something as instrumental as class, and lives are now actually defined by individual identity, lifestyle choice and patterns of consumption. It became fashionable in some academic circles to describe class analysis as rather simplistic, even vulgar, and vaunted post-modernists like Jean-Francois Lyotard and Jean Baudrillard ostentatiously pronounced the death of the meta-narrative. In the context of 'hyperreality' and 'hypercommodification', according to the prophets of post-modernism, not only class but also the 'social' evaporates into irreducible individual differences which reflect a myriad of identities and lifestyles which are encoded in flexible networks and language games. Indeed Ulrich Bech referred to class as a 'zombie category' because 'the idea lives on even though the reality to which it corresponds is dead', as Bech famously claimed, 'community is dissolved in the acid bath of competition' (Heath, 2009: 21, 24).

For some experts, class was replaced by 'politics of recognition' which completely excised capitalism from the analytical agenda – the idea of class simply ceased to be of serious empirical or theoretical significance (O'Kane, 2002). Influential sociologists like Anthony Giddens (1994), therefore, downgraded class in deference to 'lifestyle' and 'taste'. According to Giddens the links between class and social engagement had reduced dramatically in the context of 'high modernity', which meant the increasing salience of lifestyle choices in terms of social identity.[2] This academic re-evaluation of class was referred to as the 'cultural turn', and the new hypothesis focused on individual identity meant that in the era of multiplicity and personal choice, shopping was as important as class (Crompton and Scott, 2005).

Some prominent sociologists such as Jan Pakulski and Malcolm Waters (1996) went even further and talked explicitly about the 'death of class' (Crompton, 1998: 9). They argued that, despite some surviving remnants, 'classes are dissolving', and 'the most advanced societies are no longer class societies'; indeed 'we are witnessing the death of class society as a historical formation' (Ibid.: 4, 147). They argued that although inequality persisted, specific class identities were challenged by new associations and social movements such as those prioritizing the new gender-, eco- and ethno-centred politics. All of which was, according to Pakulski and Waters, 'good news' (Ibid.: 7). Stylized consumption was seen as the predominant form of self-expression and the chief source of individual identity and social differentiation (Ibid.: 121). Consequently,

> identities are therefore based no longer on location in neigh-bourhood, kin or class but on an inward gaze on the self. Material success is the consequence of individual performativ-ity, reflexively established in the competitive arenas of the ed-ucational and occupational markets. Class milieu can no longer form (Ibid.: 124).

In the new era, class analysis had become an anachronism, impo-tent and unable to cope with the sheer diversity of social actors, indeed 'the intellectual armoury of class theory is about as use-ful for the contemporary social and political scene as a cavalry brigade in a tank battle' (Ibid.: 152).[3] Pakulski and Waters observed that 'class appeals and class rhetoric are on the wane even among the true believers of the far left' (Ibid.: 147). In the context of the collapse of communism, the apparent diminution of the working class and the decline of trade unionism, identity politics offered a new and apparently 'radical' agenda. The focus on ethnic, sexual and gender identity effectively seduced the liberal-left intelligent-sia into abandoning class analysis, while 'New Labour' began to see the very notion of class itself as a toxic relic to be jettisoned in the effort to win over floating voters in marginal constituencies.

Thus, it was felt that identity, which used to be rooted in stable and secure working class communities, was now atomized and cast adrift as anonymous individuals developed personal identities which cut across the conventional demarcation lines of social class. Interestingly, this was an analytical position which originally secured some purchase in and around the British Communist Party and its theoretical magazine *Marxism Today*. As Stuart Hall (1978: 8) suggested, the conventional Marxist idea of class was becoming redundant: 'a Marxism which has not purified its own traces of reductionism and economism is going to be unable to understand the domain of culture and the complexity of capitalist social formations'. A new wave of post-Marxists emerged in the 1980s to suggest that the working class could no longer perform its historic function as the motor of progressive social change and that the notion of proletariat was an outdated encumbrance which should be written out of the political script. A broad rainbow alliance of new social movements was the new (only) way forward for the left according to the Marxist revisionists because the material conditions had been transformed (Hall, 1990: 172; Townshend, 1996: 251). The idea that there had been a qualitative, epochal transformation in social conditions in capitalist societies therefore led to the belief that 'the old visions of the Left have literally been overtaken by history' (Hall and Jacques, 1990: 16; see also Hall, 1978; Virdee, 2010).

A new 'cultural politics' was developed on 'the left' and the way opened up for the articulation of a variety of alternative approaches, as Hebdige (1990: 92–93) proclaimed: 'new political agendas and priorities are being forged on the ruins of the old and there seems little likelihood that a new set of universal values or objectives will emerge to bind us all together "beyond the fragments" into one progressive bloc'. Some analysts argued that socialism needed to foster diversity and focus on rights and responsibilities, thereby creating a new 'socialist individualism' (Leadbeater, 1990: 137), whilst others asserted that the left had to recognize 'the degree to which political activity and effort involves a continuing process of making and re-making ourselves' which 'must rightfully be available for anyone to make up as they go along' (Brunt, 1990: 151). Others, such as Mort (1990), emphasized consumer consumption as a source of power and pleasure, whilst Mulgan (1990) even called into question the idea of a single truth, and drew on Taoism, Buddhism and Hinduism to emphasize the need to create social 'harmony'. As Mulgan said, 'it should be the very hallmark of a genuinely radical movement that it is prepared to distrust even its own predispositions' (Ibid.: 388). Despite the self-denying absurdity of Mulgan's ruminations, it was clear that for many on the left 'class' was seen as failing basic epistemological and empirical tests of adequacy and theoretical rigour – class was dead and the ghost of Marx was exorcised. Thereafter class became 'the problem that dare not speak its name' (Sayer, 2005: 224) whilst identity and subjectivity became the watchwords of a new explanatory discourse. In effect this ideological recalibration represented a full-scale retreat by the 'left' in the face of the rising tide of neo-liberalism, and those refusing to relinquish their attachment to Marxism were stranded on the remote archipelagoes of Trotskyism.

However, the consequence of this radical emphasis on cultural politics was, overall, socially conservative. Indeed 'through this linguistic measure, the moral ugliness of poverty turns, as if by the touch of a fairy's wand, into the aesthetic appeal of cultural diversity' (Bauman, 2011: 46). Capitalism had no difficulty facilitating multifarious identities, nor indeed with dividing classes into discrete ethnic communities, genders or sexual orientations since it had the capacity to commercialize such categories and was perfectly capable of exploiting the differences highlighted by cultural diversity. The new notions that emphasized (sub)cultural difference, which produced 'progressive' political movements, were actually sustained by the monetary demand for a commodifiable counter-cultural text – gay lifestyle, black consciousness or sisterhood became the essence of the new political dispensation, although the outcome was hardly equitable (Milner, 1999). The solutions supplied to eliminate discrimination, for example, were ultimately individualist and consumerist, rather than contained within an analytical framework which required meaningful structural social change or a significant redistribution of resources. Despite their apparent success, the new social movements did not pose a challenge to the class basis of post-Fordist capitalism (Milner, 1999: 166). Racism, patriarchy and homophobia are not merely superficial social epiphenomena but constitute genuine forms of oppression and injustice which are best dispatched into the dustbin of history – however, the desire to accomplish this task was undertaken in such a way as to facilitate the continued domination of capital. In short, the social landscape shifted somewhat, sometimes in very positive ways, but the contours in terms of *class* have remained very much the same. Hence, 'identity politics will eventually be better understood as an effect of, rather than an alternative to, post-modern late capitalism' (Ibid.: 8).

In fact there are much greater dangers lurking beneath the surface of cultural identity politics. For example, in prioritizing the (multi)cultural approach to politics based on the specificity of ethnic identity, there is always a risk of scoring some spectacular own goals. We might note that the word 'equality' was commandeered by the most prominent advocates of multiculturalism as a concept for use in inter-ethnic disputes to secure equitable status, rather than as a description of desired material outcomes within communities. Thus, the meaning of the word was obfuscated and, as Bauman (2011: 42) says, 'when the poor lock horns with the poor, the rich have every reason to rub their hands with glee'. Indeed the new 'radicals' have been content to embrace multiculturalism as a political agenda and transformative method (rather than a desirable social outcome). Hence, the focus has been on cultural and ethnic identity and the need for inter-communal recognition and tolerance rather than a redistribution of resources.

In this process the 'white' working class has been portrayed as simply another marginalized minority and a community which has lacked social skills to secure the requisite resources in the new cosmopolitan, multicultural utopia. The focus on the politics of culture meant that the white working class remained isolated, alienated and vulnerable to being characterized as an irredeemably racist ethnic category (despite the fact that the working class has always been multicultural; Todd, 2014). This approach, constructed around conceptions of ethnicity, not only underscores the process of demonization identified earlier, but the emphasis upon a specifically 'white' working class resonates with those ideologies which have an entirely different agenda. The language of ethnic identity is familiar to all those who have studied British National Party (BNP) policy documents. The BNP of course portrays the 'white working class' as a beleaguered indigenous people trying to preserve their ethnic heritage against encroachment from minority communities, but to some extent the acceptance of the 'white working class' as a category allows racial populists to swim with the tide. In effect the ideological territory staked out by the multiculturalists has inadvertently made it easier for the ideas of right-wing populists and racists to gain traction because the vocabulary of ethnic and cultural identity suits their ideological requirements. Hence, cultural politics in the age of austerity has (albeit inadvertently) helped to spawn the new racial populism of UKIP.

Embracing and celebrating cultural heritage is a perfectly legitimate activity or aspiration, and certain ethnic groups have a distinctive history in terms of being subjected to discrimination, exploitation and racism, and have quite understandably responded to protect themselves and their interests. However, as a form of political praxis, multiculturalism often prioritizes pluralism and the celebration of difference (rather than the need for material equality), which can erode the capacity for collective working class agency (Virdee, 2010). Although the gains that have been made as a consequence of the politics of creed have been (in some cases) tangible, they are inevitably partial and can be detrimental to working class mobilization. Yet multiculturalism has been assimilated as conventional wisdom by the liberal left, despite the obvious fact that the poor white working class share many problems with the poor from ethnic minority communities (Sveinsson, 2009: 2). As Bottero (2009: 7) says, 'if we really want to understand disadvantage, we need to shift our attention from who fights over the scraps from the table, to think instead about how much the table holds, and who really gets to enjoy the feast'.

Culture, agency and the desubordination of the working class

Despite ideologically motivated efforts to deny, obscure and obfuscate social reality, class is back on the agenda – the 'age of austerity' has seen to that. Indeed if we adopt a global perspective, there is a distinct pattern of increasing proletarianization (Wright, 2000: 262; Mason, 2008). Globalization, technological advance, industrialization in the South and marketization in the East 'has doubled the size of the global working class' (Mason, 2008: 278). Moreover, global inequality is increasing rapidly and during the era of austerity the super-rich are the only social category that has benefitted in material terms; indeed Rothkopf (2008: xv, 5) has referred to the 'age of asymmetry' and the emergence of a new global elite of billionaires. According to the UN, while the richest 1 per cent of the earth's population continues to capture more wealth, the number of undernourished people is increasing (Rothkopf, 2008: 318; Therborn, 2012: 14 and 2013). A recent Oxfam report titled *Working for the Few* reveals that the eighty-five richest people on earth have as much wealth as the poorest half (3.5 billion) of the world's inhabitants (Wearden, 2014). As Beresford (2013: 14) points out, the super-rich, the cheerleaders for unfettered capitalism, now constitute a global 'overclass' and 'it is under the auspices of political leadership closely associated with this "overclass" that the politics of austerity have been implemented in the form that they have'.

Yet the multicultural identity theorists are incapable of providing an adequate analysis of this process, and conventional cultural politics cannot offer any viable alternative. Having moved away from the economic determinism of vulgar Marxism the political identity crisis on the left led only to the egoistical abomination of 'designer socialism', while the free-thinking post-modernist, far from being an insightful iconoclast, has become the newest form of irredeemably functional apologist for capitalism, offering nothing but the dreary pretence of radicalism. Bedazzled by the bright and sparkling new cyber world of individual autonomy, self-composing biographies and multiple identities the post-modernists, who became obsessed by 'the narcissism of small differences' (pace Freud), failed to see the contours of the new global class divisions emerging on the horizon (Lawler, 2008: 4).

In the context of the 'age of austerity', which has exposed the naked class interests served by the economic system, those 'new world' sociologists and political activists who deny the reality of class are revealed as not simply self-serving and/or morally vacuous, but they increasingly resemble the tortured technophiles searching for UFOs, or the sad Californian 'Heaven's Gate' cultists who claimed that they were going to join a space ship trailing the Hale-Bopp comet! They might as well be discussing how many angels are able to dance on the head of a pin – few will listen and even fewer will care, because class has already moved back to centre stage (Milner, 1999: 175).

Nevertheless, there is still a sense in which class is 'an embarrassing and unsettling subject' because it raises questions of relative 'value', 'merit' and 'worth' (Sayer, 2005: 1). Indeed, people may fear the issue because 'class' makes people confront the reality that social disparities are built into capitalism (Ebert and Zavarzadeh, 2004: 135). However, such sensitivity notwithstanding, the continued salience of social class evidently means that some of the older explanations of class, culture and inequality retain their conceptual power and heuristic value. Contemporary cultural politics certainly cannot be divorced from the study of ideology as the means by which ruling class hegemony is replicated, and 'there are indeed essential processes and structures which, although they may not be observable at the level of surface appearances, have a real causal efficacy for contemporary social existence and its cultural forms' (McMahon, 1999: 213). The mode of production and the cash nexus exert a powerful influence upon the general processes of social, political and intellectual life, as Engels (1981: 301) observed: 'it is not possible for a single human sentiment or opinion to remain untainted'. Whilst the conceptual frame of economic sub-structure and its deterministic influence on the superstructure might be too simplistic, it retains an essential essence of truth, and while those two entities might not be self-contained with fixed properties – interaction is clearly dynamic, complex, uneven, reciprocal and sometimes internally contradictory – *some* form of determination is discernible and must remain central to any adequate analysis (Williams, 1992: 83, see also 137–38), economy matters.

The idea of 'hegemony' is particularly useful in this context because it helps explain social process, structures, and cultural content. Hegemony denotes the means by which the values and beliefs supportive of the ruling class pervade society, creating a kind of value-laden common sense structured in the interests of those with wealth and power (Watkins, 1999). As Gramsci argued, ruling class hegemony was maintained not only by the coercive instruments of the state but also by their more opaque dominance inherent in the institutions and processes of civil society. In this way domination and subordination saturate the whole process of living, not just in terms of political, economic and social activities, but in the substance of lived identities and relationships, which inevitably affect expectations, perceptions and values, although this is an active process which has to be continually renewed, modified and defended. As Williams (1992: 118) said:

> the true condition of hegemony is effective *self-identification* with the hegemonic forms: a specific and internalized 'sociali-zation' which is expected to be positive but which, if that is not possible, will rest on a (resigned) recognition of the inevitable and the necessary.

This is the crucial point with regard to 'austerity' pursued by the Coalition – there might not be enthusiastic acceptance, but there is evidently a resignation that it (or something very similar) is un-avoidable. People identify with the purpose despite the fact they did not precipitate the crisis and are, indeed, the primary victims of its seemingly inexorable logic. It is not that people's beliefs in their own motives are false but that their perceptions of the so-cial world surrounding them are demonstrably erroneous – it is, a 'miscognition of reality due to social causes' (Torrance, 2000: 5). Consumption, having been essentially de-coupled from the pro-cess of production, enables capitalism to conceal forces that deter-mine its existence, hence the real nature of the economic system remains un-comprehended and class society is disguised, whilst consciousness and culture are saturated by the ideological power of capital. That realm of 'civic freedom', so prominent in liberal theory, is therefore circumscribed in such a way as to produce outcomes compatible with a dominant ideology which prefigures forms of thought and behaviour that do not pose a threat to the 'austerity agenda', still less the system of capitalist reproduction. Indeed 'a portion of the subjected subject's ego has been colonized by the actions of an anaesthetizing command' which constitutes hypnoidal interpellations 'as forms of inter-subjective imperialism' (Tedman, 1999: 69; Gibson-Graham, 2005).

The real significance of contemporary culture in the era of aus-terity is *colonialism*. The word 'culture', having evolved from the Latin *colere,* precipitated the word *colonus* and hence colonialism – therefore culture and colonialism might be described as 'mildly tautological' (Eagleton, 2000: 2). The dominant ideology has eroded working class cultural identities. The creed of unfettered capitalism, which stresses individualism, competition and greed, which emphasizes a fallacious meritocracy, has metastasized in the cells of society into a pernicious, patronizing culture which derides the working class and undermines basic cooperative values and collective action. The consequence of this consolidation of dominant neo-liberal cultural hegemony has been a form of social class 'identity theft'. As Fanon noted in another context, the cultural life of a conquered community is continually disrupted, and every effort is made to convince the colonized classes of the inferiority of their culture. In effect a kind of collective Stockholm syndrome has taken place as the subjugated population engages in the frantic acquisition of the culture of the oppressor. These subtle and sophisticated 'affirmative' processes have taken place to such an extent that the distinctive culture of the working class has been deracinated by denuding it of basic collectivist impulses and assumptions. The consequence is what social psychologists might call a 'fundamental attribution error'. Those working class cultural values, underpinned by notions of social solidarity, which have provided a protective ozone layer against damaging rays of unfettered free enterprise, have been attacked by the *necrotizing fasciitis* of capitalist culture. This process has occurred to such an extent now that in 'austerity Britain' sections of the working class are regarded as utterly worthless and, like the Biblical Samson with eyes gouged out and set in shackles, exist to be mocked and abused by those seeking to reaffirm their own superiority (New International Bible, Judges 16:21): they have become post-industrial capitalism's *homo sacer*.

However, there are some conflicting signs, some of which could denote the beginning of a new departure toward resistance and de-subordination, and this is precisely what makes cultural politics in austerity (ideology) so pertinent to class consciousness. The 'moving equilibrium' of hegemony always exhibits a contradictory character and contains elements that can be mobilized in different directions at any given historical moment, and capitalist 'common sense' is constantly vulnerable to interruptions and counter-mobilizations – 'although ruling ideas may be dominant, they are not thereby uncontested' (Milner, 1999: 26; Savage, 2012).

Clearly it is important not to put the cart before the horse – the solutions to the imposition of 'austerity' are political and economic (rather than cultural). Class identities are inhibited or stimulated by political organization, and they are forged in the heat of ideological battle as well as the everyday experience of social life. Given this fact, the emphasis on political praxis must acknowledge that multiculturalism, despite its seductive normative dimension as a desirable social outcome, is an essentially liberal political perspective and is a strategy designed for a terrain mapped out by the enemies of the working class. Even the Coalition government can, in practice, accommodate many of its preconceptions, precepts and policy preferences (see HM Government, 2010 which talks about 'equality at the heart of government', the 'equality duty' and 'promoting diversity').

In reality, an undifferentiated, postmodern 'identitarian' version of multiculturalism has not only furnished a strategy which fights on a social and ideological battlefield acceptable to capitalism and its political class, but it is also a territory which has the capacity to unleash far more dangerous reactionary forces. In essence, the emphasis on cultural politics in the post-modern era has, to a significant extent, simply reinforced the tendency to fracture specifically working class social identities and thereby facilitated the dissemination of the dominant orthodoxy. Although 'imagining the possibility of another way of living together is not a strong point of our world of privatized utopias' (Bauman, 2005: 117), in the age of austerity it is self-evidently more productive to focus upon what unites us as humans rather than what divides us. Moreover, that common identity of interests is undoubtedly increasing because what happens to workers in Mumbai has a real and practical relevance to ordinary people in Manchester, and there are similarities and shared priorities which transcend the (albeit significant) cultural specificity of ethnic identity, religion, language and so on. It is upon the common experience of exploitation and disempowerment that politics should be constructed, rather than any exaggerated account of cultural difference. It is time to recognize and re-assert the fact that redistribution of wealth is more important than cultural recognition and diversity.

Notes

1 Collins makes a decent point but draws the wrong conclusion. He blames, principally, the post-war planners for destroying the fabric of working class communities and only touches upon the real culprit, Thatcherism.

2 In his withering critique, Milner (1999: 91) is correct to point out that Giddens' text *Beyond Left and Right* would be more accurately titled 'between' left and right. The penetration of neo-liberal ideology is clearly evident in Giddens' (2009) textbook where he states unequivocally that 'more than 75 per cent of the 1,000 richest Britons in 2007 made their own wealth rather than inheriting it' (Ibid.: 450–51). Of course the notion of millionaires 'making their own wealth' is a preposterous fiction.

3 The weakness of the Pakulski and Walters (1996: 112, note No. 1) thesis is nowhere more clearly illustrated than when they tackle

education. They argue that 'a system of inequality based on educational credentials is non-economic, and therefore cannot properly or usefully be conceptualized as a class system' and 'to the extent that people use educational qualifications to cross class boundaries, those boundaries are without substance'. This constitutes an extraordinary misunderstanding of the role of (especially elitist private) education as a positional good which reflects and reinforces class position.

Bibliography

Andrews, G. (2013). 'The return of social class?' *Sociology Review*, April, 16–19.

Atkinson, W. (2012). 'Economic crisis and classed everyday life: hysteresis, positional suffering and symbolic violence'. In: W. Atkinson, S. Roberts and M. Savage, eds., *Class Inequality in Austerity Britain*. Basingstoke: Palgrave Macmillan.

Atkinson, W., Roberts, S. and Savage, M. (eds.) (2012). *Class inequality in austerity Britain: power, difference and suffering*. Basingstoke: Palgrave Macmillan.

Basham, P. and Luik, J. (2010). *The war on working class culture*. London: Democracy Institute.

Bauman, Z. (1982). *Memories of class: the pre-history and afterlife of class*. London: Routledge and Kegan Paul.

Bauman, Z. (1991). *Modernity and the Holocaust*. Cambridge: Polity Press.

Bauman, Z. (2005). *Work, consumerism and the new poor*. Berkshire: Open University Press.

Bauman, Z. (2011). *Culture in a liquid modern world*. Cambridge: Polity Press.

BBC News Online (2007). 'What is working class?' Available at: http://news.bbc.uk.

Beresford, P. (2013). 'From "underclass" to "overclass"?' *Sociology Review*, February, 12–15.

Bottero, W. (2009). 'Class in the 21st century'. In: K. Sveinsson, ed., *Who Cares About the White Working Class?* London: Runnymede Trust.

Bragg, M. (2012). *Class and culture parts 1–3*. BBC February 24, March 2 and March 9.

Brunt, R. (1990). 'The politics of identity'. In: S. Hall and M. Jacques, eds., *New Times: The Changing Face of Politics in the 1990s*. London: Lawrence and Wishart.

Collins, M. (2005). *The British working class*. Channel 4, July 10.

Crompton, R. (1998). *Class and stratification: an introduction to current debates*. Cambridge: Polity Press.

Crompton, R. and Scott, J. (2005). 'Class analysis: beyond the cultural turn'. In: F. Devine, M. Savage, J. Scott and R. Crompton, eds., *Rethinking Class: Cultures, Identities and Lifestyles*. Basingstoke: Palgrave Macmillan.

Devine, F. (1996). 'The "new structuralism": class politics and class analysis'. In: N. Kirk, ed., *Social Class and Marxism: Defences and Challenges*. Aldershot: Scholar Press.

Devine, F., Savage, M., Scott, J. and Crompton, R. (eds.) (2005). *Rethinking class: cultures, identities and lifestyles*. Basingstoke: Palgrave Macmillan.

Duggan, E. and Owen, J. (2014). 'Millions of British children's futures "written off by poverty"'. *Independent*, May 28.

Eagleton, T. (2000). *The idea of culture*. Oxford: Blackwell.

Ebert, T. and Zavarzadeh, M. (2004). 'ABC of class'. *Nature, Society and Thought*, 17(2): 133–42.

Engels, F. (1981). *The condition of the working class in England*. London: Granada.

Equality Trust (2011). 'Income inequality: trends and measures'. *Equality Trust Research Digest*, No. 2, 1–8.

Gibson-Graham, J. (2005). 'Dilemmas of theorizing class'. *Rethinking Marxism*, 17(1): 39–44.

Giddens, A. (1994). *Beyond left and right: the future of radical politics*. Cambridge: Polity Press.

Giddens, A. (1998). *The third way: the renewal of social democracy*. Cambridge: Polity Press.

Giddens, A. (2009). *Sociology*. Cambridge: Polity Press.

Hall, S. (1978). 'Marxism and culture'. *Radical History Review*, 18 Fall: 5–14.

Hall, S. (1990). *The hard road to renewal: Thatcherism and the crisis of the left*. London: Verso.

Hall, S. and Jacques, M. (eds.) (1990). *New times: the changing face of politics in the 1990s*. London: Lawrence and Wishart.

Hayes, M. (1994). *The new right in Britain*. London: Pluto.

Heath, A., Curtis, J. and Elgenius, G. (2009). 'Individualization and the Decline of Class Identity'. In: M. Wetherell, ed., *Identity in the 21st Century: New Trends in Changing Times*. Basingstoke: Palgrave Macmillan.

Hebdige, D. (1990). 'After the Masses'. In: S. Hall and M. Jacques, eds., *New Times: The Changing Face of Politics in the 1990s*. London: Lawrence and Wishart.

HM Government (2010). 'The Equality Strategy – Building a Fairer Britain'. London: Government Equalities Office.

Hobsbawm, E. (1978). 'The forward march of Labour halted?' *Marxism Today*, September, 279–86.

Hoggart, R. (1973). *The uses of literacy: aspects of working class life with special reference to publications and entertainments*. Harmondsworth: Penguin.

Jeffries, S. (2012). 'Why Marxism is on the rise again'. *Guardian*, July 4.

Johnson, B. (2013). 'We should be humbly thanking the super-rich, not bashing them'. *Telegraph*, November 17.

Johnson, J. (2012). 'Culture is a class issue'. Centre for Labour and Social Studies. Available at: www.classonline.org.uk.

Jones, O. (2012). *Chavs: the demonisation of the working class*. London: Verso.

Kirk, N. (1991). '"Traditional" working-class culture and the "rise of Labour": some preliminary questions and observations'. *Social History*, 16(2): 203–16.

Laclau, E. and Mouffe, C. (1987). 'Post-Marxism without Apologies'. *New Left Review*, 166, 79–106.

Lawler, S. (2008). *Identity: sociological perspectives*. Cambridge: Polity Press.

Leadbeater, C. (1990). 'Power to the person'. In: S. Hall and M. Jacques, eds., *New Times: The Changing Face of Politics in the 1990s*. London: Lawrence and Wishart.

Leys, C. (2014). 'The British ruling class'. *Socialist Register*, 108–37.

Lynch, R. (2014). 'Bank Governor warns of increasing inequality'. *Independent*. May 28.

Marx, K. (2004). *The eighteenth Brumaire of Louis Bonaparte*. New York: International Publishers.

Marx, K. and Engels, F. (1979). *The communist manifesto*. Harmondsworth: Penguin.

Mason, P. (2008). *Live working or die fighting: how the working class went global*. London: Vintage Books.

McMahon, C. (1999). 'Marxism and culture'. In A. Gamble, D. Marsh and T. Tant, eds., *Marxism and Social Science*. Basingstoke: Macmillan.

Miliband, R. (1985). 'The new revisionism in Britain'. *New Left Review*, 150 March–April.

Milne, S. (2012). *The revenge of history: the battle for the twenty-first century*. London: Verso.

Milner, A. (1999). *Class*. London: Sage.

Monbiot, G. (2013). 'It's business that really rules us now'. *Guardian*, November 11.

Mort, F. (1990). 'The politics of consumption'. In: S. Hall and M. Jacques, eds., *New Times: The Changing Face of Politics in the 1990s*. London: Lawrence and Wishart.

Mulgan, G. (1990). 'Uncertainty, reversibility and variety'. In: S. Hall and M. Jacques, eds., *New Times: The Changing Face of Politics in the 1990s*. London: Lawrence and Wishart.

Mulholland, H. (2012). 'George Osborne has unveiled a millionaires' budget, says Ed Miliband'. *Guardian*, March 21.

O'Grady, P. (2013). *Paul O'Grady's working Britain*. BBC 1, August 15, 22.

O'Hara, M. (2014). *Austerity bites*. Bristol: Policy Press.

O'Kane, J. (2002). 'Capital, culture and socioeconomic justice'. *Rethinking Marxism*, 14(2): 1–23.

Pakulski, J. and Waters, M. (1996). *The death of class*. London: Sage.

Resnick, S. and Wolff, R. (2005). 'The point and purpose of Marx's notion of class'. *Rethinking Marxism*, 17(1): 33–37.

Rothkopf, D. (2008). *Superclass: the global power elite and the world they are making*. London: Little Brown.

Rutherford, J. (2008). 'The culture of capitalism'. *Soundings*, 38, 8–18.

Savage, M. (2000). *Class analysis and social transformation*. Buckingham: Open University.

Savage, M. (2012). 'Broken communities?' In: W. Atkinson *et al.*, eds., *Class Inequality in Austerity Britain*. Basingstoke: Palgrave Macmillan.

Sayer, A. (2005). *The moral significance of class*. Cambridge: Cambridge University Press.

Sayer, A. (2012). 'Facing the challenge of the return of the rich'. In: W. Atkinson *et al.*, eds., *Class Inequality in Austerity Britain*. Basingstoke: Palgrave Macmillan.

Scase, R. (1992). *Class*. Buckingham: Open University Press.

Smith, M. (2013). 'Media depictions of the poor'. *Sociology Review*, February, 30–32.

Sunday Times (2014). 'Rich List'. Compiled by Philip Beresford. May 18.

Sveinsson, K. (ed.) (2009). *Who cares about the white working class?* London: Runnymede Trust.

Tedman, G. (1999). 'Ideology, the State, and the Aesthetic Level of Practice'. *Rethinking Marxism*, 11(4): 57–73.

Therborn, G. (2009). 'The killing fields of inequality'. *Eurozine*, 1–10. Available at: www.eurozine.com.

Therborn, G. (2012). 'Class in the 21st century'. *New Left Review*, (78) November–December: 5–29.

Therborn, G. (2013). 'Global inequality: the return of class'. *Global Dialogue*, 2(1). Available at: www.isa-sociology.org/global-dialogue.

Thompson, E. P. (1981). *The making of the English working class*. Harmondsworth: Penguin.

Ticktin, H. (2006). 'Political consciousness and its conditions at the present time'. *Critique*, 34(1) April: 9–26.

Todd, S. (2014). *The people: the rise and fall of the working class*. London: John Murray.

Torrance, J. (2008). *Karl Marx's theory of ideas*. Cambridge: Cambridge University Press.

Townshend, J. (1996). *The politics of Marxism: critical debates*. London: Leicester University Press.

Virdee, S. (2010). 'Racism, class and the dialectics of social transformation'. In: J. Solomos and P. Hill-Collins, eds., *The Sage Handbook of Race and Ethnic Studies*. London: Sage.

Watkins, E. (1999). 'Gramscian politics and capitalist common sense'. *Rethinking Marxism*, 11(3): 83–90.

Wearden, G. (2014). 'Oxfam: 85 richest people as wealthy as poorest half of the world'. *Guardian*, January 20.

Westergaard, J. and Resler, H. (1977). *Class in a capitalist society: a study of contemporary Britain*. Harmondsworth: Penguin.

Wilkinson, R. and Pickett, K. (2010). *The spirit level: why equality is better for everyone*. London: Penguin.

Williams, H. (2010). 'The Rich gets richer: Barclays chief Rich Ricci lands £18m windfall'. *Independent*, March 20.

Williams, R. (1992). *Marxism and literature*. Oxford: Oxford University Press.

Wright, E. O. (2000). *Class counts*. Cambridge: Cambridge University Press.

7 The European Union project, social movements and alienation

David Berry

> Our real objective is to enable a society to live at the highest pos-
> sible level of historical action instead of blindly passing through
> crisis and conflicts.
>
> (Touraine, 1981: 149)

The French sociologist Alan Touraine once undertook research
in order to understand the structural formation and ideological
role of social movements in relation to changes in society at many
distinct levels. This interest ranged from the profound to more
subtle, nuanced changes in empirical composition, to abstract
formation and alterations in social awareness (consciousness).
Touraine argued that social movements were defined by certain
internal characteristics and outward objectives beyond the static
order of the prevailing status quo. For Touraine this meant that
not all 'political groupings' or 'political parties' could legitimately
be characterized as a social movement, and, as we'll see, Touraine
argued that something profoundly 'radical' was at the centre of
defining the essential characteristics of a social movement coupled
with a deep-seated desire to produce alternative outcomes to the
established order.

It's worth bearing in mind that the term 'radical' is often, and
wrongly, singularly associated with the revolutionary left (see
Berry, 2006) but the reality is far more complex; the term 'radical' in fact can be applied to many different political philosophies
ranging from left to right political positions and all the varied perspectives they entail; it also depends on the specific historical context and perhaps more importantly, the object of radical intentions.
Thus, when we apply the term 'radical' within a particular or actual epochal process, we can at least recognize that at its heart is
a desire to move beyond the status quo, to challenge established
norms and create an alternative system. The Bolsheviks did so in
1917 and so did revolutionaries in the 1848 European revolutions

or indeed the newly developing Merchant class that sought to usurp the old Feudal order; even for Central and East Europeans, Thatcher was seen as a radical for offering a different vision of society to the old Stalinist regimes. For our purposes, to understand Touraine's idea of social movements we therefore need to bear in mind the political, economic and cultural context in which radical is being applied.

To avoid any confusion, I will refer to movements of various kinds as 'political groupings' and inquire whether any can be characterized as a social movement in the way Touraine argued. I will then draw on Touraine's concept of social movements to tease out what differences exist between various political groupings with contrasting ideologies and assess the importance of such differences that exist for us in order to appreciate Touraine's work in the present context of 'austerity' and the production of 'cultural politics'.

Perhaps the most telling point of Touraine's work is that the key characteristic of a social movement under his specific-time analysis was that they were opposed to capital and further that 'alienation' underpins the rationale of social movements that seek to throw off the shackles of oppression and the alienated order. This appears to suggest that then, and certainly now, social movements were primarily characterized as left-leaning, but when we closely scrutinise the empirical data across Europe's 'political groupings' collectively today, the right-wing/far right-wing often share such opposition to capital in its present guise and seek to create a community of difference that places the collective over the individual; perhaps the main differences are the strategies and certainly the objectives and outcomes, and I will further analyse and discuss this as I proceed.

Clearly, across Europe during the current period of austerity, a variety of political groupings have emerged, and we see how cultural politics is at the heart of such development, affecting the shape of the European landscape at all levels. These groupings, including broad left and right, oppose not only austerity but also the European Union project (EUP) in its present form, governed by neo-liberal political philosophy.

Economic austerity is a policy that operates on many levels within the EUP, but non-leftist groupings are more concerned with prioritizing another feature of the EUP, namely free movement of citizens and immigration rather than austerity, although they are closely linked. A few questions to consider are: Can we categorize non-leftist groupings as social movements, and if not, why not? And furthermore, what is the significance of not doing so? Do the political groupings of various ideological persuasions signify the fragmentation of the EUP's policy of European integration and longer-term vision of Europe? What impact is cultural politics having on the EUP in the age of austerity?

A core objective of the EUP is *integration* between European nation-states on economic and legal spheres. The degree of 'intended integration', governed by European-wide policy and governance – governmentality when we use Foucault as a reference point – undoubtedly varies between these spheres of influence within national settings. The preferred promotion of the economic and legal spheres takes precedent over but impacts upon social, political and cultural networks. Without doubt the impact, perceived or real, of the 'unintended consequences' of economic integration and legal harmonization have shaped and altered national perceptions and actualities of indigenous social, political and cultural landscapes across the European Union, in unison, it must be added, with wider processes connected to globalization.

This complex network of spheres measured in terms of integration or harmonization in the case of legal frameworks, differ significantly, for example, from the economic and political–based system developed in the Americas, principally the North American Free Trade Agreement (NAFTA) that was set up in 1994, becoming the world's largest free trade zone area. The development of NAFTA was principally based on economic expansion (rationale), legal statutory frameworks, requirements and political will, but with little to no emphasis on cultural factors other than the idea that economic links were seen to possibly foster closer cultural ties at a higher political level, but certainly not a type of *cultural integration* which has become a central feature of the *theory of Europe*.

A consequence of the creation of NAFTA – free-market-based ideology – was that it forced the European Union (EU) to reassess and intensify the economic rationale of its policy objectives and thus to further re-evaluate key issues, such as culture, identity and philosophical values which helped rationalize and legitimize the EU's bureaucratic authority. For many the economic rationale would dominate all other spheres – hence, the governance of economic austerity as a rational response to the crisis in capitalism governed by neo-liberal thinking and moreover the opposition to austerity by political groupings within the EU that offers alternatives to the dominating ideology. As we shall see later in this chapter, the outcome of austerity, as an ideological weapon, has subsequently created a dialectical[1] moment across Europe, which has emerged within the realms of the base-superstructure model.[2]

One principal concern, both historically and contemporary forwarded by various groupings with ideological differences within the EUP, is the idea that the economic necessities to compete with NAFTA, and more recently China, would vastly reduce cultural and political differences despite the fact that such differences were often a cause of war and conflict in Europe. Such concerns over cultural integration, assimilation and the possible negation of cultural difference differ according to political ideologies from right to left, the former more concerned with loss of cultural and national identity, particularly when we factor in immigration, which is seen in recent times by right-wing and far-right-wing groupings as adding to the demise of cultural and national identity.

More recently, the economic imperatives of the Union, specifically to increase neo-liberal economic rationality in the age of austerity, have focused the left's concerns with an increasingly marginalized oppressed and exploited working class, seen more prominently in Greece, Portugal and Spain[3] and more recently in the UK with the election of the left-winger Jeremy Corbyn as leader of the Labour Party.[4] The fact that the economic gains of European capital, prior to austerity within the EU, failed to effectively reduce high levels of poverty and social inequalities has become a central concern of the left; in other words, the left's concerns are embedded within the age of austerity but placed in context of the broader failure of capital itself. It's just that political groupings aligned to the left have raised conscious levels and deepened a sense of realization that austerity is an ideological weapon to re-adjust capital at the expense of workers and, perhaps more importantly, when the crisis rescinds – if it does – the left fully understand that any subsequent boom will be limited and skewed once more towards the ruling classes in terms of both surplus for business and legitimization of existing political governance under prevailing neo-liberal winds. Austerity as ideology is seen as a neo-liberal reaction by states to the collapse or crisis in capital detrimentally affecting workers with decreases in social welfare funding, public services, crisis in housing, increases in student fees and increasing levels of unemployment to varying degrees across European states.

Right-wing fears over cultural integration, immigration, assimilation and/or the negation of cultural differences and traditions within Europe, heightened during austerity, have equally produced political groupings opposed to the EUP despite claims by the major players in the EU that cultural integration was never a foreseeable objective, preferring economic and political union as objectives. The right's response is largely to argue that cultural integration has been surpassed by immigration, and therefore the 'unintended consequences' of economic and political union is the demise of distinct national and cultural differences.

Whatever the arguments over whether the EUP is able to fully integrate in cultural terms is presently of no interest, but there is no doubting that the consequences – unintended or otherwise – and perceptions of the EU's reaction to NAFTA is far beyond the economic, which has embraced social, political and cultural spheres, and this is mainly the reason why some political groupings and established parties have come to reject the EUP as it currently stands. Culture and, more specifically, 'cultural politics' are at the centre of reactions through cultural practice, which ranges from the stabilization of hegemony to forms of resistance to hegemonic conditions.

Resistance and rejection on cultural grounds are stark amongst far-right and right-wing nationalist groupings such as Jobbik (Hungary), Golden Dawn (Greece), Front National (France), the United Kingdom Independence Party (UKIP; United Kingdom), Freedom Party (Holland), Freedom Party (Austria), Progress Party (Norway), Danish People's Party (Denmark), Sweden Democrats (Sweden), True Finns (Finland) and the Northern League (Italy). In Germany, Pergida has emerged in the former East Germany with mass demonstrations taking place in Dresden against Islam, and the oldest nationalist grouping, the National Democratic Party of Germany, continues to exist despite attempts by the German Government in 2003 to close the party down.

Existing alongside right and far-right political groupings are left-wing and left-leaning populist groupings such as Syriza (Greece), Podemos (Spain), the Five Star Movement (Italy), New Left Bloc (Portugal), Labour Party (UK) and the Green Party across Europe with its left-leaning political programmes for change; to make matters even more complex, Syriza currently has Green Party members amongst its ranks, along with Maoists, Trotskyists, etc. Taken as a whole, these political groupings are currently reconfiguring the European political and cultural landscape which may have profound impacts throughout Europe in relation to the direction and vision of the European project because many of these groupings are grassroots movements or, in the case of the UK Labour Party, becoming so, including the participation of citizens directly affected by the harsh economic measures of austerity; in sum the sphere of cultural politics across Europe is active, signifying an intense struggle over cultural hegemony.

The European Union project (EUP)

When the Treaty of Rome was signed in 1957 and finally presented on January 1, 1958, it formally established the European Economic Community (EEC). The signatories were West Germany, Belgium,

Luxembourg, France, the Netherlands and Italy and the essential rationale of the document was, at this initial period, the *economic integration* of states in order to begin the process of a European Common Market. By 1993, one year before NAFTA, the word 'economic' – as in European 'Economic Community' – was formally removed in the Maastricht Treaty, and in 2009 at the Treaty of Lisbon, the Treaty of Rome was renamed Treaty on the Functioning of the European Union (TFEU).

The core principle underpinning the EUP, 'integration', is related to another principle – namely, 'unification' – which is often pejoratively referred to as the overriding objective of the EUP by many within the Euro-Sceptic camp, such as Front National, UKIP and other smaller movements on the right/far-right. Established right-wing parties across Europe use integration disparagingly at times by perceiving both principles as inherent contradictions of the EUP and indeed as threats to the philosophical principle that historically underpins the rationale of the European Union, namely liberalism and the rights of individuals; the Front National places less emphasis on liberal individualism, preferring to emphasize the protection of the established national culture and traditions as a defence against European Union objectives.

Currently, left-wing and left leaning populist groupings referred to above oppose the notion of integration and unification – as defined by established European institutions and policy – and certainly oppose the principle of liberal philosophy that has given way or panders towards neo-liberal-based capitalist economics. Both integration and unification are important to understand in the context of the EUP because unification is often misused primarily by right and far-right groupings, and integration is seen not as an end in itself but rather as the means to achieve unification or full integration. Integration thus perceived is often seen as going beyond legal harmonization and economic standards which obliterate difference rather than incorporating differences of distinct nations. In the short term, unification in the European context is not a particularly useful term to use in order to understand the current process of European development because clearly integration dictates current narratives on European objectives.

Often missing from formal debates concerning integration are concerns over whether it includes or *should* include the cultural sphere of influence, including identity politics. Clearly this latter perspective with an emphasis on *should* or *ought*, entails a discussion away from economic, political and cultural perspectives towards moral philosophy which envisages a community of citizens as a justification of civilization. But one clear example of cultural integration as the *dominant value* is based on the Judeo-Christian order, which in right-wing circles is used – explicitly or otherwise – as a defence against Islam and immigration.[5]

Even though formal EU statements concerning integration presupposes the allowance of national and cultural differences amongst states, it is based however on free-market principles governed primarily by neo-liberal and corporatist ideology which, as discussed at the beginning, is seen to create unintended consequences that directly affect the cultural and social spheres. If cultural politics/practice is driven by *thought* that transcends dominant narratives by offering difference, the political philosophy counter to that is neo-liberalism as *the* basis of EU policy.

It is true however that many EU documents recognize that large corporations pose a threat to political democracy and citizenship within the EU, but the reality is that there has been a failure within Europe – despite its rhetoric otherwise – to empower citizens to challenge the authoritative norms of corporate capitalism; the EU's policy towards media literacy – a contradiction on a huge scale – is a case in point. That said, it is also clear that threats to the economic rationale, broadly capitalist with degrees of state intervention to assist 'public policy' is seen to be a general threat to its survival by existing powers and that ideological variations, amongst both right- and left-wing groupings, contravenes the European project under established norms; Syriza is currently a case in point, and Podemos is currently establishing oppositional ideologies to the dominant forms, which seek to undermine established norms with a view to offering a different concept of integration and unification.

The EUP's broad objective was to create a stable, sustainable and just system, but it is – inevitably – subject to laws of movement and contradiction central to the thesis on dialectics, which are out of its control, although austerity is an attempt to control such instabilities. The contradictions within the EU have helped forge alliances whose rationale is diametrically opposite corporate neo-liberal logic that persists with such illusions as the right of individuals and contradictions over free movement of goods that create parity amongst nation states. The fact that austerity has different meanings and consequences in Greece and Spain as opposed to Germany and Holland, as examples, is proof of the failure of integration in the broadest sense of the word.

Whilst Rome may not be burning internally quite yet,[6] the EU and NATO for that matter, have concerns externally to contend, particularly with Russia, whose geo-political objectives seek to further disrupt the fragmentation of European politics, evidenced by Russia's failed attempt at developing a relationship with Greece, a country that did not support economic sanctions against Russia.

The fact that Greece rejected Russian advances and succumbed to German-led austerity measures only seeks to uphold the idea that the EUP is unstable and fragile. The new type of narrative governed by Syriza, with the addition of right-wing ideologies, disrupts current dominating narratives concerning cultural politics evidenced by concerns from the European Cultural Foundation which was founded in 1954, stating in 2015 that 'Over the past four years, we set out to uncover new *Narratives for Europe* at a moment when the prevailing narratives seemed to have lost their resonance'. In a separate document titled 'Connecting Culture, Communities and Democracy' the European Cultural Foundation states: 'We bridge people and democratic institutions by connecting local cultural change-makers and communities across Europe because we firmly believe that Europe can be powered by culture'.

A Europe 'powered by culture' isn't an unreasonable proposition; however, cultural politics and dialectics dictate uncertainties over prevailing economic and political philosophical forms and frameworks such as free-market ideology and neo-liberalism of which the European Cultural Foundation are firmly rooted.

The European form of 'governmentality'

During 1978–79 the French philosopher Michel Foucault gave a series of lectures at the Collège de France concerning government practice and rationality producing his concept of 'governmentality' in the process. Sennalart's (2008: 1) edited text on the lectures detail what Foucault described as the 'art of government', which is, in part, an exercise of power through processes of discourse and rationality that is an 'exercise of political sovereignty' (Ibid.: 2). Foucault argued that he wasn't particularly interested in the actual practice of government, but rather 'the reasoned way of governing best, and at the same time, reflection on the best possible way of governing' (Ibid.). Foucault's aim was to understand how the process of rationalization of governing emerged and was disseminated as a legitimate sovereign body. Governmentality in sum then is the entire process of the art of governing, of thinking and enacting an 'idea'. We can take Foucault's concept and apply it towards the 'idea' or the 'project' of the European Union as a form of rationalization towards objective goals. But it is one that foments contradictions between Foucault's interest concerning 'neo-liberalism' and European-wide public policies which seek to restrain neo-liberal and free-market ideology in favour of citizens and what we may loosely refer to as the 'common good'.

Foucault lectured on the theme of the 'Appearance of a governmental rationality extended to a world scale', so is it possible we can reduce this theme to the 'European scale' whilst clearly contextualizing it within global neo-liberal structures? If so, such *rationalities of scale* will be fomented through discourse and the process of rationalization, and much of what Foucault spoke is a continuation of the work by the German Sociologist Max Weber and his account of 'calculated rationality' and 'bureaucratic authority'; *integration as logic* works on this level. It's clear to see how the 'idea' of the EUP is manifested by policy, discourse and power through the institution's bureaucratic lexicon of language that dominate culture as the authoritative narrative; such narratives and governmentality are currently being challenged by social movements and political groupings.

Equally, as demonstrated by the Italian writer Umberto Eco (*The Guardian*, 2012), we can see that 'crisis' and 'austerity' begins to undermine the prevailing narratives, discourse and governmentality that has historically dominated governing policy within Europe:

> When it comes to the debt crisis ... we must remember that it is culture, not war that cements our ... identity. Today, we've been at peace for 70 years ... The United States needed a civil war to unite properly. I hope that culture ... will do the same for us.

Eco's comments are to be understood in direct relation to European cultural identity which for Eco cements relations between different cultural contexts. Eco further argues that prior to the debt crisis European identity was 'shallow' and that the debt crisis threatened the vulnerability of European identity. It is a fact that the economic and ideological austerity has forged new meanings within cultural politics that is fragmenting whatever social cohesion and cultural identity existed, although the notion of European-wide cultural identity is complex and contested. Eco's use of the word 'shallow' is supplemented by this caveat: 'I am using an English word that is not the same as the Italian word *superficiale*, but which is somewhere between 'surface' and 'deep'. We must change this, before the crisis strips it [Europe] of everything'.

But the crisis has eroded whatever sense of social and cultural cohesion that previously existed with increased alienation of subjects and conversely – and dialectically – substantially increased forms of solidarity amongst alienated European citizens; this is a direct consequence of the forces contained within cultural politics – the cultural space with no formal rules, only conformity or confrontation, each depending on economic and social conditions. Moreover, as previously discussed, the crisis has revealed to the left at least, the failure of capital to resolve social inequalities pre-austerity.

New cultural politics and social movements

> A crisis cannot give the attacking forces the ability to organise with lightning speed in time and space; still less can it endow them with fighting spirit. Similarly, the defenders are not demoralised, nor do they abandon their positions, even among the ruins, nor do they lose faith in their own strength or their own future (Antonio Gramsci, *The Prison Notebooks*).

The form of EU governmentality and the 'culture' of which Eco spoke of which 'cements' European identity is under threat as a new formation of cultural politics and outcomes develop across Europe never to be reversed; their impact will be profound, and the future is uncertain. Since the banking collapse/crisis in 2007/08 and the entrenchment of economic austerity across the European political landscape, political groupings opposing established European norms have grown and developed into powerful political forces which are challenging established power. The revolutions that occurred in 1989 and the subsequent enlargement of the European Union have failed as a project to harmonize cultures.

What we know of Syriza in Greece, New Left Bloc in Portugal, Podemos in Spain, UKIP and the Labour Party in the United Kingdom and the Front National in France is that they are all in the process of reconfiguring the cultural political landscape and are effectively challenging existing regimes of power within both national boundaries and the broader European political landscape; the type of power that Foucault argued that was central to his theory of 'governmentality' is under threat in the European context.

Foucault's theory of governmentality allows us to understand the complex relationship between governors and governed with the former idealized for our purposes within governing legislature of the European Union. Such discourses of power can be evaluated in Foucault's terms as forms of control and discipline, but such discourses or ideological processes are always contingent on the relative epochal structures of which subjects are constructed; in other words, subjectification for Foucault was not universal.

The context of austerity throughout Europe has produced contrasting reactions to the European project governed by the European Union, first evidenced in voting patterns across Europe in the 2014 European elections – elections which, under normal circumstances, are seen as either irrelevant or uninteresting but under such historical circumstances they became a beacon of change. For example, in Greece the hitherto tiny left-wing Syriza party (Coalition of the Left) won the European election, gaining an impressive 26.60 per cent of the votes, coming first, with the neo-fascist party Golden Dawn coming third with 9.38 per cent ahead of the last refuge of Stalinism, the KKE (Communist Party of Greece) with 6.07 per cent. The cultural and political landscape of Greece has been in transition since 2010 when both the European Union and the International Monetary Fund (IMF) provided £88 billion to shore up the Greek economy; Syriza had, in this context at least, risen from an obscure small political party to outright winners.

Kouvelakis (2011: 27) asked the following question in relation to the Greek situation: 'How has the unfolding crisis affected the political landscape?' Referring to opinion polls, Kouvelakis argued that the polls suggested 'an enormous distrust of almost all political parties'. 'Almost' was the crucial word in this context, because in reality the preference for Syriza was due to an 'enormous distrust' of the *mainstream political parties* that had governed Greece for so long and a corrupt system that was a component of the EUP.

Despite this shift in cultural politics with the context of the European elections, the centre-right Greek party, New Democracy, was the dominant force in the Greek Parliament, despite its past association with corruptive practices and a highly damaged political, economic and social system. This system was the preference of the EU, the European Central Bank and International Monetary Fund (IMF); the Troika of which symbolized the corrupt character of the Greek establishment propped up by capital in the broadest sense was guilty at the very least by *association*.

At the time of writing Kouvelakis argued that the 'fragmented left' (Ibid.: 29) indicated the left's inability to 'intervene strategically in the political situation', namely refusal by the KKE to consider an alliance with Syriza. The 2014 European elections indicated a shift towards Syriza perhaps recruiting votes from the KKE who in the Greek general election of 2012 gained 8.48 per cent of votes winning twenty-six seats in Parliament. This is compared to the drop to 6.07 per cent in the European elections. But crucially, Syriza, who won 16.79 per cent of the vote in the general election of 2012, jumped to 26.60 per cent in the European election suggesting votes gained from the established parties. Kouvelakis said this:

> In truth, the KKE leadership, like that of Syriza, make use of a radical but disembodied discourse, one eye always on the polls. They seem content with the role of passive repositories for popular rage, a shared position which has created a strange complicity, beyond the virulent polemics. In both cases, albeit for opposing reasons, what is included is the idea

of an alternative built on *transitional objectives*, responding concretely to the crucial problems raised by the crisis (my italics; Ibid.: 31).

The 'transitional objectives' is based on creating a different form of economy, in the first instance, and the overall context isn't entirely that far removed from the politics employed by the German left-wing parties during the period of economic collapse of the Weimar Republic when the crisis of capitalism enveloped Germany with the left refusing to unite. Statistically the shift in voting patterns were significant, although one can argue that the European elections raised different issues and grievances to a national election, but such shifts in the European elections do not always inform us of the trajectory of any given national consciousness and it is, after all, the latter which has become a crucial element in the production of cultural politics and the changes that have since emerged from shifts in consciousness over a long period of time.

The normally uninteresting European elections in 2014, in fact, turned out to be one of the most decisive indicators for Greek politics when Syriza was elected to power in the general election of January 2015, and for the record Kouvelakis was wrong in terms of Syriza's emergence. Syriza won a staggering 149 seats in the Greek parliament (36.3 per cent) just 2 short of the votes required to have an overall majority. Syriza invited the right-wing Independent Greeks Party to form a coalition government; the only political position they had in common was that they were both 'anti-austerity'. The KKE, who took fifteen seats (5.5 per cent), remained outside – on every occasion I have taken part in demonstrations in Greece both Syriza and the KKE march separately – Golden Dawn lost one seat reduced to seventeen seats (6.3 per cent) but were placed third.

In Spain, a new left-wing movement Podemos emerged out of the 15-M social movement gaining 7.97 per cent in the European elections (2014). The ruling Partido Popular (PP) won the elections in Spain with 26.06 per cent with the main opposition the PSOE (The Spanish Socialist Workers Party) winning 23.00 per cent. But less than a month later, public support for both of the latter two parties dropped considerably with Podemos on 15 per cent, PP on 30 per cent and the PSOE on 22 per cent. Podemos was founded only two months prior to the European elections in March 2014 as a tiny formation. In June 2015, Ahora Madrid (Now Madrid), a collection of leftist groups under the leadership of former judge and communist Manuela Carmena, marginally lost to the Conservative Partido Popular in the Madrid municipal elections but joined forces with the Socialists to gain control of Madrid.

In France the right-wing Front National (FN) was first with 24.95 per cent; the Five Star Movement with its 'citizens activists' was second in Italy with 21.15 per cent, and in the United Kingdom, UKIP (United Kingdom Independence Party) beat the three main political parties winning with 26.77 per cent of the vote. The European elections, however, reflect the rise of contrasting ideologies to established norms, and the emergence of movements and political parties in such a relatively short space of time – more critical for Podemos perhaps – isn't only a rejection of the European project from differing political standpoints but more crucially, overall, critical reactions to the failure of capital, presented as 'austerity' across the European landscape.

Touraine's concept of social movements

It's clear from the previous discussion that the degree of opposition to the EUP is both varied in ideologies across the political landscape. But the crucial question is this: do the various groupings and political parties which have emerged, and/or strengthened in the case of the Front National and UKIP, constitute social movements in the way Alan Touraine envisaged? Moreover, does it matter whether we categorize some groupings as social movements and others not? Consider this extract taken from *The Observer* (May 31, 2015), article titled 'Ex-Communist, retired judge, blogger... the woman now poised to run Spain's capital':

> Ahora Madrid is not a political party she [Manuela Carmena] explains, but rather a coalition of leftist groups, which includes Podemos and thousands of citizens. 'It's a platform of people who have come together to change things'.

Similarly, activists supporting Corbyn's Labour Party leadership in the UK set up a campaigning group called Momentum, and this is what the Media Advisor of Momentum James Schneider said on the BBC's *Daily Politics* (Friday, November 20, 2015) in response to the question 'Are you the party within?'

> No we are not the party within. ... What we are trying to do is two things. We are trying to build popular power in the country, and we are trying to make the Labour Party more like a social movement, more embedded in communities, and more able to engage with social movements and campaign groups at community and national level.

In 1981 the French sociologist Alan Touraine wrote *The Voice and the Eye: An Analysis of Social Movements* which as the title states was, amongst many things, an attempt to evaluate and understand the internal and external logic of social movements, how they emerged, how they developed organically, and how they were ideologically positioned vis-à-vis the established order.

In order for us to grasp Touraine's interest in social movements, we can turn to the works of Antonio Gramsci, particularly Gramsci's concepts of 'hegemony', 'war of position' and 'war of manoeuvre', although strangely, Touraine makes no mention of Gramsci whatsoever in *The Voice and the Eye*. What Touraine was attempting, despite the absence of Gramsci, was a clear analysis and understanding of not only how social movements emerged and the dynamics which drove them, and how they were *positioned*, but importantly how social movements were attempting counter-hegemonic strategies to the prevailing class powers.

Raymond Williams details counter-hegemony in *Marxism and Literature* as evidence of working class consciousness pitted against dominant ideology, which is a mode of critical thinking, opposition and non-compliance. In sum, counter-hegemonic strategies are a crucial part of what Gramsci termed a 'war of manoeuvre', which is when social movements move against what Touraine called a 'class adversary', which for Touraine was pivotal to distinguishing between a genuine social movement and a pressure group and groupings with internal inclinations towards the economics of capital; it wasn't all-out class war – which for Gramsci was 'war of position' – but the possibilities of the latter developing were there and contingent on social and economic conditions. For our purposes, the 'war of manoeuvre' is the important phase of development to understand.

Touraine's book was met with mixed responses from the academic world – nothing new perhaps – but in my view it remains an essential text for a sociological understanding of the emergence of social movements in late capitalism and, more specifically, in relation to austerity across Europe and, perhaps more importantly to assess, in contemporary Europe whether there are faults with Touraine's analysis. Before I proceed further, I want to ask the following question: Are there differences, subtle or otherwise, between 'social movements' as defined by Touraine and groupings and/or pressure groups which inhabit the current European landscape and to which appear to share or have similar characteristics in structure, organization and outlooks?

If we use the term 'opposition' for one moment, it is true to state that generally speaking, as discussed in the previous section, there is opposition to the EUP today which is directed by broad and diverse political groupings including right, far-right, left-wing and populist movements. But do they represent the type of social movements which Touraine was so concerned with? And further, what difference does it make whether they are defined as social movements if they are all characterized as 'oppositional' groups?

To answer these questions, we need to understand what Touraine meant by social movements and what the consequences are in the context of the EUP, if we accept Touraine's definition. So what exactly is Touraine's (1981: 77) definition of social movements? It is this:

> The social movement is the organized collective behaviour of a class actor struggling against his class adversary for the social control of historicity in a concrete community.

Although this quote is very important, to leave it at that would certainly be an injustice to Touraine's extensive work. Thus, an additional concept which Touraine used to analyse and understand social movements was 'solidarity' and as Martell and Stammers (1996: 128) state: 'Solidarity is situated at the very heart of this period of Touraine's intellectual work' concerning his analysis of social movements. Moreover, Touraine offers a unique notion of 'conflict' which we must use in relation to 'solidarity'. When Touraine (1981: 77) says this: 'The idea of social movement should ... be preferred to that of conflict' and then this: 'Society is conflictual production itself' (Ibid.), it is tempting to think in relation to the first quote that perhaps Touraine abandoned conflict as a defining element for describing social movements, and in relation to the second there appears to be a contradiction at play.

This isn't so because Touraine is thinking in terms of a specific modality of conflict which, importantly for Touraine, is counter to the neo-liberal notion of conflict wrapped up or presented as 'competition'; this for Touraine was conflict that emerged from the internal motions of free-market ideology. This type of conflict for Touraine is 'external' to the ideological imperatives of social movements that situate class, and class conflict, at the centre of thinking and action; this is why Marx's idea of *praxis* is so important for Touraine. The 'internal' conflict is the organic and authentic effort produced by the class-based movement which threatens its 'adversary'; not a natural adversary, but one that has developed from the ashes of feudalism, developing further through the period of industrialization and then as forms within what Touraine called 'post-industrial society'. This latter context is *the* context of Touraine's analysis of the formal development of social movements. One could add that the modern idea of 'grassroots movements' – seen as popular

formations on the Internet under the guise of citizen journalism/
activists (the Occupy movement, for example) – resonates with
Touraine's concept but is not identical to it.

As Touraine articulates later in his book, 'A social movement
represents a particular form of struggle, *but the most important
one*' (my italics; Ibid.: 85) and lists four important conditions essential for the logical understanding of such formations, which are:

1   The first Touraine calls *committed population* ('worker or peas-
    ant struggles');
2   Struggles require 'organization' not simply mere opinion;
3   'It must fight against an adversary'
4   Conflict should represent 'social problems concerning the
    whole of society' (Ibid.).

It's worth stating that point 4 sets out to distinguish the differing
motives between social movements and pressure groups; the latter, according to Touraine, merely saw conflict in specific rather
than general terms. In other words, it was limited in interests and
numbers and, more importantly, in outcomes because social benefits were greatly reduced. This is not to argue that pressure groups
and their campaigns are to be de-valued, on the contrary, but it
was for Touraine a heuristic device to separate the two groups and
to help us understand the dynamics of a social movement.

A central element of Touraine's thinking revolves around the
concept *historicity* evidenced in the title of Chapter One, which
is, 'Men make their own history', a play of sorts on the following
quote from Marx in the *Eighteenth Brumaire of Louis Bonaparte:*

> Men make their own history, but they do not make it as they
> please; they do not make it under self-selected circumstances,
> but under circumstances existing already, given and transmit-
> ted from the past.

In the context of Marx's thought on movement and dialectics –
although Touraine doesn't use the term 'dialectics' – he nevertheless argues that society, and movement/change, is determined
by the struggle between competing forces over *historicity* or, as
Touraine put it, 'class struggle' (Ibid.: 29).

Alienation and post-industrial society

Dewey once argued that 'men are not isolated non-social atoms,
but are men only when in intrinsic relations' to one another, and
the state in turn only represents them 'so far as they have become

organically related to one another, or are possessed of unity of purpose and interest' ('The Ethics of Democracy', *EW*1, 231–2). Marx's concept of alienation is evoked here along with the idea that 'Social movements are actors that by definition challenge power' (Raschke, 1991, in Britta Baumgarten and Ullrich, 2012: 1) particularly when alienation is confronted.

We can't fully understand Touraine's later work concerning so-cial movements unless we assess his work published ten years earlier in 1971 which was *The Post-Industrial Society: Tomorrow's Social History: Classes, Conflicts and Culture in the Programmed Society*. Touraine's book essentially argued that a new type of so-ciety had emerged out of the previous industrial form, and it was a society, Touraine claimed, that was suffocating people or, to use the language from the book cover, 'strangling us'. In particular it's vitally important to understand Touraine's analysis and thinking towards *alienation* and the role alienation plays in the production of and defining characteristics of social movements.

A central element of Touraine's work was to argue that new social relationships had developed as a consequence of the shift from industrial society towards post-industrial society and further to understand the process of social conflict in this new society. Touraine argued that social conflict was posed in terms of a class war between owners of the means of production and workers, and this was a simple framework of how social conflict emerged; this in sum was a classical Marxist understanding of how social conflict occurred in class structured systems with clear boundaries of demarcation.

Touraine argued that these clearly defined boundaries between industrialists/capitalists and workers had been obliterated in the new post-industrial society, which he called 'programmed society' which was primarily governed by technocratic authority. So why is this earlier text important to review and to understand in the context of social movements across Europe in the age of austerity? The answer, put simply, is Touraine's emphasis on the concept of 'alienation'; a concept, it must be recalled, that was central to hu-manist Marxist thinkers but largely rejected by scientific Marxists, such as Loius Althusser, because for Althusser 'alienation' was nothing more than ideology.

The importance of Touraine's (1971) work was based on his break from traditional Marxist analysis of social conflict stated here:

> The method I choose to follow is different: it will question first of all the social and cultural orientations of a society, the na-ture of the social conflicts and power struggles through which these orientations are worked out, and what it is that the ruling

social elements repress that provokes social movements. My analysis will not focus on the inner workings of the social system but on the formation of historical activity, the manner in which men fashion their history (Ibid.: 4).

What is interesting about Touraine's work is that despite the rich complexity of the post-industrial 'programmed society', the notion of alienation remained a central defining feature of dialectical movement. The previous industrial society had been defined by Marxists in mainly class terms or rather the conflict between workers and industrialists, and for Touraine this dichotomy was no longer useful for understanding social conflict in post-industrial society.

We can find the first references to alienation in the Economic and Philosophical Manuscripts of 1844 where Marx argued that 'Estranged Labour' is a product of the Capitalist Mode of Production. Estranged labour or alienation are concepts commonly associated with the early period of Marx – the later Marx, it has been argued, was less enthusiastic about the concept of alienated labour, but there are traces of alienation in the later writings of Marx, which proves he hadn't abandoned the theory in its entirety. The early/later periods are often conceptualized in terms of a move away ('break') from 'Humanism' to a 'Scientific' mode of analysis, and nowhere is this more clearly articulated than in the works of the French philosopher Louis Althusser who had argued that Marx's scientific analysis of capitalism was a rejection of ideology.

The discussion on estranged labour/alienation (estrangement), is complex and it is important to highlight associated concepts such as commodity fetishism, objectification and reification – the latter a key concept introduced by the Hungarian philosopher Georgy Lukács. Under the heading 'Estranged Labour' in the *Manuscripts*, Marx is critical of political economy for failing to understand the exploitative relationship between private property and labour and begins his analysis on the 'economic facts', stating:

> The worker becomes all the poorer the more wealth he produces, the more his production increases in power and size. The worker becomes an ever cheaper commodity the more commodities he creates. The *devaluation* of the world of men is in direct proportion to the increasing *value* of the world of things. Labor produces not only commodities; it produces itself and the worker as a *commodity* – and this at the same rate at which it produces commodities in general.

Marx argued that in the productive process of industrialized capitalism, the worker becomes 'estranged' from the product she/he produced and that this form of 'objectification' further estranged the workers not only from themselves but also from those around them. The objects the worker produced (products) were means by which industrialists gained profit and in return offered a wage, a partial and relatively small amount vis-à-vis the total profit, despite the empirical fact that production is essentially the activity of labour; a product of the worker is destined to produce surplus value (profit) – thus, like the object, labour also is a means to an end.

Objectification thus embraces both the individual and product, and in this form the product of the capitalist mode of production is purely measured in economic terms – it is alien to the actual lives of workers, and its use is purely measured not in social terms but in monetary or 'exchange value'. There is 'spinoff', a reward industrialists claim, which is a wage and that is one of the most controversial aspects of capitalism, for the means of production and ownership are equally estranged from labour bound up in the liberal ideology of 'private' over 'public property/ownership'.

The controversy over alienation is based on the idea that Marx argued that under capitalism workers were removed from their true nature because they were incarcerated or what is termed 'bonded labour'; it's akin to acting against your will. Liberal philosophy differs where generally it posits the idea that human nature is based on the idea of individualism which guarantee rights, and Hegel further argued that pursuing individuality was a natural state of affairs; he referred to this as humans seeking 'recognition' and Fukuyama later used this as the reason for the collapse of Stalinism in 1989 because it was natural and therefore unstoppable. So on the one hand we have unnatural-alienated labour pitted against a natural state of affairs, and Marx was questioning what was seen and remains as 'natural', 'rational' and 'legitimate'.

To make an empirical analogy, the current UK Green Party's belief – which I would argue currently encompasses elements of the internal class-based dynamics of a social movement – and its concerns for the 'common good' is close to Marx's ideas, although the Greens would tax the wealthy and introduce *redistributive justice* as a means to achieving the 'common good' rather than, as Marx had argued, move towards socialism then communism based on the common ownership of the means of production. Any theory on human nature is bound to be contentious, but it is important to bear in mind that Marx wasn't prescriptive about what actually constituted human nature; rather Marx was arguing that workers weren't able to shape their nature freely under the conditions of their existence according to the laws of capital, and the laws of capital are primarily shaped by economic necessity at any price.

It's worth noting that Althusser offered a scathing critique on alienation and Marxist Humanism in 1964 in an imaginative piece titled 'Marxism and Humanism' in the *Cahiers*, beginning: 'Today, Socialist "humanism" is on the agenda' – note the quotation marks on humanism, which was to emphasize the contempt Althusser held for humanism – and Lukács – but as we'll see, the clarity of his scientific preference over humanism would be muddied later in his life. Althusser detailed the two stages of Marx's thinking on humanism from 'liberal rationalist humanism' to Feuerbach's theory and sums it all up, thus:

> History is the alienation and production of reason in unreason, of the true man in the alienated man. Without knowing it, man realizes the essence of man in the alienated products of his labour (commodities, State, religion). The loss of man that produces history and man must presuppose a definite pre-existing essence. At the end of history, this man, having become in-human objectivity, has merely to re-grasp as subject his own essence alienated in property, religion and the State to become total man, true man.

But for Althusser, humanism was nothing more than a pointless piece of ideology – socialism, on the other hand, was scientific until in 1976 in his response to John Lewis in the *Elements of Self-Criticism* Althusser acknowledged that his assessment wasn't quite correct, but he refused to call it an 'error' but rather a 'theoreticist deviation' in regards to the definite 'break' by Marx from early to later periods. Althusser said this:

> I wanted to defend Marxism against the real dangers of *bourgeois* ideology: it was necessary to stress its revolutionary new character; it was therefore necessary to 'prove' that there is an antagonism between Marxism and bourgeois ideology, that Marxism could not have developed in Marx or in the labour movement except given a radical and unremitting *break* with bourgeois ideology, an unceasing struggle against the assaults of this ideology. This thesis was correct. It still is correct.

The harsh reality for Althusser was that elements of the early 'humanist' Marx stubbornly continued in residual forms in his later works, crucially in *Das Capital* and resurrected in the works of Touraine. I admire Althusser for many reasons, not least because he tirelessly attempted to shift Marxism towards the scientific away from an illusory bourgeois ideology as he perceived it, but I have always felt that this was always a false dichotomy. To use his term, there can never be a 'break' in conceptual thought; the whole history of ideas is a continuation of the past into present forms of which residual historical forms/concepts persist albeit with subtle changes. We can see this in the writings of Marx, where Marx used 'estranged labour' and 'alienation' shifting towards 'commodity fetishism' which is central to the Marx in his later period of *Capital* but retaining alienated labour within the idea of commodity fetishism.

Georgy Lukács observed this continuation – not 'break' as Althusser mistakenly observed – when the former produced what is in my view one of the greatest contributions to Marxist theory, namely Lukács's theory of 'reification'; even the Althussarian Etienne Balibar acknowledged this contribution towards Marxist theory. Anyone wishing to understand this complex concept and its relationship to alienation and/or commodity fetishism should read *Marxism and the Proletariat: A Lukáscian Perspective*, by Stephen Perkins. Chapter Five is a superb explanation of the three aforementioned concepts and the subtle nuances relating each whilst containing new moments of the thoughts of Marx.

The commodity fetishism of Marx – the science of economics – was for Lukács, as Perkins explains, the concrete form of the abstract alienation, thus, the continuation of thought in a different form. Lukács's theory of reification relies heavily on alienation and observes the relationship between object and subject in bourgeois society which turns social relations into a process of objectification. Workers alienated from the product they produce and workers alienated from themselves creates a social consciousness which is hindered by the compulsion to produce goods, and it is the one reason that Lukács is correct to have placed false consciousness into its right place by arguing that reification limits the horizons of thought.

As Perkins quite rightly argues, the pawprints of Georg Simmel are everywhere to be found in the theory of reification – bourgeois culture imposing itself upon consciousness becoming reality impeding the development of the 'soul', of intellectual creativity, of culture. What Simmel saw as a 'crisis of culture', Lukács saw as a crisis of humanity, and the only way to reverse alienation was to actively confront the process of reification; like Marx, this was to be achieved by the awakening of the proletariat towards their emancipation and establishment of the true 'species-being'. If alienation has achieved anything, it is the legitimization and rationalization of the bourgeois notion of the 'individual'. Marx had noted in his early period how civil society, as opposed to political society, had established the individual as the most potent form of ideology, and it was perhaps the greatest obstacle to establishing communism of which the species-being was central.

In his work *For Marx*, Althusser argued that reification was no more than ideology when he famously spoke of the epistemological break of Marx. As briefly detailed, the 'break' never happened, but was Althusser correct nevertheless to argue that reification was ideology and, if so, that it establishes and resolves nothing? Not when it directly reflects actual working lives and actual thinking in relation to the production of objects and all that follows, and finally when it relates to the negation of critical action, and this is why alienation abstracted through commodity fetishism remains the critical point for change.

Touraine's (1971) use of alienation then is a clear rejection of Althussarian Marxism and the continuation of Marx's works vis-à-vis alienation through to commodity fetishism clearly stated here:

> Today, it is more useful to speak of alienation than of exploitation; the former defines a social, the latter merely an economic relationship. A man is not alienated because his 'natural' needs are crushed by a 'dehumanized' society, by work on an assembly line by urban congestion, or the mass media. Such expressions only give rise to vague moral philosophy. ... Alienation must be defined in terms of social relationships (Ibid.: 8).

And finally:

> A man is alienated when his only relationship to the social and cultural directions of his society is the one the ruling class accords him as compatible with the maintenance of its own dominance. Alienation means cancelling out social conflict by creating dependent participation (Ibid.: 8–9).

It's important to note that for Touraine, whilst alienation was oppressive, it nevertheless sowed the seeds for change. Whilst he said this: 'Ours is a society of alienation ... because it seduces, manipulates, and enforces conformism' and this: 'Alienation means cancelling out social conflict by creating dependent participation' (Ibid.: 9), he also said this:

> ... social conflict is inaugurated when the battle against this alienation begins and the marginal segments of society reject their assigned role, become conscious of their dependency, and begin to act with their sights focused on themselves and their self-determination (Ibid.: 10).

Thus, the rejection of 'dependent participation', 'alienation' and the production of alternative narratives towards dominant ideologies are the bedrock of defining a social movement of which Touraine sought to explain and understand via his 'sociological intervention' ten years later.

Alienation rooted in life under capitalism propels agents to action because alienation is *suffering* and, as both Schopanheaur and Horkheimer[7] argued, suffering is the basis for action and change. But does alienation, so often used in Marxist circles under industrial conditions, change in form and substance in post-industrial/ programmed society where if anything the emphasis in individualism is even greater?

Taking Greece, Spain, Italy, Portugal and the UK, including radical Green agendas, as examples, it seems that the post-industrial system is turning back in on itself towards protest and opposition so indicative of industrial society; the contradictions are delicious. Marx's analysis of the types of contradictions inherent in industrial society was an attempt to understand the dynamics of social systems and the emergence of class struggle and here we are in the post-industrial epoch, or what Alan Touraine called the 'programmed society', witnessing the very social dynamics that Marx observed. Post-modernists must have taken to the hills for their silence is deafening as the emerging social movements defy their perverse logic.

Conclusion

Touraine's 'sociological intervention' is urgently required to fully understand the 'new' form of cultural politics of which social movements are located, not only in terms of the opposing narratives to the EUP but also for their alternative narratives to the political groupings associated with right and far-right ideologies. Groups defined as social movements are left-leaning because they not only seek to oppose the established rationale of neo-liberalism but are clearly 'class adversaries' of the elite, and their emergence can be located in the many realms and forms of alienated labour. Touraine's research and sociological intervention in the 1970s was an attempt to understand the position and role of social movements in post-industrial 'programmed society' which had replaced the workers' movements so indicative of industrial society. Touraine's earlier work, particularly his emphasis on alienation, in my view, provides the context for his later work on social movements, and his later work provides a context for our understanding on the development of social movements across the European landscape – and elsewhere – in the age of austerity and to the way social movements and opposition in general across the broad political spectrum are redefining a 'new' cultural politics.

Notes

1 Both Hegel and Marx argued that 'dialectics' is governed by movement, by 'critical thinking' and 'action'. Two quotations that may help are, 'Dialectics attempts to perceive movement as a contradictory unity of opposites and attempts to comprehend the dynamics of social relations in society' (Berry, 2004: xiii), and 'The working class in every country lives its own life, makes its own experiences, seeking always to create forms and realise values which may originate directly from its organic opposition to official society, but are shaped by its experiences in co-operative labour' (James, 1984: 76). 'Movement' and 'transformation' are central to understanding the dialectic and whilst Marx argued that as method the dialectic would observe 'what exists' (Marx, 1976: 103), it would also condition thinking of what may evolve.

2 The base-superstructure model has been heavily criticized for being a crude and reductionist theory which essentially maintains that the 'economic base' of society governs thinking which manifests within the superstructure. What this means is that culture, social, political, and theological issues are determined or conditioned by the form of economic rationality of any given system. Marx saw the economic element as a central driving force of 'motion'; in other words it is given priority which shapes other spheres of society. For our purposes, the base-superstructure model is useful for understanding opposition to 'austerity' and the dialectical movement and transformations that may occur from opposition to austerity measures and the crisis in capitalism.

3 During the 2015 general election in the United Kingdom, three political parties/social movements placed the 'people' or 'workers' at the centre of their manifestos, stating that austerity within the United Kingdom was detrimental to workers and was immoral in the light that the UK is the sixth wealthiest nation in the world. The three groupings are the Scottish National Party (SNP), Plaid Cymru (Wales) and the Green Party, all of which to some degree share the concerns of Syriza in Greece and Podemos in Spain.

4 An estimated number of 100,000 new members, including myself, joined the Labour Party as a result of the possibility that Corbyn would become the leader of the Labour Party, and when Corbyn won a further 50,000 joined.

5 Evidenced at a higher political level by the Hungarian political leadership during the refugee crisis in 2015.

6 During an interview with Paul Mason (Channel 4 News, June 4, 2015), the Greek negotiator and top-ranking Syriza member Euclid Tsakalotos informed Mason that if Europe was not prepared to re-think its 'vision' then it had no future. The interview took place on the eve of the latest, expected debt payment from Greece to the International Monetary Fund (IMF), which Greece refused to make.

7 See 'Max Horkheimer: Issues concerning Liberalism and Culture' in *Revisiting the Frankfurt School: Essays on Culture, Media and Theory* (2012), edited by D. Berry. Aldershot: Ashgate Publications.

Bibliography

Althusser, L. (1964). 'Marxism and Humanism'. In the Cahiers, *Ecole Normale Supérieure*.

Althusser, L. (1973) *Essays in self-criticism*. 'Réponse à John Lewis'. Available at: https://cesarmangolin.files.wordpress.com/2010/02/althusser-essays-in-self-criticism.pdf.

Althusser, L. (2005). *For Marx: radical thinkers*. London: Verso.

Eco, U. (2012). 'Umberto Eco: "It's culture, not war, that cements European identity"'. *The Guardian*. Available at: http://www.theguardian.com/world/2012/jan/26/umberto-eco-culture-war-europa.

European Cultural Foundation. Available at: http://www.culturalfoundation.eu/story/.

European Cultural Foundation. Available at: http://www.culturalfoundation.eu/thematic-focus.

James, C.L.R. (1984). *At the rendezvous of victory*. London: Allison and Busby Ltd.

Martell, L. and Stammers, N. (1996). 'The study of solidarity and the social theory of Alain Touraine'. In: J. Clark and M. Diani, eds., *Alan Touraine*. Falmer Press: London.

Marx, K. (1852). 'The Eighteenth Brumaire of Louis Bonaparte'. Available at: https://www.marxists.org/archive/marx/works/1852/18th-brumaire/ch01.htm.

Marx, K. (2007). *Economic and philosophical manuscripts of 1844*, translated by Martin Milligan. New York: Dover Publications.

Perkins, S. (1993). *Marxism and the proletariat: a Lukascian perspective*. London: Pluto Press.

Sennelart, M. (ed.) (1978). *Michel Foucault: the birth of biopolitics, lectures at the Collège de France, 1978–1979*. Basingstoke: Palgrave MacMillan.

Touraine, A. (1971). *The post-industrial society: tomorrow's social history: classes, conflicts and culture in the programmed society*. New York: Random House.

Touraine, A. (1981). *Voice and the eye: an analysis of social movements*. Cambridge: Cambridge University Press.

8 Cultural politics and anti-austerity movements in Spain

Towards a comprehensive strategy of change

Joan Pedro

The suffering generated by the politics of so-called 'austerity' in Spain, together with the country's history, political tradition and socio-demographic characteristics, has led to growing questioning of the implementation of such policies. What in Spain is called 'the social majority' has confronted austerity as a form of increasing economic oppression established through political authoritarianism against the will of the population, including the voters of parties that have approved severe measures of cuts in social spending after promising otherwise in electoral campaigns.

The politics of austerity have created great suffering among the Spanish popular classes who, moreover, are not responsible for the economic collapse in recent times. This Orwellian strategy has not been successful in achieving a hegemonic position over society as citizens have organized and mobilized to confront austerity economics and ideology and have proposed an alternative vision for political action. By placing the concept of power relations at the centre of the analysis, cultural politics is understood here as a contested space in which meaning is introduced in society and the material relations are co-configured (Berry and Theobald, 2006; Fenton, 2015; Freedman, 2014; Klaehn, 2010; Mosco, 2009; Pedro, 2016a; Goss, Pedro and Gould, 2016). In this battle, a plurality of factors comes into play; both complementary and opposing forces interact in a manner that confers a hegemonic position to elitist economic and political blocs which have been systematically challenged by counter-hegemonic forces.

This chapter, therefore, focuses on the confrontation between economic and political elites on the one hand and critical, social and political organizations on the other. It first addresses the general characteristics and consequences of the implementation of austerity policies in Spain, as well as its specific effects in education and housing. Second, this chapter focuses on the resistance to austerity and the general proposals posed by the 15-M (or *Indignados*) movement and the Podemos party, together with an analysis of the concrete struggles to defend public education and the housing sector from austerity. These two case studies will show the economic and ideological interests behind the implementation of austerity. Regarding the housing sector, this means that public housing is privatized in a way that limits human rights while it provides high profits for market speculators. Regarding education, the politics of austerity is operating as a method to augment the corporate and political control of knowledge to the detriment of its critical edge and emancipatory value for the common good.

The implementation of austerity in Spain: economic and cultural dimensions

Austerity is already being applied in most parts of the world (90 per cent of the world population) as a specific socioeconomic model for the reorganization and further expansion of the global capitalist system in the current historical period (Ortiz and Cummins, 2013). It can thus be said that austerity has been a successful programme in generating bottom-up transference of wealth that has further enriched the dominant class through the impoverishment of the majority of the population.

The success of this economic programme is inevitably linked to its failure as a social model, and this failure explains the development of protest movements. In this regard, austerity also plays a fundamental cultural role as a discourse oriented to increasing the political and ideological control of the population. Economic and cultural change work in synergy as austerity produces an oppressive material reality that promotes the type of frameworks conducive to discourses that further justify austerity and practices that limit the possibilities of building a democratic and egalitarian alternative. The imposition of austerity is an attempt to provide legitimacy and rationality to the idea that there is no alternative, that the only logic acceptable is austerity.

In economic terms, austerity can be understood specifically as a programme of socioeconomic adjustment at a macro level, based on the reduction of social public spending, lower wages and the establishment of higher taxes for the middle and lower working classes. This programme is justified by the European Union (EU) and Spanish political and economic elites as the necessary means for reducing debt and deficit so that economic growth and employment can be generated.

As Navarro (2015) and Torres (2013a; 2013b) have shown, empirical evidence on the application of austerity points to the opposite conclusion: debt and deficit have continued to grow and inequality has soared both in Spain and other countries. Spain has not become more competitive in the global market and it has not been able to attract sufficient productive investment. Job creation is testimonial and precarity in the working conditions is intensifying; jobs are being split between more workers with temporary and low-wage contracts. Unpaid overtime hours are commonplace, and demand of goods and services has contracted with economic activity and reduced state income has led to an expansion in debt. Consequently, higher debt level is used as a justification and excuse for further cuts in social provisions, impacting negatively on large sections of the Spanish populace.

Temporary short-term growth of GDP in Spain is often used as an argument to legitimize austerity measures, neglecting the fact that GDP is a very limited variable of analysis, which includes criminal activities that will probably stop expanding in the near future. Moreover, GDP is connected to the global economy and essentially reflects the increased accumulation of capital by corporations and financial institutions as a result of the policies of austerity.

The imposition of austerity measures by the economic and political elites of both the EU and Spain meant breaking with the previous social consensus which agreed that the role of the state is to provide protection for society and deliver basic public services that assure human needs. In Spain the financial crisis was transformed into a social and economic crisis for the majority of the population through the transfer of public wealth to the banking system. Austerity applies only to citizens and not to the financial sector that was bailed out with funding. The high levels of corruption, accompanied by ostentatious consumption, of the political rulers provide clear evidence of the perversion of the term 'austerity' when applied by elites.

The cuts have been very damaging not only for the general functioning of the economy but especially for the fundamental rights and living conditions of the majority of the population, with the higher cuts being applied to health, education, housing, community services, unemployment protection, pensions, the environment and culture, while the monarchy, political advisors or the military and security sectors have been less affected.

Ideologically, these cuts in social spending have been justified by an alleged excess of spending that would have been fundamental in the economic crash. Spaniards were told that they 'had lived above their possibilities'. While there certainly had been a lot of squandering of public money – particularly by the *Partido Popular* (PP), the party that has applied cuts in social spending more intensely – this argument is flawed as the State had surplus (not deficit) and debt was only 25 per cent of the GDP before the crisis erupted in 2007 compared to 100 per cent in 2016. Lots of activism and political pedagogy was required for victims of innumerable frauds not to feel guilty and manage to empower themselves through collective organization and solidarity.

The political, economic and media elites of Germany and Spain that have promoted the imposition of austerity as an unavoidable policy, have argued that the origins of Nazism can be found in the reaction against hyperinflation that was produced by the expansion of public spending and deficit. According to Navarro (2016) this interpretation is historically incorrect: Hyperinflation (1921–23) was produced by the increase in printing money to pay for war reparations, and it was not inflation that determined the rise of the Nazi Party but austerity policies (1930–32) that included cuts in public spending and salary reduction, which created discontent.

The flawed arguments being used are part of the cultural war the elites use to promote fear, moral panic, subordination and obedience. This cultural war further allows tilting the power relations between capital and labour very much in favour of the dominant classes. The austerity model promotes competition between workers in a context of job scarcity, low state protection and attacks on solidarity; it is every person for him- or herself! Both austerity discourse and its materialization promote the type of selfish individualism that erodes solidarity bonds. The individual who has been marginalized from political and economic decision-making processes is persuaded to set the blame on other marginalized and exploited individuals and social groups: The attack of the upper classes against a social majority is hidden behind the criminalization and vilification of refugees, migrants, Muslims, other national workers who compete for the few job opportunities, poor people with (minor) public benefits, leftists who want to 'destroy everything' and other usual scapegoats.

Austerity also reduces the bargaining power of workers vis-á-vis the corporate class as it is accompanied by attempts to pass labour laws that reduce or eliminate collective agreements in search of so-called 'flexibility' (precarity) that allegedly generates more jobs and economic growth. However, austerity and precarity contribute to high unemployment rates and thus to the development of an *industrial reserve army of labour* comprised of desperate people who willingly accept jobs in conditions of semi-or outright slavery.

The result of austerity and its coalescent cultural war is that many individuals belonging to the working class engage in conflict and view themselves as adversaries instead of allies who share common ground. The lack of a sense of commonality, together with the atmosphere of fear which has been generated and the miseducation promoted by the mainstream media and increasingly by the educational system, lead to a sociological Stockholm syndrome that makes the aggressed individual identify with the aggressor group. The perpetrators of inequality and suffering deploy a discourse which presents them as the guarantors of the stability and order that they themselves have broken. Moreover, the victims are guided to believe in a naïve affirmation of the self, independently of other people, and in a chimerical individual salvation.

Spanish society has resisted individualized marginalization to a great extent and has organized and mobilized massively to confront austerity measures and propose alternative routes of action. But the attack on ordinary citizens has been multi-dimensional and difficult to resist. Austerity has been accompanied by the bursting of the housing bubble, huge unemployment levels, lack of opportunities for the youth, high corruption and the perception of impunity, the politisization of the judicial system, home evictions, the selling below market price of city council homes to vulture funds like Goldman Sachs, the abandonment of the patients of Hepatitis C, authoritarian-style government reforms and a long list of abuses by the government, banks and other corporations. In addition, the specific form of Spanish capitalism is usually defined as crony capitalism, as it is based on public servants discretionarily granting licences and other privileges to their families, friends and contacts in the corporate and media sectors. All of these elements would come to fray in May 15, 2011, with the formation of mass mobilizations in Spain not witnessed since the years of *transition* to democracy.

Austerity and housing

Housing is no longer a right in Spain with more than 350,000 families forced out of their homes. The BBC reported in February 2014 that 'hundreds of families in Spain are evicted every day, after falling behind on mortgage payments – and under Spain's draconian laws they must continue paying off the loan even after the home has been repossessed' (Ash, 2014); this mortgage law has been enormously beneficial to banks that control a significant part of the housing market.

The issue has many problematic dimensions, but austerity has *the* central role. An immediate solution proposed is to provide alternative public housing to people who have been evicted. However, and as a consequence of the historically limited welfare state in Spain and the ongoing cuts in social spending, only 2 per cent of the houses are public when the EU average is 9 per cent, with

17 per cent in France and 32 per cent in Holland (García and Espinosa, 2016). Public investment would thus be required to expand the public stock and provide a house to those who loose it. In addition, some regional governments have sold – way below market price – huge stocks of public houses to vulture funds controlled by Goldman Sachs, which are raising the prices tenants agreed with the city councils, engaging in dubious methods and forcing further evictions. A solution proposed by the PAH (Platform for People Affected by Mortgages) would be to change the law so that people are not obliged to continue paying the mortgage after the eviction. The EU's top court ruled against the mortgage law in 2013, but the Spanish government (PP) retained the legal standing.

State-private connivance has continued to provoke daily evictions, even if the number has been reduced. The national government has not offered any solution and has even blocked proposals of mild reform. Instead, the official narrative on the evictions presented it as an unavoidable drama that people who had gained a mortgage contract with the bank should now face difficulties alone. No mention was made to how the political powers and banks benefited greatly from the housing and mortgage bubbles and the massive existence of fraudulent contracts, speculation, corruption, extremely high prices of houses and low salaries, sky-rocketing unemployment rates provoked to a great extent by austerity and the neo-liberal policies implemented by the two main parties.

The strategy is to blame victims who feel ashamed to speak about the problem affecting their lives. But, as developed in the section on alternatives to austerity, in 2009 the PAH started to meet the people and pedagogically explain what was happening. What became apparent is that the problem can be solved with political will to change the law and finish with austerity by increasing public funding of housing.

Austerity and education

Spanish education is marked by both the international/European transformations and Spain's specific socio-historical reality. The Spanish university system is part of the European Higher Education Area, also known as the Bologna process (1999–), which allegedly plans the development of a so-called knowledge society (Pedro, 2016b). But nothing appears more contradictory to the development of a knowledge-based society than the politics of austerity. In practice, austerity is being employed as a strategy to transform the university system according to the directions marked by the capitalist market (i.e. by the preponderance of exchange value over use value). Very clearly, a reduction in the public funding of education leads to more difficulties to function properly and accomplish society's expectations, thereby opening the way to justify further privatization.

The application of austerity in Spanish universities includes a decrease in public funding, higher tuition fees, reduction of grants and the introduction of bank loans that lead to student debt. This essentially means that education is ceasing to be considered a public good and instead turned into a business that produces commodities in search of profit. Precarisation, de-professionalization and disciplining of teachers, business management, external control or enhanced marketing and public relations are commonplace (Alegre-Zahonero and Fernández-Liria, 2004).

The right-wing government of the *Partido Popular* has abandoned the idea of ensuring equality of access to university through necessary public funding. The resulting increase in costs for students and the reduction of grants adversely affect the possibilities of the working class to complete the educational process. The number of students and graduates has thus been reduced, veering to a university for economic elites, something easily understandable from the point of view of the dominant groups: if everybody has access to higher education, it ceases to have a differential value which grants prestige, value and allows obtaining high-level jobs. Economic elites no longer need a mass of middle managers; on the contrary, in a context of systemic unemployment in which the labour market is unable to accommodate a significant portion of graduates, their existence in large numbers is an element of competition. More equality of opportunity may equal more difficulties for elites to maintain a privileged position and assure high profits. More educated people also entail more possibilities of questioning the established order in a critical way and perhaps of transforming it. The famous axiom that knowledge is power acquires a specific meaning in the present context; it is power based on the monopolization of knowledge (and of title) against those who are excluded.

In a context of public austerity, students with limited resources are offered an alternative: indebtedness. In Spain, as in the US and England, the conditions have been set so that many families are forced to ask for bank loans to finance their studies. This has opened a niche market for the penetration of the financial sector in higher education. The debt establishes a relationship of asymmetrical power that creates a dependency and can generate various kinds of personal problems, while it is also very damaging for the economy potentially developing into a new financial bubble.

The fact that austerity is used as a multi-level strategy for the commodification of education can be readily observed in the rise of financial education, with statements such as 'stimulating a positive change in attitudes and beliefs about finance' and 'sensitizing individuals to supplement the public pension', according to the Bank of Spain and the National Commission of the Stock Market (CNMV-BdE, 2013: 12–20). At a time in which pensions are being reduced, education is instrumentalized for the promotion of private plans and a marketized ideology.

This commodification directly affects the disciplines and perspectives that tend to be considered unprofitable as they no longer appear among teaching and research priorities. In other words, the focus on marketable knowledge means that the humanities and the critical social sciences are increasingly neglected. These disciplines, with their emphasis on critical, historical, holistic, transformative and ethical reflection of human affairs, are the fundamental requirement for a democratic and egalitarian society. In other words, humanist thinking is contrary to austerity. Humanistic reason leads us to think that the pensions of hardworking people and all other public services that constitute social and human rights should be assured by a progressive tax system and control of tax-eviction. Austerity in education, understood as a fundamental element of marketization, has not gone uncontested. The next section provides an analysis of the strategies of resistance to austerity and how they are being applied in the education and housing sectors.

Strategies of resistance to austerity

In 2011 the ideological hegemony of the dominant classes was progressively eroding, however, it had still not made its physical presence in the public sphere. The mass media were still upholding the great agreements based on austerity of the two-party system of PP-PSOE. Social movements were analysing the situation and organizing, but their power was limited. Traditional left-wing parties and trade unions were viewed as part of the problem and were incapable of relating positively to ordinary citizens.

However, responses to austerity eventually materialized when citizens attempted to reassert democracy and reimagine visions and strategies for political and social change geared toward socioeconomic equality. For example, the idea of holding referendums to reinstate sovereignty and decide collectively about the nation's future is currently expanding. The mobilization and collective processes for the generation of political and economic demands have also allowed for opening up dialogue which can act as a pedagogical instrument for the politization of citizens who may become more aware of the stakes and may further engage in politics. Proposals have been made of auditing public debt, increasing citizen participation in politics, increasing the minimum wage, a universal basic income, solving the problem of home evictions, raising the taxes of the rich and redistributing wealth in some possible measure.

So-called austerity soon became to be identified with *Austericide* with the 15-M movement and Podemos becoming the most visible social forces fighting against austerity. At the same time, the struggle against evictions (PAH) has been paradigmatic, and one of its leaders – Ada Colau – has become the mayor of Barcelona. The mobilization in defence of public education by the Green Tide in face of austerity has also been very strong. None of them have been fully successful in putting an end to austerity, but they have promoted cultural shifts, cultural politics and the advancement of struggles which may be of deep interest for the development of an anti-austerity strategy. The following analysis assesses some of the key strengths and limitations of the strategies that have been developed so far. This analysis is oriented to drawing a conclusion on the general lines that the collective strategy of resistance against austerity and social change may take.

The irruption of the 15-M

The 15-M or *indignados* movement developed against the marginalization and exploitation of citizens by economic and political powers provided an initially short number of demands that transformed into a very long list of measures for social transformation that were not applied in the short term but achieved social legitimacy that has opened new political spaces from where to confront austerity. While it certainly has limitations, the importance of 15-M can be found in the novel method developed to confront authoritarian structures and cuts in social spending through a deep connection of sociability and socio-political change. This allowed for the creation of new political sentiments and methods for reclaiming the public sphere as a space for hope, mutual support and the development of alternative politics. The 15-M movement attempted to recuperate politics and the economy for the people. While the new movements and projects have not succeeded so far in stopping the march of austerity, it has given hope to citizens in their own capacity to intervene in history and transform the socio-political reality.

The Spanish phenomenon shared many elements with the movements in the US and the UK. For example, as Giroux (2012: para. 8) explains, the promotion of a politics of educated hope that combines critique and the proposal of alternatives – i.e. by 'illuminating the anti-democratic forces and sites that threaten human lives, the environment and democracy itself', and 'at the same time, its visionary nature cracks open the present to reveal new horizons, different futures and the promise of a global democracy'. This is a pedagogical and performative practice that reminds citizens that the power of the dominant classes ultimately relies on the acceptance of ordinary citizens who thus have the capacity of reducing elite power and orienting the social relations in a more humanistic and less capitalistic direction. In this view, individual freedom and responsibility should be tightly connected to collective solidarity in the process of democratic and egalitarian social change. According to Giroux (2012: para. 21):

> Freedom and justice, in this instance, have to be mediated through the connection between civic education and political agency, which presupposes that the goal of educated hope is not to liberate the individual *from* the social – a central tenet of neoliberalism – but to take seriously the notion that the individual can only be liberated *through* the social.

In this vein, a substantive innovation was set in motion in February 2011: *Estado de Malestar* (State of Unrest) was a call through the digital networks to people from all ages and ideologies to join once a week in the squares with the common desire to express their outrage against the political and financial systems. There was no systematic articulation of demands or proposals because a prior step of expression, affection and identification was required.

This transversal, non-identitarian approach was also fundamental in the development of *Democracia Real Ya* (Real Democracy Now), which called for the May 15 demonstration, only after holding a process of dialogue and contacts through the Internet that helped to obtain the support of more than 600 organizations. In a post-hegemonic context in which the consensus was crumbling, an alternative proposal for hegemony did not exist yet; the key lied in focusing on the unifying elements for the multitudes to visualize the idea that 'We are not merchandise in the hands of politicians and bankers', but instead demand 'Real democracy now', one based on participation and the defence of the interests of the social majority. The fact that the call came from a social movement that was not aligned with any political party, trade union or ideology, but at the same time was not apolitical, was an important factor in the success of the demonstration.

The shout 'they do not represent us' demonstrated that the spiral of silence in Spanish society had definitively been broken and that the power of the two-party system and crony capitalism to impose austerity was being irreversibly damaged by popular power and a progressive change of mentalities. But, as has already been described, the dominant class broke the social consensus through its abuses of the population, something which was reflected in the new languages being developed, for example, in a phrase which disarmed the accusation of being 'anti-system' (which is always related to negative and violent radicalism) by holding that 'we are not anti-system, but the system is anti-us'. The indignation against the social suffering and lack of future if the so-called political class remained in power was combined with the hope for changing the situation, thereby reminding the population of the fundamental idea that we can change our conditions of existence, that 'it depends on us'.

This essential combination of anger and hope (Pedro, 2016a) was materialized in the occupation of the public squares all throughout the country (habitually occupied by corporations and commercialism) following the lead of Tunisia and Egypt. The 15-M movement employed the method of the assembly-type dialogue for mutual solidarity and decision making based on consensus with the aid of digital technologies. What was defined as a creative laboratory of ideas allowed the opening of a process for collective intelligence to generate and share common knowledge in a process of participation, more horizontal relations, cooperation, feedback, enhancement, learning and self-transformation. Without these processes no consensual proposals would have been appropriate for political and economic change.

The combination of theory and practice acted as a force of public pedagogy that allowed them to envision the possibility of change after the proclaimed *End of History* – particularly as austerity was starting to be justified as necessary and unavoidable – by providing certain ideas to understand reality and some material evidence of the possibility of change in which many people joined together to exemplify that 'yes, we can'. It meant a disruption in the normal state of history, an extraordinary moment characterized by the deterioration of the hegemony of the ruling classes and by a belief in the possibility of change when ordinary citizens engage in the transformation of reality. The predominant idea that there is no alternative and that nothing can be done was put into question by a renewed feeling of solidarity and mutual trust.

The creative and cooperative use of new media platforms allowed more public discussion and the questioning of dominant frameworks through alternative framing of messages, particularly by contributing to transform individual frames of reference in collective and interpretative frames (Martínez-Avidad, 2011). However, there did not seem to be sufficient reflection on the limitations of social networks, the vertical processes of communication that take place on the Internet and the critiques of techno-utopianism (Pedro, 2016a). A variety of actions were undertaken, such as hundreds of time banks to counter the effects of austerity through a time-based currency for exchanging services and knowledge or the creation of both physical and digital networks to paralyse the normal functioning of Bankia, a corrupt financial institution that was bailed out with public funding.

The 15-M movement could not retain its strength and influence in society over time and seemed to vanish from the media and public discussion. However, its spirit was diffused through society, leading to experimental actions like the 2015 virtual march in which thousands of holograms of people surrounded Congress to protest against the so-called Gag Law, which criminalizes social activism against austerity and limits freedom of speech.

Post-15M mobilization focused more specifically in the resistance against austerity policies being applied to fundamental public services and took the form of *Mareas* or Tides. Following the diffused spirit of 15-M, the Green Tide initiated the struggle in defence of public education (see the section on 'Resistance and alternatives to austerity in education'), the White Tide defended the universal health system against austerity cuts, the Blue Tide started promoting the view that water is a common good and a public service, the Yellow Tide campaigned for the protection and funding of the public system of libraries and many more, leading to the development of the Multi-Colour Tide that acts as a coordinator. Also the Marches of Dignity placed centre stage a fundamental humanist concept to reclaim the satisfaction of the basic needs and rights; we are humans – not a commodity upon which the powerful can impose austerity.

Podemos moves centre stage

In spite of all the mobilizations and collective thinking, the capacity to confront austerity and change Spanish political and economic reality remained very limited. As Rentea and Pedro (2015: para. 13) note: 'a broader strategy was needed: the struggle for social change required now an agent for institutional change, one capable of embarking on the electoral route'.

It is in this context that Podemos was born with the perspective of bringing into Parliament the ideas of the social movements for a new politics. Not only that, Podemos was conceived as a vehicle for becoming government. The new party would amalgamate the social discontent and build a counter-hegemonic political bloc in the form of a *movement party* based on transparency, new financing mechanisms, transversal appeal, open procedures for the formulation of programs and candidates' lists, and the defence of social and economic rights.

Podemos ran in the December 2015 general elections, presenting itself as a social-democratic party willing to take the role of confronting austerity and improving equality through neo-Keynesian economics that the traditional socialist party had abandoned after embracing austerity and neo-liberalism since Zapatero's second term. For many citizens, Podemos was perceived to have had the courage to confront the EU dictates and the impositions of the Spanish ruling class. When Christine Lagarde, president of the IMF, said that pensions should be further reduced due to the 'problem' of people living too long, Podemos' Juan Carlos Monedero brought the voice of the street and responded jokingly that Lagarde could start by giving an example and dying. Of course, he later explained that he does not wish her death but that he hopes Lagarde lives for 150 years, with a €450 pension.

One of the fundamental strategies of Podemos to combat austerity and create social change is its use of media. Podemos used the cracks in the social consensuses to create a space on national television and express in an intelligent and direct way the outrage and hopes of much of Spanish society and dialectically defeat their political and journalistic adversaries. Podemos contends that television is still the most powerful media outlet to engage in political pedagogy and transmit emotion. In its discourse it attempts to align itself with the prevailing common sense while also contributing to expanding and modifying it in the direction of egalitarian socio-political transformation.

Podemos has argued that in this historical period, left-wing identities have become secondary but that many of its aspirations are still felt by society and require a re-conceptualization and a new language and image. Podemos has emphasized national-popular dimensions and has followed a plain-folk approach to relate closer with social majorities, thereby overcoming a traditional flaw of the left, and create unity for the opposition of *el pueblo* against the *casta* (caste, understood as political and economic elites who use their position to obtain further benefits, especially through state-market interrelations like the revolving doors or discretional granting of public contracts). In a context of fragmentation in which social classifications are becoming more impure and movable, Podemos attempts to provide the political structure and the charismatic leader that may allow to electorally unify different types of people and contribute to build a new cultural hegemony with a *pueblo* that also needs to be progressively constructed (Cano, 2015).

Television is considered central to the construction of hegemony, but it follows a one-way flow of information model, which is why Podemos has also promoted a creative and participatory use of new media technologies for discussion, sharing of ideas and democratic decision making. However, it has not addressed the problematic elements of media technologies such as the irrelevant overabundance of information being shared in some platforms or the processes of online communication that follow a vertical model in which the participants may become mere organs for the diffusion of ideas provided from the upper echelons.

In Madrid, the city council, formed by an alliance of different forces that include Podemos, is transforming the conception of the functions of new media technologies in a way that is not in the interest of high-tech giants that benefit from lax fiscal obligations and state support. As Paul Mason (2015: para. 11) has noted, the city's model is based on openness (for example, free, open software), the common good, democratic participation, critical reflection about access to power and policy defending the right that data generated from public services should be publicly owned: 'Instead of asking: which of the city's grids and networks do we want to automate and connect, Podemos-backed major Manuela Carmena asked advisers: What are the social problems we want technology to solve?'. Following this philosophy, the city council of Madrid has enabled an online platform for developing a participatory budget.

At the time of writing, the political situation in Spain is uncertain. Podemos has options of holding the vice presidency and four ministries under a government of PSOE but new elections will probably be needed. In any case, the short story of Podemos is one of success but also of problems and difficulties. For example, the relations with social movements have deteriorated. One can observe contradictions between the more radical or leftist discourse of social movements and the more pragmatic approach of political communication of Podemos, between the need to seek efficiency through an *electoral war machinery* and the need for democratic participation, between centralization and decentralization, above and below, unity and plurality, representativeness and non-representation, between the short and the long term or between the rules of institutions and assembly procedures. In addition, difficulties have occurred in reconciling solidarity and autonomy, the demands and interests of different geographic locations in cultural terms, according to their size and their more urban or rural character. Podemos has, however, made recent moves to try to satisfy the demands of the movements that claim the spirit of the 15-M.

Podemos may be absorbed by the system now that it is in parliament; it may be incapable of delivering what it promises in the context of the EU and the power of financial institutions so that hope may turn into disappointment and disbelief, facilitating a new period of *End of History* in which society does not substantially engage in politics anymore. But the audacious project it has initiated may also help to generate new ideas, act as a fundamental agent of public pedagogy and institutional transformation, win important battles and tighten the connections between communication and education, and both of them with a project of broad social change. Together with the 15-M, Podemos has already acted as a ceasefire against neo-fascism, and in the future it attempts to make an alliance with Italy, Portugal, ideally with France and other countries to pressure the EU to allow a reduction of deficit at a slower pace and eventually build the sufficient collective power to end with the model of austerity. Podemos and its allies may succeed in using the margin of political action to actually make a change in people's lives, but only the future will tell.

Resistance and alternatives to austerity regarding the right to housing

Ada Colau's Platform for People Affected by Mortgages (PAH) started to call for assemblies in 2009 and became a symbol of resistance and humanity when it surrounded the homes of people who were going to be evicted, providing solidarity, empowerment, pedagogy and psychological comfort. The anti-evictions movement soon grew, bringing into practice the principle that 'we are people taking care of people'. This meant building strength and hegemony at a grassroots level in a context of social emergency.

The anti-evictions movement confronted the feeling of guilt that the political, economic and media powers had induced. People who had been evicted and people who had resisted evictions with collective support turned into activists positively impacting upon the process of Spanish cultural politics. They managed to shift media and public discourse in a way as to clearly establish the conception that housing is a human right that is being violated in Spain, even though the problems generated have simple solutions. Activists counteracted the discourse of austerity and explained that evictions were the result of the corrupt practices of politicians and banks. They explained that public funding was being given to the banks that were evicting them, and that those same banks now owned by the state had a huge stock of empty houses that could be used to solve the social emergency without creating any damage to the economy. They expressed that the media, banks and political elites pushed people to buy a house instead of wasting money in rent. They have managed to stop more than 1,000 evictions and raised public awareness. They staged demonstrations outside the homes of politicians and bankers and occupied empty blocks of houses owned by banks and the state.

The PAH amassed 1.5 million signatures that allowed it to present a 'popular legislative initiative' as contemplated by the Spanish law so that Parliament would discuss and vote to get rid of the mortgage law that forces people to continue paying their mortgage after losing their homes. The PP government, with Parliamentary majority, rejected the proposal.

Ada Colau appeared before a parliamentary committee on mortgages and provided a response to some false comments made by the representative of the Spanish Banking Association that is now part of the collective memory of the social struggles. In a courageous, emotional, rational and very human way, Colau called him a criminal (Ash, 2014). Her voice and image resonated with the anger and anxiety of the streets that tell the truth very directly because they suffer the ugly truth of evictions. The video of the intervention went viral, and both Colau and the PAH attracted massive support in society, in the social media and even in part of the traditional media.

Social activism played a fundamental role in developing a counter-narrative and fostering solidarity, but it lacked sufficient power to effectuate change in the face of growing political authoritarianism that dismissed activists as a violent crowd. Amnesty International launched its first campaign against evictions in June 2015, but central government remained irresponsive.

Ada Colau is currently the major of Barcelona after being elected as part of a citizen coalition. Just like Manuela Carmena in Madrid, Colau promised to solve the problem of evictions and govern in favour of the people. PAH and other social activists are happy with the new intentions but feel dissatisfied with the depth of the changes introduced and the small number of public houses that have been put at the disposition of evicted families (García and Espinosa, 2016).

The problem has not yet been fully resolved, and the situation for many families is poor. Future governments will have to face the tensions between their promises and the difficulties and limitations of their position for the exercise of transformative power; a change in the mortgage law can be approved only by the central government, and the resources are very limited after years of austerity and corruption. Building a network of powers at a local, national and European level is essential in the long term but families demand an immediate solution.

Social activists have noted that around 3.4 million houses are empty in Spain and that many of them are owned by public entities, especially public banks that were rescued by the state which the PP has proposed to privatize. Activists argue that all these houses should be included in a park of public housing either at state, regional or local level in order to comply with the law and human rights (García and Espinosa, 2016).

It is perhaps too early to judge the new city councils, but it seems clear that in spite of all their limitations and contradictions, they are trying to find viable solutions. For example, there have been 340 evictions in Barcelona during Colau's first year in the mayor's office, but 110 of those families have been provided with alternative housing. The stock of public houses has been doubled to 455 in Barcelona and other measures are being implemented, such as imposing fines on real estate companies and banks that evict people without providing the option of social rent.

The questions are obvious: will local governments use their limited power to confront the economic elites that are imposing social cuts for the majority? If so, can they succeed? The struggle in defence of education analysed in the following section may provide further clues for the development of a winning strategy.

Resistance and alternatives to austerity in education

The spirit of the 15-M permeated a variety of educational processes. For example, it helped to revitalize the student and teacher protest movement against the Bologna university model that was being installed and the critique of the marketization of universities, of cuts in public funding and of lack of democratic participation in the establishment of reform.

Mobilization took different forms. The Green Tide unites all platforms and associations in defence of public education. The collective *La Uni en la Calle* (The Uni in the Street) has organized classes in a variety of public places and discussed the state of education in a context of fiscal austerity, its importance for society and the possibility of promoting a different educational model and alternative pedagogical practices. The experience resulted in a collective book by the participants that was published by a cooperative of journalists and readers called *La Marea*. *University against the Crisis* expressed support for the protest movements and attempted to contribute to build more democracy and end the market policy that imposes austerity. In particular, it criticized the veiled objective of ongoing austerity reforms to deteriorate education and research as well as equality of opportunity to progressively privatize the university system.

Formal education has also been a priority for Podemos with the resolution proposed by the Circle (citizen assembly) of Education being the most voted on by the Citizens Assembly. The document is based on the defence of public education as a right and not as a business. It advocates for the derogation of a reactionary educational law (LOMCE) and calls for an open assembly-type process of dialogue for all stakeholders to participate in an integral transformation of education through a new law and the immediate increase of public funding to assure the universality of free-of-charge education, de-commodification, secularization of schools, pedagogical change according to educational realities, university autonomy from economic and political powers and the establishment of mechanisms which guarantee decent working conditions. According to the Resolution, education is understood as a tool for a free and autonomous citizenship with critical capacity to build a new society based on equality, justice and the development of human personality that contributes to a happy life and the expansion of dignity.

Salazar-Alonso (2015: para. 12), spokesperson for the Podemos group in the Madrid Assembly and member of the Green Tide, has noted that the party's vision for education is 'openly opposed to the ruinous policies of privatization in education' that have been promoted through austerity policies. It opposes cuts in public funding, marketization, the establishment of competition as the supreme criterion and of turning education into a mere dispenser of an *acritical* workforce. According to Salazar-Alonso 'faced with the rise of selfish individualism and the depletion of social resources and rights', Podemos 'proposes a model promoting inclusion, diversity, collaboration and openness to the community as fundamental to its success' (Ibid.: para. 13). To this end, Podemos has promised to immediately increase public funding of education to the EU average if it reaches government.

Conclusion

As Podemos' Jorge Moruno (Moruno and Delclós, 2015: para. 1) stated, 'it takes a lot to get very little, but there is no other option… we must open a new way, without the means to do so. We are in the belly of the whale'. The sociohistorical analysis of anti-austerity movements that has been developed in this chapter points to the need and possibility of developing a comprehensive strategy of operations at different levels. Further activist networks can be developed to increase participation and build unity around the defence of all public social services through the establishment of a progressive tax system and tight control of tax evasion and other consensual reforms that are deemed necessary to redistribute wealth and assure increased funding and the good functioning of public services.

The forces opposing the politics of austerity and promoting change still lack sufficient power to change the course of action imposed by the EU and national governments. The emerging cultural hegemony has to be further developed through a combination of cultural and material interventions that allows bringing in wider sectors of society that are not currently engaged in social change.

The possibilities of traditional mass media and digital media can be further explored to share the message that public services are inalienable as they assure the satisfaction of human rights. Counter-discourse is necessary to explain that it is not true that there is no alternative to austerity, but that instead there is no political will by most of the governments and economic elites. In this regard, it is fundamental to keep alive the flame of hope, without falling into illusions that may lead to frustration and disenfranchisement.

However, history shows us that acting in the cultural sphere alone is a reductionist strategy that does not allow addressing the multi-level restrictions on egalitarian change. The strategy against austerity also requires citizen intervention in the material sites of conflict and social struggles where people acquire political consciousness and develop networks of resistance: in workplaces, on the streets, in organizations, at festivities, sports events, neighbourhoods, popular theatres, institutions, etc.

The 15-M movement, the anti-evictions movement and other social and educational movements have shown the power of sociability, creative communication and collective intelligence and action to empower citizens and bring back the feeling that if people organize they can confront austerity policies. Podemos and the confluences of change are attempting to expand this citizen power into institutional power, to symbiotically promote further citizen empowerment and build sufficient strength to democratize politics and transform the economy in a more egalitarian direction. The capacity to effectuate the meaningful changes that society is demanding will depend on the capacity of the different anti-austerity forces to come together in an alliance of social movement, political parties and wider sectors of society for the transformation of political institutions, economic policies, the media and human relations.

Bibliography

Alegre-Zahonero, L. and Fernández-Liria, C. (2004). 'La revolución educativa. El reto de la Universidad ante la sociedad del conocimiento'. *Logos. Anales del Seminario de Metafísica*, 37, 225–53.

Ash, L. (2014). 'Ada Colau: Spain's anti-eviction crusader'. BBC. Available at: http://www.bbc.com/news/magazine-26228300 [Accessed June 19, 2016.].

Berry, D. and Theobald, J. (2006). *Radical mass media criticism. a genealogy.* London: Black Rose.

Cano, G. (2015). 'Podemos: the challenge in Spain'. openDemocracy. Available at: https://www.opendemocracy.net/can-europe-make-it/ germ-n-cano/podemoschallengeinspain [Accessed June 14, 2016.].

CNMV-BdE (2013). *Plan de Educación Financiera 2013–2017.* Madrid: CNMV-BdE.

Fenton, N. (2015). 'Left out? Digital media, radical politics and social change'. *Information, Communication and Society*, DOI: 10.1080/1369118X.2015. 1109698.

Freedman, D. (2014). *The contradictions of media power.* London: Bloomsbury.

García, B. and Espinosa, M. (2016). 'Sin casas no hay solución'. Diagonal. Available at: https://www.diagonalperiodico.net/global/29464-sin-casas-no-hay-solucion.html [Accessed June 22, 2016.].

Giroux, H. (2012). 'The Occupy Movement and the politics of educated hope'. *Truthout.* Available at: http://truth-out.org/opinion/item/9237-the-occupy-movement-anthepolitics-ofeducatedhope [Accessed May 18, 2016.].

Goss, B., Gould, M. and Pedro, J. (2016). 'Introduction: washed up on the shores of neoliberal globalization'. In: B. Goss, M. Gould and J. Pedro, eds., *Talking Back to Globalization: Texts, Practices and Interventions.* New York: Peter Lang.

Klaehn, J. (ed.) (2010). *The political economy of media and power.* New York: Peter Lang.

Martínez-Avidad, M. (2011). 'Redes alternativas de comunicación, framing y la construcción del poder político'. *Obets. Revista de Ciencias Sociales*, 6(2): 269–91. Available at: http://rua.ua.es/dspace/handle/10045/20546 [Accessed June 22, 2016.].

Mason, P. (2015). 'We can't allow the tech giants to rule smart cities'. *The Guardian*, October 25. Available at: http://www.theguardian. com/commentisfree/2015/oct/25/we-cant-allow-the-techgiantsto-rule-smart-cities [Accessed June 22, 2016.].

Mosco, V. (2009). *The political economy of communication,* Second revised edition. London: Sage.

Murono, J and Delclós, C. (2015). '"Our situation is Quixotic and Machia-vellian": an interview with Podemos' Jorge Moruno'. OpenDemocracy. Available at: https://www.opendemocracy.net/can-europe-make-it/ carlos-delcl-s/our-situation-is-quixotic-and-machiavellian-interview-with-podemos [Accessed June 22, 2016.].

Navarro, V. (2015). 'El enorme daño causado por las ineficaces políticas de austeridad'. *Público.* Available at: http://www.vnavarro.org/?p=12232 [Accessed June 4, 2016.].

Navarro, V. (2016). 'Los orígenes del nazismo antes, ahora y después'. *Público.* Available at: http://www.vnavarro.org/?p=13038 [Accessed June 4, 2016.].

Ortiz, I. and Cummins, M. (2013). 'The Age of Austerity – a review of public expenditures and adjustment measures in 181 countries'. Initiative for Policy Dialogue and the South Centre. Available at: http://

policydialogue.org/files/publications/Age_of_Austerity_Ortiz_and_ Cummins.pdf [Accessed June 22, 2016.].

Pedro, J. (2016a). 'A Conversation with Natalie Fenton: Resocializing the Political and Re-politicizing the Economy'. In: B. Goss, M. Gould and J. Pedro, eds., *Talking Back to Globalization: Texts, Practices and Interventions*. New York: Peter Lang.

Pedro, J. (2016b). 'A history of the globalization of universities: European higher education area viewed from the perspectives of the enlightenment and industrialism'. In: B. Goss, M. Gould and J. Pedro, eds., *Talking Back to Globalization: Texts, Practices and Interventions*. New York: Peter Lang.

Rentea, S. and Pedro-Carañana, J. (2015). 'Introducing this week's theme: "Smile at the Indignados": Podemos' struggle for a new politics'. openDemocracy. Available at: https://www.opendemocracy.net/can-europe-make-it/simona-rentea-joan-pedrocaraana/introducing-this-week-s-theme-smile-at-indignados-podemos-struggle [Accessed June 14, 2016.].

Salazar-Alonso, C. (2015). 'Podemos on education: the education "we can" have'. Available at: https://www.opendemocracy.net/can-europe-make-it/cecilia-salazar-alonso/podemosoneducation-education-we-can-have [Accessed June 15, 2016.].

Torres, J. (2013a). 'La verdadera cara de la austeridad'. *Sistema Digital*. Available at: http://juantorreslopez.com/impertinencias/la-verdadera-cara-de-la-austeridad/ [Accessed April 18, 2016.].

Torres, J. (2013b). 'Austeridad y control del conocimiento'. *Sistema Digital*. Available at: http://juantorreslopez.com/impertinencias/austeridad-y-control-del-conocimiento/ [Accessed June 21, 2016.].

9 The sweet smell of success

Spanish football as the antidote to austerity since 2008

Jim O'Brien

The impasse in Spain following the December 2015 national elections has highlighted the political, economic and cultural uncertainty and volatility which has touched all aspects of Spanish society since the global economic crash of 2008. The impact of the crash resulted in a deep and prolonged period of austerity with significant consequences for the Spanish state. The protracted nature of the negotiations between potential coalition partners during the interim government and its precarious survival since the elections has highlighted the constitutional crisis and raised critical questions of legitimacy for the governance of contemporary Spain. It has also brought into sharp focus deeply embedded historic and traditional concerns around the complex interplay of language, ethnicity and alternative nationalisms at the core of fragile and interlocking cleavages in the representations of nationhood and national identity within the Spanish political landscape (Solís, 2003; Vincent, 2010).

The dual impulses of resurgent nationalism fashioning renewed campaigns for separation and independence, most markedly in Catalonia, fused with the shift away from the two-party consensus which has dominated national politics in Spain since the transition to democracy in the late 1970s following the death of Franco (Encarnación, 2008; Vincent, 2010) has led to the assertion that the Spanish state is currently in the midst of a second transition, in which new political groupings such as Podemos[1] and Cuidadanos[2] have challenged the old orthodoxy in the political shift towards a multi-party democracy (The Spain Report, January–April 2016). In doing so, they have opened social class divisions as one of the key dynamics underlying Spain's austerity. If the seminal transition of the 1970s was driven by the desire to fashion a stable democracy out of the ashes of the Franco dictatorship and underpinned by the 'Collective Amnesia' or 'Pact of Forgetting' (Encarnación, 2008), the political ramifications of what has been termed Spain's *second transition* were foreshadowed by the cultural and historic implications of the Zapatero administration's Law of Recorded Memory (2007). This contentious process challenged the constitutional settlement of 1978 in opening many of the wounds of Spain's tortured political past (Ibid.) and exposed the paradoxes and limitations of a document which is essentially bound by the specific expediencies of its contemporary landscape (Tremlett, 2012).

Since 2008, the cohesion of Spain's democracy at the heart of the European Union has witnessed economic meltdown, with record levels of unemployment, mass protest and demonstration against the political and social consequences of austerity. Indeed, the leadership of Podemos has suggested that the north-south divisions within the European Union are part of the cause of, rather than the solution to, Spain's austerity. These sentiments are far removed from the halcyon days of 1982, when Felipe Gonzáles spoke about Spain's 'historic re-orientation with Europe' at the start of the process of accession to membership (Junco and Shubert, 2000; Iglesias, 2015). A juxtaposition of these interwoven developments have called into question Spain's future existence as a sovereign, unitary nation-state, with the legitimacy and coherence of its governing elites being challenged by age-old tensions between nation and region and new movements for political change (Castro, 2013; Iglesias, 2015). Not for the first time in its turbulent history, the Spanish nation is at another crossroads.

The pluri-national consensus of the 'Banal Nationalism' (Billig, 2004) secured and projected by the 1978 Spanish Constitution, led to the balanced cultural diversity and ethnicity of the 1980s and 1990s and created the political settlement and democratic stability at the foundations of economic growth and increased prosperity underpinning Spain's rapid transformation from dictatorship to democracy (Junco and Shubert, 2000). The separatist ethnicities of cultural politics had been largely muted and contained, with the notable exceptions of the ETA armed and Batasuna political struggle for independence in the Basque Country, together with the political groupings and manifestos for more autonomy in Catalonia (Conversi, 2000; Solís, 2003).

Sport, in particular football, had traditionally played a key role within the cultural dichotomy of Spain, since its embryonic development as a modern nation-state in the last decades of the nineteenth century (Riordan and Kruger, 2003). As football gradually gained supremacy over more indigenous and traditional sports during the 1920s and 1930s, its first boom period in evolving to a mass spectator professional sport (Goldblatt, 2008; Burns, 2012), it became a site and metaphor for the expression and articulation of cultural synergies and divergences (O'Brien, 2013). The emergence and growth of the game as a reflector and definer of mass culture is rooted in football's foundations in the Basque Country and Catalonia in the 1890s (Ball, 2011) following its folkloric genesis in Andalusia during the 1870s (Bretnell, 2009; Burns, 2012). The growth of football in the regions of Spain fused with a cluster of socioeconomic developments and political and cultural changes to signpost modernity and a decisive break with Spain's imperial past (Junco and Shubert, 2000). Most significantly, the game's formative period both embedded it at the core of oscillating tensions between centre and region and located it within Spanish political culture (Goldblatt, 2008; Burns, 2012). Throughout the twentieth century, as Spain embraced monarchy, dictatorship, republic, civil war, Francoism and democracy, the beautiful game has been manipulated and exploited by differing guises of the central Spanish state for propagandist purposes to manufacture consent and fashion a sense of national consensus and identity whilst being utilized as a safety valve to contain aspirant alternative nationalisms (Crolley and Hand, 2006). It has also acted as a catalyst for the articulation and symbolic ritualism of local and regional cultural and political identities, especially in Spain's historic communities of the Basque Country, Catalonia and Galicia (Burns, 2009; Quiroga, 2013).

The backdrop to this chapter is the recognition of the seminal role of football's folklore, symbols and iconography in the representation of cultural politics in Spain. The first section seeks to contextualize the principal factors which have shaped and defined Spanish football's cultural lexicon. A consideration of these aspects provides some insight into the interlocking synthesis between the Spanish game's historic development and political associations to carve a distinctive cultural space. At the core of the chapter is an examination of Spanish football's cultural influence and significance during the nation's austerity period. The 2008 crash came at a time when La Selección,[3] the Spanish national team, was about to embark upon a period of unrivalled success. The achievements of La Roja[4] in winning three successive tournaments (The European Nations Cup 2008 and 2012, and the FIFA World Cup of 2010) was set against the bleak and stark contrast of economic recession and political fragmentation. During the same period, the commercial impulse and globalization of La Liga, which had evolved since the 1990s, had catapulted Spanish Club Football, most particularly through the successes of FC Barcelona and Real Madrid at National and European levels, to high-profile exposure across a plethora of global media platforms and audiences (Hanlon, 2013; Hunter, 2013).

This section evaluates the apparent paradoxes and contradictions between the successes and excesses of Spanish football at global, national and regional levels since 2008, with the debate articulated around the construction, representation and ethical ramifications of the relationship between elite-level Spanish football and its contemporary cultural space. The chapter concludes by assessing the implications of the role of Spanish football in 2016 in order to reflect on its interface with the complex dynamics of change in the new political order. The tension between football's secure, traditional cultural position and the potential challenges to this by new political actors is considered. Furthermore, in the post-2008 era the extensive and accelerated use of visual and social media as the prime mode of mediatized communication has been a key facet in linking the iconography of football with the contemporary processes of mass political communication adopted by Podemos and other forces of change (O'Brien, 2013; Iglesias, 2015).

Spanish football and mass culture: some key contexts

> Spanish football's remarkable rise and popularity rested on its capacity to combine fierce national, regional and urban identities and conflicts within a single footballing culture.
>
> (Goldblatt, 2008: 212)

The relationship between Spanish football and mass culture operates on a number of levels. This symbiosis is rooted in the historical landscape of the Spanish state in the late nineteenth century. The year 1898 aptly illustrates the divided sensibilities which came to shape the cultural landscape of modern Spain. For Imperial Spain, this was the 'Year of Disaster' in the wake of the loss of Cuba as the last colonial remnant of the Golden Age (Junco and Shubert, 2000). Madrid's hegemony at the centre of affairs had been compromised by both political factionalism and the loss of status brought about by the demise of empire so that the genesis of a modern European state struggled to secure legitimacy whilst lagging behind the socioeconomic developments of other nations (Vincent, 2010). Moreover, 1898 witnessed the culmination of political and cultural renaissance in the historic communities of the Basque Country, Catalonia and Galicia, giving rise to the nascent surge in regional and separatist sentiment, so that the birth of the PNV[5] in the Basque Country and the emergence of political cleavages in Catalonia threatened the fragile coherence of Spanish national identity.

Within this fractious dichotomy between centre and region, football was initially imported into the regions of Spain to manifest a distinct sense of locality and cultural separation from the centre. Within this milieu of industrialization, urbanization and demographic change, the historic foundation of Spanish football's regional axis took place, from Athletic Bilbao (1894) and Real Sociedad (1905) in the Basque Country, to FC Barcelona (1899) and FC Español (1901) in Catalonia (Ball 2011). The genesis of these clubs was firmly rooted in the political and cultural movements of the time, constructed around social class and the dialectic of modernity. In the Basque Country, Athletic Bilbao and Real Sociedad soon became culturally assimilated as contrasting representations of Basqueness (Rivas, 2012; O'Brien, 2014) to define and locate the clubs' Cantera[6] as a potent symbol of cultural purity, with the enduring legacy of Athletic's 'Basques Only' policy maintaining this reference point of ethnic separatism (Burns, 2012; O'Brien, 2014); in Catalonia, FC Barcelona and Español were embedded in the complex political and cultural fabric of Barcelona from the outset (O'Brien, 2013). Football developed later in Madrid, mirroring the capital's struggle to maintain its status as the nation's capital in the midst of rapid change. This overt politicization of the sub-cultural matrix of the game continued into its development as a mass spectator sport with a growing media profile in the boom period of the 1950s, first through radio and subsequently via television, when football was utilized for the first time as an antidote to austerity in the grim reality of life in Franco's Spain during the period (Viñolo, 2009).

If Spanish club football is rooted in constructions of cultural identity based on language, locality, and community to fashion a folkloric pattern of alliances and rivalries, the Spanish national team's capacity to engender a sense of 'Spanishness' and national identity has been problematic since 'La Selección' (Ball, 2011) participated for the first time in the Antwerp Olympics (1920). Drawing on the cultural and sporting legacy of La Furia Española created by the team's legendary success in the competition, the national side has been a barometer for the political and cultural cleavages between nation and region (Burns, 2012). The historic growth and expansion of the game has been subject to political intervention, exploitation and manipulation by differing political regimes. During the 1950s and 1960s in particular, the Franco dictatorship became adept at utilizing the burgeoning mass appeal and spectacle of football to manufacture consent and secure national unity in framing mass populism around the game's deep cultural roots in Spanish society (Duke and Crolley, 1998). This was achieved by a juxtaposition of the appropriation of cultural heritage of the fabled values associated with La Furia (team spirit, courage, hard work and physical strength) to represent archetypal Spanish values.

The power and capacity of football to act as a social drug of mass diversion and escapism was a seminal facet of the regime's exploitation of the game. Under Franco, football played the key role of both engendering a sense of national identity and acting as a safety valve to contain supressed nationalism in the regions, most particularly in the Basque Country and Catalonia (Ibid.). The state's use of the game to define a sense of cultural homogeneity was manifested in two key ways. In respect of La Selección, the success of 'the New Spain' in defeating the Soviet Union in the final of the European Cup of Nations in front of El Caudillo at a flag-waving Bernabéu stadium in June 1964 was carefully orchestrated by the regime to represent the ideological victory of fascism over communism, and stimulate patriotic sentiment around the construction of a vibrant, economically progressive nation, emerging peacefully from the austerity of the 1950s (Ball, 2011; Quiroga, 2013). This was matched by the dictatorship's adoption of Real Madrid, tapping into the glittering achievements of the club in winning five successive European Cups between 1956 and 1960 (Burns, 2012). The team was culturally embedded to symbolize positive iconography in fulfilling a quasi-ambassadorial role, providing a high-profile respite from Spain's international isolation (Ball, 2011).

Football was pivotal to Francoism's attempts to manufacture cultural cohesion and national identity; it also played a critical role in both the transition to democracy in the late 1970s and in Spain's subsequent political and cultural development as a democratic society embracing a rich tapestry of regions, languages and cultural diversity (Ball, 2011; Tremlett, 2012). During the volatile uncertainty of the transition, it acted as a focal point of national cohesion through the maintenance of club competition at national level, suggesting that the vibrancy of local and regional rivalries, embedded in the game's traditional enclaves, was able to deflect from political turbulence to engender a sense of normalcy (Montalbán, 2005). Moreover, the game was in the vanguard of change in this period, signposting the aspirant resurgent regionalism within the historic communities and paving the way for the successes of Real Sociedad, Athletic Bilbao and FC Barcelona during the early 1980s (Duke and Crolley, 1998).

As competitive two-party politics became firmly established as the modus operandi for Spain's democracy at the national level during the 1980s, and a cluster of regional parties re-emerged to establish a measure of equilibrium, football shifted away from the juxtaposition of state and alternative nationalisms which had defined its niche in the Spanish political and cultural lexicon. During the Spanish economic boom of the 1990s and the post-millennium period, the game's traditional link with state power was challenged by commercialism, globalization and enhanced mediatization (Crolley and Hand, 2006; Lopis Goig, 2009). The impacts of both deregulation and technological change altered the cultural dichotomy in which football was framed so that the period witnessed a blurring of its folkloric hegemony. The seismic effects of the Bosman Ruling (1995)[7] coupled with shifting patterns of consumption meant that by 2000 the political and cultural nuances of football were becoming more fluid in their representations of 'Spanishness', 'Basqueness' and 'Catalanism'. In the immediate post-millennium years, the game mirrored images of Spain itself: brash, diverse and increasingly affluent but with lingering uncertainties on the vexed questions of national and regional identities, coupled with growing inequalities between the haves and have-nots (Tremlett, 2012). Football later exposed these paradoxes when the alluring bubble of success burst.

Football, culture and austerity in Spain since 2008

> The feel good factor generated by the World Cup victory of La Roja translated into a more enduring popular support for the Spanish National team than at any other time in history, not just because of its success but because of the quality of it... and the image of togetherness they and Del Bosque conveyed.
>
> (Burns, 2012: 362)

In its historic context, football has acted as a barometer for the shifting sands of Spain's political landscape and is deeply rooted within the cultural labyrinth of Spanish society. The paradoxes and dualisms surrounding both club football and the national team serve as a catalyst for constructions and representations of cohesion and consensus, fragmentation and diversity. Apart from the specific circumstances of the Franco period, La Selección has struggled to reflect any coherent or consistent pattern of Spanish nationhood (Duke and Crolley, 1998; Ball, 2011). Spain has no national stadium, with the national side generally alternating its matches between Madrid, Valencia and Seville. It rarely plays in Barcelona and has not played in Bilbao since 1968 (O'Brien, 2014). The historic antipathy and indifference of the regional heartlands of the Spanish game to the national team illustrates the sense of cultural dislocation between centre and region and is in contradistinction to the rich tapestry of football's folkloric rivalries and cocktail of vibrant passions within the Basque Country and Catalonia (Ball, 2011; Burns, 2012). It also maintains and perpetuates historic political divisions in spite of the burgeoning globalized boom in Spanish football during the 1990s and early

2000s. Until relatively recently, the iconography embellishing La Selección was imbued with the twin spectres of the curse of El Fatalismo[8] and the historic memory of being indelibly associated with the Franco regime itself (Ball, 2011). During the post-Franco settlement and Spain's transition to democracy, football reflected both the resurgent regionalism and nationalisms of the 1980s and the contested nature of Spanish cultural identity.

Within this complex mosaic of competing political and cultural forces, even Spain's hosting of the 1982 World Cup (Paradinas, 2010; Glanville, 2012), projected as an overt symbol of the nation's international reintegration through the potent cultural symbolism of the game in securing and reinforcing legitimacy and national identity, was problematic. The event, framed as testimony to the success of 'The Pact of Forgetting' in promoting a unified modern nation at the heart of Europe, merely served to reflect the deep schisms and divisions in Spanish society (Ibid.). The underachievement of the team, the slavish adherence to the outdated values of La Furia Española, the antipathy of supporters in Valencia and Madrid towards a squad composed largely of Basque and Catalan players was intensified by the severity of press criticism. These factors highlighted the fragility of the central Spanish state in the post-Franco period. The negative and backward-looking imagery of the marketing campaign adopted to promote the Spanish World Cup, with the much derided figure of 'El Naranjito'[9] at its centre reflected a wider set of political and cultural cleavages (Paradinas, 2010).

During the 1990s, Spanish football was on the cusp of radical change and in cultural flux. The traditional orthodoxy of state nationalism and control, spawning the cultural values of La Furia Española associated with La Selección (Ball, 2011), was gradually challenged by the corporate nationalism of emerging media landscapes catapulting the Spanish game into new audiences and patterns of consumption (Crolley and Hand, 2006; Lopis Goig, 2009). These processes assisted in defining the contemporary cultural and political landscape in which Spanish football became couched; a pastiche of competing arenas of state and corporate nationalisms resulting in a post-modernist fusion of the global and the local, the regional and the national, the fan and the consumer. Within this complex set of variables, the cultural nexus of Spanish football became more fluid than the bedrock of deeply rooted folkloric traditions. For a time, La Selección remained attached to the norms and mores of La Furia, perennially reinforcing the image of the national team as underachievers or even failures in international competitions (Ball, 2011). Changes within football itself, towards a more technically pure and tactically sophisticated model, witnessed a shift in the cultural identity associated with the national side.

This trend began in the 1980s when La Selección reverted to its original national colours of playing in red, rather than the blue adopted under Franco. This juxtaposition of overt and more subtle cultural developments became more evident from 2006 with the appointment of Luis Aragonés as coach of La Selección, when the values of La Furia were jettisoned in favour of those of La Roja. This process built on the foundations established by Johann Cryuff at FC Barcelona, where La Masia[10] had been established to refashion La Cantera as the lynchpin of the club's subsequent playing style and success (Hunter, 2013; O'Brien, 2013). The synergy between tactical evolution, cultural reframing and the synthesis of club and national identities first bore fruit in the success of La Roja in winning the European Cup of Nations by defeating Germany 1–0 in Vienna (July, 2008). This marked the first success of La Selección in an international tournament since 1964 (Burns, 2012; Quiroga, 2013).

The impact of this success had political and cultural ramifications for Spain itself in 2008. First, it allowed the negative stereotyping around the national team and the perception of it as the representation of Francoism, Centralism and Madrid to be replaced by the positive fluidity and diversity of 'La Roja' (Ball, 2011; Hunter, 2013). This was subsequently emphasized by the slick Marketing and Public Relations campaign adopted by Adidas in the build up to the South Africa World Cup in 2010, which sought to link corporate strategy with a contemporary sense of patriotism in order to maximize successful profiling of 'La Roja'. The slogan underpinning the advertisement, Nace de Dentro[11] attempted to exploit a commercially manufactured sense of identity to promote a corporate culture of nationhood through attachment to the team's success. Second, the team's iconography tapped into the notion of a pluralist, coherent, prosperous and unified Spain at the core of the 1990s and post-millennium boom (Hooper, 2007). The political establishments were swift in seeking to use the success of the national team to define a culturally homogenous sense of contemporary Spanish identity, within a mature, stable democracy. If football had been a potent symbol of Spain's historic regionalism and cultural diversity, the first success of La Roja in 2008 seemed to suggest a new consensus and cohesion around the contemporary dynamics of La Selección, in which alternative nationalisms had been expressed and contained through the post-1978 constitutional settlement of devolved power, maintaining a balance between the region, the state and the nation (Burns, 2012; Quiroga, 2013).

In retrospect, the flourishing of La Roja in 2008 constituted a high water mark for football's capacity to represent cultural symmetry in

Spain. The subsequent successes of La Selección in winning Spain's first World Cup in Johannesburg in July 2010 and in retaining their European Crown in Kiev in July 2012 was set against the backdrop of economic meltdown and political protest and fragmentation, which stood in stark contrast to the national side's success. The period of austerity since 2008 brought into focus the cultural paradoxes and ambivalences between the high-profile success and positive iconography surrounding Spanish football at national and club levels with the harsh realities and consequences of recession. The historic centre-region tensions underpinning the game's complex mosaic of identity re-emerged within a contemporary political and cultural matrix to raise seminal questions about Spanish football's cultural role in the political dynamics of austerity (Quiroga, 2013).

The cultural heartbeat of Spanish football's regional identity resonates most strongly in Catalonia and the Basque Country. Since the genesis of the game as an integral component of the cultural renaissance which took place in the historic communities during the 1890s (Conversi, 2000), football has acted as a cultural custodian preserving and maintaining, through its rituals, rivalries and iconographies the distinctive ethnicities around constructions and representations of 'Catalanism' and 'Basqueness' (O'Brien, 2013; 2014). In Catalonia, the folklore, history and status of FC Barcelona since its foundation in 1899 have been inextricably linked to the complexities of the debates around Catalanism *per se*. In one sense, the club has acted as a force for cultural assimilation and cohesion to fuse the indigenous manifestations of Catalan culture and politics with the cyclical swathes of immigrants and migrants into Catalan society, to fashion a 'broad church' (Burns, 2009) or 'civic religion' (Moltalbán, 2005) of social inclusion. This role has dovetailed with the club's political status as a site of opposition to the centralizing forces of Madrid and the Spanish state (Duke and Crolley, 1998). From the exile of the team's players during the Civil War, to being virtually the sole means of clandestine protest against the suppression of the Franco regime (Tüñon and Bray, 2012), FC Barcelona's mission of being 'Més que un club' (Burns, 2009) was implicit and subsequently articulated as an expression of the club's cultural and political identity. In a historic context, a middle-class, entrepreneurial elite have generally established a top-down hierarchy for maintaining its power and influence in Catalan society (Tüñon and Bray, 2012). The dualism between FC Barcelona's cultural role and its political function is at the core of questions surrounding the club's representation of contemporary Catalan identity (Miravitlaas, 2013). These questions were given a sharper profile by the contrasting fortunes of FC Barcelona as Catalonia itself lurched into austerity from 2008 onwards.

In football terms, the club's rehabilitation and modernization began during the 1970s with the Núñez presidency and the landmark signing of Johan Cryuff (Burns, 2009). The subsequent foundation of La Masia as the academy for the development of the club's future players stressed the symmetry between the team and the emergence of the historic mores of La Cantera as a focal point of identity and the inculcation of Catalan cultural values (O'Brien, 2013). This juxtaposition evolved into Guardiola's all conquering side from 2008/09, in which a generation of exceptional players, including Valdés, Puyol, Xavi, Iniesta, Busquets and Messi, formed the nucleus for the tiki-taka brand of football which encapsulated the team's nomenclature and identity (Burns, 2009; 2012). It also provided the majority of the national side underpinning the successes of La Roja in international tournaments. The achievements of Guardiola's Barcelona projected the complex values of Catalanism to a global audience through saturation media coverage so that the political and cultural nuances underscoring Catalanism were increasingly globalized (Hunter, 2013). This added a contemporary dimension to the archetypal tensions between Barcelona and Madrid, Catalonia and Castile, pinpointing the extent to which the club acted as a fulcrum for the city, region and nation. In a period of economic recession and political fragmentation, the function of FC Barcelona as a barometer of cultural politics became a site of increasing discussion and debate.

The successes of FC Barcelona, celebrated and ritualized by the excessive hyperbole of 'El Clásico' during the intense rivalry between Guardiola and Mourinho's Real Madrid (Relaño, 2012; O'Brien, 2013) provided an escape and distraction from the impacts and consequences of austere economic times during the same period. The collapse of the property market in Catalonia, which witnessed a 37 per cent depreciation in value from 2008 to 2013, coupled with the rise in unemployment to over 25 per cent of the workforce, fuelled protests against the austerity measures adopted by the Zapatero and Rajoy governments and tapped into historic anti-Madrid sentiment. Couched in this mould, Catalonia was paying the price for the profligacy of the centre and its failure to regulate the banks during the speculative boom period of the 1990s and early 2000s (Iglesias, 2015). These factors helped to provide the political stimulus for the upsurge in support for factions and parties advocating separation and independence from Spain, resulting in increased profile and support at the ballot box. During the boom period, support for independence and self-governance remained largely at the fringes of political opinion, suggesting that the compromises provided by the Constitutional Settlement of 1978 had secured the centre ground of moderate consensus for devolved power within a unitary Spanish state.

Whilst the economic indicators and trends remained positive, football broadly reflected the political consensus and confidence of a maturing democratic society, in which the game channelled regional and local rivalries into a legitimized representation of folkloric traditions. From 2008, the increased prevalence of the politics of direct protest through the anti-austerity indignados demonstrations (Ibid.) foreshadowed the erosion of consensus and the subsequent emergence of new political parties in the shape of Podemos and Cuidadanos, which found a groundswell of support in Spain's troubled regions. These developments in the Spanish political landscape also reverberated in Catalan politics, in which the implications of austerity and recession became embedded in the historic and cultural legacy of suppressed nationhood (Conversi, 2000; Castro, 2013). The paradox between the high-profile globalization of the success of FC Barcelona since 2008 and the economic meltdown and political fragmentation in Catalonia impacted significantly on the role of Spanish club football during a period of austerity. In respect of FC Barcelona, the shift from boom to bust in Catalonia coincided with the presidency of Joan Laporte (Hanlon, 2013).

The Laporte presidency of FC Barcelona (2003–10) was characterized by an erosion of the industrial/entrepreneurial typology which had historically defined the majority of previous incumbents of the office. With his background as a lawyer, his controversial period in office saw the club simultaneously embrace a more radical Catalan agenda whilst abandoning some of its cherished historic symbols in order to maintain a leading position within the global football elite (Hanlon, 2013). Consequently the flowering of the generation of players imbued with the cultural values of La Masia and La Cantera coincided with the club's leadership, locating it within the upsurge of separatist sentiment, simultaneously representing an articulation of Laporte's own political ambitions. Moreover, the anti-Spanish rhetoric, which increasingly came to the fore during the period, highlighted FC Barcelona's more public support for the populist Catalan political agenda. This posture was diametrically at odds with the commercially and public relations driven policies underlying the club's adoption of a partnership with UNICEF (2006) and its subsequent affiliation with the Qatar Foundation (Ibid.). The implementation of these policy goals offended traditionalists as they implied that the club was 'selling out' by jettisoning the cherished legacy and potent ethnic symbolism of the club badge on the altar of global capitalism. The pragmatic opportunism at the core of the Laporte presidency masked the ambivalences at the core of FC Barcelona's contemporary political and cultural identity (Hanlon, 2013; Miravitlaas,

2013), underscoring the tension between its global corporate reach and its roots as a repository for Catalan nationalism.

In the wider context of economic austerity and political change since 2008, FC Barcelona has reflected the broader dichotomy between the apolitical, social force of the game as a binding nexus of civic consensus and its contemporary political nuances in a period of volatility and uncertainty (Tüñon and Bray, 2012) within the global marketplace of elite club football (Lopis Goig, 2009). These processes raise seminal questions pertaining to the role of football as a source of cultural power and influence. For FC Barcelona, the contradictions stemming from its pivotal institutional function in the fabric of Catalan society is illustrated by the increased profile of the club as a site of political protest and cultural affirmation during the presidencies of Rossell and Bartomeu since 2010. From the historic symbolism of the chants of 'Independencia' which ring out around the Camp Nou at every home match to commemorate the events of 1714, to the mass display in November 2015 of the non-constitutional Catalan 'Estelada' flag in protests against UEFA's ban and fine for the club concerning the prevalence of political symbols in the stadium, factional elements, mass populism and banal nationalism have all found their voice. In the contemporary idiom, FC Barcelona has become a significant arena for discourse within the complex mosaic of Catalan politics, challenging the club's historic capacity to act as a force for social and cultural inclusion (Burns, 2009).

If the folkloric legacy of football locates FC Barcelona within the cultural inclusiveness of Catalanism, the game's articulation of cultural politics in the Basque Country reveals a divergent, distinctive iconography. As previously noted, the fusion between football, politics and Basque identity is rooted in the seminal socioeconomic developments of the 1890s. Since then, expressed primarily through the interlocking histories of the region's two major clubs, Athletic Bilbao and Real Sociedad, the game has been critical in maintaining cultural cohesion around the representation of distinctive ethnicities of 'Basqueness' and supressed stateless nationhood (Rivas, 2012; O'Brien, 2014). The iconography of folkloric rivalry is etched into the deeply embedded manifestations of La Cantera shaping the identity of both clubs. In respect of Athletic Bilbao, the institutional and cultural profile of the club has been shaped by its adherence to a 'Basques only' policy throughout most of its history (Ibid.). Its wealth and status in Basque society, derived from the iconic symbolism of 'San Mamés', nicknamed 'the Cathedral' as the first purpose built football stadium in Spain, to the success of its players in never having being relegated from La Liga, has allowed it to perpetuate the myths of ethnic purity and the resonance of exclusivity as cultural custodian throughout oscillating periods of economic boom and austerity in the Basque Country. Moreover, it has acted as focal point of unity for many of the divergent strands of political factionalism to project the international profile of Basque nationhood (O'Brien, 2014). The club's traditional style of play; direct, physical, courageous and whole-hearted, is commensurate with wider Basque social and cultural mores, so that the historic identity of the club perpetuates the sense of locality, region and separateness from Spain. This provides Athletic Bilbao with a significant cultural legacy (Rivas, 2012; O'Brien, 2014).

The alternative metaphor for Basque identity emanates from Real Sociedad. This debate is bound up in territorial definitions of what constitutes the Basque homeland. For Athletic Bilbao this has tended to reflect the historic claims to the French Basque Country, Pamplona and the wider credentials of the Basque diaspora internationally, whereas for Real Sociedad a narrower provincial construction historically applied (Rivas, 2012; O'Brien, 2014). More recently, whilst Athletic has sought to maintain its 'Basques Only' policy by a rather fluid interpretation of Basque ethnicity, Real has fluctuated between abandoning the practice and subsequently seeking to reintroduce La Cantera at the core of the club's identity. This shows that the inter-relationship between football and Basqueness is a complex, evolving dynamic, fusing tradition with the contemporary implications of migration and globalization (Rivas, 2012). Furthermore, in spite of rivalry based on football and cultural politics, the two clubs acted as the embodiment of kindred spirits as the site of alternative nationalist sentiment during the Franco Regime, a safety valve for the wide spectrum of clandestine Basque ethnicity (Ibid.). Throughout the years of repression and austerity in the 1940s and the 1950s, football carved a distinctive hue within the manufactured consent of Franco's unitary, centralized Spanish state (Vincent, 2010).

The latter years of Francoism and Spain's transition to democracy in the late 1970s coincided with an upsurge in the armed struggle of ETA to secure separation and independence for the Basque homelands and a split within nationalist sentiments between those groups advocating direct, violent action to achieve these objectives in contradistinction to the political goals of Batasuna (Junco and Shubert, 2000; Vincent, 2010). The role of football as a conduit for Basque nationalism in its myriad forms is ambivalent and contested, and the region's clubs have historically stopped short of any public endorsement of the methods employed by ETA. Nevertheless the fact that La Selección has not played in Bilbao since 1968 is explained both by concerns in Madrid over security issues and the anti-centralist sentiments which exist in the cultural identities of the region's major clubs (O'Brien, 2014). Cast in this light, the potent symbolism of the first Basque derby in the post-Franco era in March 1976 witnessed the spectacle of the respective captains of Athletic Bilbao and Real Sociedad coming onto the pitch together carrying the hitherto circumscribed Basque flag, followed by the playing of the previously banned Basque national anthem (Ball, 2011). This celebrated ritual not only pushed the game into the vanguard of social change; it also underscored the cultural power of the region's historic clubs to fashion and, articulate, the political aspirations of supressed nationhood. Furthermore, much as it had done in the bleak austerity of the 1950s, football came to embellish a positive set of cultural values during the resurgent regionalism of the early 1980s, when both Real Sociedad and Athletic Bilbao won La Liga, marking a renaissance in the traditional heartlands of the Spanish game (Rivas, 2012; O'Brien, 2014). Athletic's success in winning a league and cup double in 1984 marked the culmination of this period, the team's achievement celebrated by the players sailing through the heart of Bilbao on the historic barge, La Gabarra. This spectacle, witnessed by hundreds of thousands of flag-waving Basques, came during the 1980s recession when the traditional industries of the Basque Country were in decline, ushering in a period of austerity, with rising inflation and unemployment. Football, through the successes of the region's two major clubs, once again brought the contested and divergent strands of Basque ethnicity together as an expression of solidarity in the midst of political volatility and economic scarcity.

The protracted nature of ETA's conflict with the central Spanish state reached a political impasse with the cessation of armed hostilities in November 2011. From the onset of austerity in 2008, the Basque economy has proved to be a little more resilient than its Catalan counterpart in resisting the most severe consequences of recession (Tremlett, 2012; The Spain Report, January–April 2016). Whilst the historic political antipathy to the centre and the region's special customs or los fueros[12] remain intact as the focal points of Basque political culture and the various factions of the separatist movement have a potent cross-section of political support within the complex mosaic of contemporary Basque politics, in the post ETA period a political vacuum exists, indicating that the groups seeking independence lack the coherence, maturity and structure of those elements espousing separatism in Catalonia. This suggests that football has even more potency as cultural custodian in bringing together the diverse elements of Basque society (Rivas, 2012; O'Brien, 2014). Moreover, constructions of Basqueness are changing in response to the demographic consequences of globalization so that since 2009, Athletic Bilbao has witnessed the first black players emerge through the ranks of La Cantera. This is a far cry indeed from the early writings of Sabino Arana, the founding father of the PNV. As both the global economy and the fluidity of population movement impacts on the vortex of contemporary football, the game maintains its distinctive niche as a metaphor for alternative ethnicities as a counterpoint to the cultural and political homogeneity of 'Spanishness'. The recent and astonishing success of FC Eibar in reaching the elite level of the Spanish game is testament to the cultural power of football as the antidote to austerity, challenging the traditional duopoly of the Athletic Bilbao-Real Sociedad axis in the process. The club evolved out of the post-Civil War era, when the town was developed to stimulate industrial growth for the Spanish economy; for most of its history, it has existed in the lower echelons of regional Spanish club football, drawing its Cantera from the local industrial landscape. Since 2011 it has progressed through the leagues so that it currently sits in the top half of La Liga. This football miracle, of the rise of a club with a tiny budget and a small stadium competing with the elite clubs of the global game, coincided with the meltdown of the Spanish economy and the ripple effect of this in the Basque Country. Its success demonstrates the post-industrial cultural politics of football in enabling FC Eibar to fashion a positive, distinctive iconographic identity within the landscape of austerity. The fact that most of the club's players came from the club's academy and live in Eibar itself connects the traditional nexus of locality to engender a specific context of community within the globalized consumption of the La Liga brand.

The relevance of football at both the macro level of the national team and through the embedded micro tradition of its clubs to constitute a key source of cultural politics and identity is pivotal within the perennially contested notions of Spanish nationhood. During periods of austerity in particular, the typologies of the Spanish game have been exploited, manufactured and projected to promote and articulate divergent political sentiments and identities. Many of Spain's largest clubs function as significant political and cultural institutions, with Real Madrid, FC Barcelona and Athletic Bilbao committed to the principle of member ownership, stressing both the adherence to democratic principles and the practice of accountability (Wagg, 1995; Goldblatt, 2008). These traditions, whether real or symbolic, reaffirm the cultural foundations of Spanish club football, to embellish that sense of community and locality at the core of their folkloric histories.

Since the 1990s, with the gradual maturation of Spanish democracy and the deregulation of Broadcast Media, La Liga has become an increasingly global brand of mass consumption, especially through the inexorably high-profile branding and commodification of the Real Madrid-FC Barcelona duopoly within the game's elite clubs, creating the contemporary phenomenon of global fandom as a distinctive economic and cultural force (Crolley and Hand, 2006). On the field of play, this has meant few challenges to the FC Barcelona-Real Madrid duopoly since 2004, with the notable exception of the success of Simeone's Atletico Madrid, culminating in the winning of the league title in 2013–14. The club's location in the industrial, traditionally working class area of the city not only serves as a striking contrast with the opulence and status of their cross-city rivals but also encapsulates the capacity of the game to fashion a positive sense of identity within the despair and aliena- tion of austerity (Levi, 2003).

The wealth, celebrity status and global cultural iconography of Real Madrid's Galacticos in the two terms of the Peréz presidency, from Beckham and Zidane to Bale and Ronaldo, coupled with the cluster of stars emerging from FC Barcelona's La Masia during the Guardiola era, (O'Brien, 2013) reflects a sense of disconnection with the harsh economic realities and political dissent which have defined Spain's austerity since 2008, as if the archetypal social drug of football exists in an inflated, protected bubble outside the strictures and norms of contemporary Spanish society. Yet as the game's embedded folkloric traditions fuel and legitimize political manipulation, corruption and excess, it also mirrors the wider dy- namics of that society in its current lexicon (Hooper, 2007; Tremlett, 2012). From the 1920s, the Spanish State at the central, regional and local level has intervened in the governance and regulation of football (Goldblatt, 2008; O'Brien, 2013). Since the transition to democracy, this interventionism has taken two main approaches; attempting to clean up and regulate the financial mismanagement, insolvency and corruption endemic to Spanish club football and acting as arbiter in the increasingly visceral disputes around the issue of broadcasting rights for the live transmission of matches, which has frequently plunged the game into a succession of media wars when these rights come up for renegotiation and renewal.[13] This pattern of state involvement, a legacy of more authoritarian times, has neither curbed financial profligacy and debt nor put a brake on media power in its control of the commodified con- sumption of the Spanish game. Indeed, as austerity strengthened its grip on the Spanish economy and political divisions intensified, football became ever more embroiled in the cultural and social divisions of austerity conditions.

Since 2008, with the specific exception of Athletic Bilbao and its limited access to the transfer market due to its historic Basques-only policy, La Liga's elite clubs have operated at staggering levels of debt, investing huge sums on salaries and transfer fees, reaching a peak in 2014 with the €100 million deal taking Gareth Bale from Tottenham Hotspur to Real Madrid. Both FC Barcelona and Real Madrid have levels of debt, only partially offset by sponsorship deals, television money and ticket sales, which would not be sustainable in practically any other business.[14] Their assets and status as cultural and political institutions, carved deep into the Spanish psyche, enables them to flourish outside the shackles of austerity. In this respect, their global fandom and branding mirrors the inequalities of the global capital market economy, in which the adulation, lifestyle and huge wealth of La Liga's stars appears grotesque and vulgar in comparison to the vast majority of the game's fans and consumers. These paradoxes are far removed from the idealized and romanticized myths and rituals surrounding the traditional cultural mores of Spanish football (Ball, 2011; Burns, 2012).

Beneath the veneer of Spanish football's recent success through La Roja and the hierarchical elites running its major clubs, the fortunes of many other clubs reflect more accurately the consequences of austerity and the deep inequalities at the core of the Spanish game. Within Spain's austerity period, Valencia, Malaga, Racing Santander, Elche and CA Osasuna have all fallen victim in one way or another to the economic and cultural costs of austerity. From unsustainable debts and impending bankruptcy, to the failure of speculative overseas investment strategies, to delayed or, non-completed stadium building and match fixing allegations, the perilous condition of much of Spanish football has been exposed. For some of the clubs involved, this has resulted in financial meltdown, sanctions and relegation. The examples of Racing Santander, Elche and CA Osasuna are significant in pinpointing the casualties of the Spanish game in recent years. The loss of status, together with the twin spectres of scandal and corruption tainting the image, integrity and reputation of these clubs as focal points of local pride and community identity go hand in hand with financial irregularity and overreach. With their current status in the lower tiers of the Spanish game, the road to recovery and success on the field may be long and difficult; as with austerity *per se*, there is no easy way back.

Football, political change and Spanish culture: contemporary perspectives

During (that) transition Spain reached a historically extraordinary, and invaluable, degree of consensus. This covered everything from foreign policy to terrorism. Most importantly, it lasted long enough for Spaniards to build a new state, with a new democratic constitution and decentralised administration. The transition, however, was not normal. It was, in fact, an exception in Spanish history.

(Tremlett, 2012: 437)

On July 10 and 11, 2010, two contrasting public demonstrations took place in Plaza de Catalonia in the centre of Barcelona. On July 10, a mass protest took place against the Constitutional Court's decision to challenge parts of the 2006 Catalan Statute of Autonomy.[15] The event witnessed a public display of political solidarity and popular protest of region against centre, bringing together the disparate strands of the burgeoning anti-austerity and pro-separatist movements under the Catalan flag. The following day the same public space in the heart of Barcelona was filled by thousands of fans celebrating Iniesta's iconic goal which brought victory to La Roja in the World Cup final in Johannesburg, with Spanish and Catalan flags woven together in celebration of the team's success. This juxtaposition of protest and celebration reflects and defines the cultural and political flux around the constructions and representations of Catalanism and Spanishness which have occurred in Spain since 2008. The protest of July 10 tapped into the economic inequalities and mounting criticism of the Madrid-based political establishment's failure to regulate the banks and property market, fuelling the subsequent mass demonstrations of los indignados, the so called 15-M cluster, in Spanish cities from May 2011. These public protests of mass political activism laid the foundations for the growth of alternative political forces in Spanish society (Iglesias, 2015). This gave added momentum to the renaissance of anti-centralism at the root of the aspiration to carve an independent political entity out of the distinctive mores of Catalan ethnicity (Castro, 2013). Paradoxically, the July 11 celebrations suggested a more cohesive shared and dual identity within the political and cultural landscape of Spain's democracy (Quiroga, 2013). This alternate construct can be traced in the leitmotif framing the foundation of Cuidadanos in projecting itself as pro-homeland, pro-country and pro-Europe. The cultural and political dynamic remains complex and fluid, as does the synthesis between football and politics.

Football's role within the volatility and uncertainty of these processes has been to be both a vehicle for recycling the local and regional political/cultural rivalries and traditions at the centre of the debates around ethnicity and identity and to constitute a focal point of political and mass populism in which the sporting and political are interdependent. The movements for political change have increasingly merged with the Spanish game to challenge the institutional mores of clubs such as FC Barcelona and Athletic Bilbao, creating ambivalence in respect of attitudes towards the emergent forces of Podemos and Cuidadanos in contemporary Spanish politics. The politicization of Spanish football continues to be a significant aspect of the contemporary debate. As recently as January 2016 FC Barcelona sent an official tweet congratulating Puigdemont on his appointment as First Minister in the Catalan government (Spain Report, January 2016). Most pointedly, the communication referred to Catalonia as 'Our Nation' in its message. In their rejection of the political consensus which has dominated post-Franco Spain, these loosely formed groups serve as a barometer for the political cleavages and economic inequalities of Spanish society.

Spanish club football continues to both mirror these tensions and to act as a distraction from them. In April 2016, the most recent instalment of the dramatic post-modern, mega-spectacle of El Clásico was broadcast to and consumed by an estimated global audience of some 500 million, across a plethora of media platforms (O'Brien, 2013). For the majority of these global consumers, this is the embodiment of the Spanish game, a stellar clash of iconoclastic rivals (Relaño, 2012; O'Brien, 2013). At the same time, another story was unfolding, far removed from the mediatized orgy of El Clásico. The plight of Recreativo de Huelva, Spain's first football club, deep in the post-industrial backwaters of Andalusia, and dating back to 1871, gradually emerged (Brentnall, 2009; Ball, 2011). Recreativo has spent most of its existence in the second and third tiers of the Spanish football hierarchy, only rarely competing with the game's elite. Yet the club is broadly respected as the folkloric birthplace of Spanish football and resonates within the idealized sentiments around the game's genesis in Spain. The club currently has debts of €20 million and teeters on the brink of bankruptcy with an uncertain future. The local community has recently mounted a campaign to try to save it from extinction. The differences between the haves and have-nots, the elite and the rest, could not be more acutely illustrated than by these two contemporary examples.

Whether any future coalition involving Podemos will be able to turn its attention to the hierarchies and elites which have traditionally run the Spanish game in order to challenge a cluster of issues from high ticket prices, which tend to exclude many fans from watching the top clubs, so that the game has increasingly become a middle-class commodity at its higher echelons to the fundamental inequality of resources at the core of the Spanish game depends on both the outcome of any future elections and the political will to become entangled in the complex mosaic surrounding the governance of football in Spain. The new deal on broadcast revenue and rights, which comes into effect at the start of the 2016–17 season, attempts to address these questions of inequality, with the expressed hope that La Liga will become more competitive and that the exodus of players to the wealthier pastures of the English Premier League since 2008 will be stemmed.[16] The capacity of the reformist impulse underpinning the rhetoric of Podemos and other groups at the national and regional level has yet to confront the vested interests which dominate Spanish club football. Whether this can be achieved by making the much vaunted socio-model of ownership, rooted in the cultural and political traditions of some of La Liga's most powerful clubs (Ball, 2011; Burns, 2012), more genuinely democratic and accountable or by adopting the Bundesliga model of ownership and regulation, which stresses a more direct line of accountability and community between the club and its supporter, is likely to be the subject of heated discussion and debate. To attempt either would be a bold move in linking the paradoxes of austerity with the privileged status that elite football has historically enjoyed in Spanish society.

As Spain's tentative and faltering recovery, since 2013, from the lowest points of austerity is threatened by the political wrangling and uncertainty in its post-electoral phase, the future is difficult to predict. At the central level, new political actors and old rivalries perpetuate the state's crisis of authority and legitimacy, whilst regional politics remains disputed and contested. These factors continue to reflect the notion that since 2007 Spain has been in the process of a Second Transition, with the 'Pact of Forgetting' at the root of the post-Franco settlement being both outdated and outmoded in its capacity to resolve the complex issues of Spanish society. On a historic and cultural level, the Second Transition was framed by the Zapatero government's Law of Recorded Memory 2007 (Encarnación, 2008; Castro, 2013), which opened many of the bitter divisions that had existed since the Civil War in its desire to finally break with the nation's Francoist past and reconcile a tortured history with the maturity of a democratic state. In a political context, the emergence of Podemos and Cuidadanos signposts Spain's Second Transition in its break with the established orthodoxy which had shaped the First Transition (Vincent, 2010). These profound cultural and political changes have underpinned Spain's period of austerity and defined the responses to it.

Had La Roja confounded expectations and won a third successive European Championship in France during the summer of 2016, with a squad that was essentially in transition, it would not only have been a fitting end to the Del Bosque period, the internecine political war for

Spain's future, and indeed for that of its contested regions would have been at least temporarily suspended, in a symbolic, somewhat muted display of unity and patriotism around the divergent constituents of Spanish nationhood. The Sweet Smell of Success would have been as potent as ever in rallying round a disparate and divided Spanish state. The failure of La Roja in its quest exposes the ephemeral nature of the beautiful game, as well as the perennial fragility of Spanish national identity. Spain's political and economic future, bound up in the impacts of long-term austerity, is uncertain. Beneath the icons, rituals and symbols of its elite, Spanish football embellishes this uncertainty. Should Catalonia and the Basque Country succeed in the separatist aspirations of their contested politics, the game will find itself at yet another crossroad. Will the stateless football nations of Catalonia and the Basque Country define Spain's disintegration by being able to fully compete as sovereign states in international competition? Will the elite clubs of FC Barcelona and Athletic Bilbao operate within the confines of these new sovereign entities? Or will Spanish football continue to be both political and apolitical as a force for cohesion and cultural integration? These questions are vexed and interrelated, and Spain's austerity since 2008 reveals the cultural power of sport in society. The hyperbole and dominance of football within this matrix gives it a continuing significance at the nexus of cultural politics.

Notes

1 The Podemos (we can) party was founded in March 2014 by Pablo Iglesias in the aftermath of the M-15 protests against inequalities and corruption; it signposts the left-wing articulation of these protests. In the European Elections of May 2015, it secured 7.98 per cent of the vote, resulting in five MEPs. It subsequently won 69 seats (21 per cent of vote) in the December 2015 elections, making it the third largest party in the Spanish Parliament.

2 The Cuidadanos (citizens) party was founded in Catalonia in July 2006. Its ideology has been described as both left and right of centre, being anti-Catalan nationalism and pro-European in its stance. In the European elections of May 2015, it secured 3.2 per cent of the vote, resulting in two MEPS. In the December 2015 elections, it won 40 seats (13.9 per cent). The President of Cuidadanos is Albert Rivera.

3 La Selección is the name historically given to the Spanish National team since 1920, revealing tensions, ambiguities and conflict surrounding Spain as a nation.

4 La Roja refers to the name given to the national team from 2006. The term was originally coined by then coach Luis Aragonés.

5 PNV – Partido Nationalisto Vasco (Basque National Party). Founded by Sabino Arana (1894).

6 La Cantera (the quarry) is a term used by clubs to define players either coming from their academies or from the local area or region. It forms part of the folkloric tradition of Spanish club football.

7 The Bosman Ruling (1995) from the European Court of Justice allowed freedom of movement at the end of contract for players, without a transfer fee being paid (article 39, EC Treaty). It followed a dispute between Jean-Marc Bosman and the Belgian Football Association.

8 El Fatalismo is a notion that reflects the historic cultural stereotyping around the national team's failures in international tournaments prior to 2008. Italy has tended to be the main perpetrator of this curse, symbolically lifted by La Roja's victory in the European Championship of 2008.

9 El Naranjito means 'the little orange'. The official World Cup mascot for 1982 was a little orange dressed in the football kit of La Selección. It both alienated alternative nationalisms and seemed to represent an unimaginative stereotype of Spanish national identity, locked into the Francoist past.

10 La Masia refers to the eighteenth century farmhouse adjacent to the Camp Nou which was developed into FC Barcelona's training academy by Cruyff in the late 1980s. The philosophy adopted produced the players which came to symbolize the style of the club and La Roja.

11 Nace de Dentro (born from within) was the shirt logo adopted by La Selección for Euro 2012. It was promoted through a huge advertising campaign video which stressed the patriotic pride of the team.

12 'Los Fueros' refers to the medieval customs of fiscal autonomy and self-rule. They are used in the Basque Country to legitimize historic and contemporary claims for independence.

13 Disputes over broadcasting rights or football's so-called 'Media Wars' have been a recurrent feature in recent years. The start of the 2011–12 season was delayed by failure to reach agreement, and similar disputes threatened the live broadcast of matches in 2012–13 and 2014–15. They invariably involved the Spanish State, football's governing bodies, the clubs, players' representatives and a cluster of media organizations.

14 During Spain's austerity, the total debt of La Liga's clubs has averaged out at between €2 to €3 billion, in spite of attempts by the Spanish Football Association and Government to reduce these levels. In 2013 measures were imposed to cut unpaid taxation by half in the period up to 2017.

15 On Saturday, July 10, 2010, an estimated 1 million people gathered in and around Plaza Catalonia to protest against the recent decision of the Constitutional Court to reinterpret or annul parts of the Catalan statute of Autonomy 2006. The following evening many thousands gathered in both Plaza Catalonia and Plaza España to watch and celebrate Spain's victory over Holland in the World Cup final.

16 The new deal for broadcasting rights is worth €2.65 million between 2016 and 2019. It followed complex and protracted discussions and copies the English Premier League 'equal distribution' model, where the monies from Telefonica, Movistar and Mediapro are shared between clubs rather than negotiated on an individual basis, as had been the case in the past.

Bibliography

Ball, P. (2011). *Morbo: the story of Spanish football.* London: WSC Books.

Billig, M. (2004). *Banal nationalism.* London: Sage.

Brentnall, R. (2009). *From a different corner: exploring Spanish football.* Leicester: Matador.

Burns, J. (2009). *Barça: a people's passion.* London: Bloomsbury.

Burns, J. (2012). *La Roja: a journey through Spanish football.* London: Simon and Schuster.

Castro, L. (ed.) (2013). *What's up with Catalonia?* Barcelona: Catalonia Press.

Conversi, D. (2000). *The Basques, the Catalans and Spain: alternatives to nationalist mobilization.* Reno: University of Nevada Press.

Crolley, L. and Hand, D. (2006). *Football, Europe and the press.* London: Routledge.

Duke, V. and Crolley, L. (1998). *Storming the Bastille: football, nationalism and the state.* London: Longman.

Encarnación, O. (2008). *Spanish politics: democracy after dictatorship.* London: Polity Press.

Glanville, B. (2012). *The story of the World Cup.* London: Faber and Faber.

Goldblatt, D. (2008). *The ball is round.* London: Riverhead.

Hanlon, T. (2011). *A Catalan dream: football, artistry and political intrigue.* London: Peak Publishing.

Hooper, J. (2007). *The new Spaniards,* 2nd edition. London: Penguin.

Hunter, G. (2013). *Spain: the inside story of La Roja's historic treble.* London: Backpage Press.

Iglesias, P. (2015). 'Understanding Podemos and More'. *New Left Review,* 93, 7–38.

Junco, J. and Shubert, A. (2000). *Spanish history since 1808.* London: Hodder Arnold.

Levi, C. (2003). *Atlético de Madrid: Cien años de historia (Athletico Madrid: a hundred years of history).* Madrid: Silex.

Lopis Goig, R. (ed.) (2009). *Fútbol postnacional (Post-national football).* Barcelona: Anthropos.

Miravitlaas, R. (2013). *La Functión Política Del Barça (The political role of FC Barcelona).* Madrid: Catarata.

Montalbán, M. (2005). *Fútbol: un religión en busco de un dios (Football: a religion in search of a god).* Barcelona: Arena Abierta.

O'Brien, J. (2013). '"El Clásico" and the demise of tradition in Spanish club football: Perspectives on shifting patterns of cultural identity'. *Soccer and Society,* 14(3): 315–30.

O'Brien, J. (2014). '"Shades of Basqueness": Football, politics and ethnicity in the Basque Country'. In: K. Dashpar, T. Fletcher and N. Mccullough (eds.), *Sports Events, Society and Culture.* London: Routledge.

Paradinas, E. (2010). *La roja en la copa del mundo (The reds in the world cup).* Madrid: T&B editiónes.

Quiroga, A. (2014). *Football and national identities in Spain: the strange death of Don Quixote.* London. Palgrave Macmillan.

Relaño, A. (2012). *Nacidos para incordiarse: un siglo de agravios entre El Madrid y El Barça (Born to bother us: a century of aggravation between Madrid and Barcelona).* Madrid: ediciónes martinez roca.

Riordan, J. and Kruger, A. (2003). *European cultures in sport: examining the nations and regions.* Bristol: Intellect Books.

Rivas, J. (2012). *Athleti: paisajes, escenas y personajes (Athletic: landscapes, scenes and people).* Barcelona: Rocabosillo.

Solís, L. (2003). *Negotiating Spain and Catalonia.* Bristol: Intellect Books.

The Spain Report, November 2015–April 2016.

Tremlett, G. (2012). *Ghosts of Spain*, 2nd edition. London: Faber and Faber.

Tüñon, J. and Bray, E. (2012). 'Sports and politics in Spain–football and Nationalist attitudes within the Basque Country and Catalonia'. *European Journal for Sport and Society*, 9(1–2): 7–32.

Vincent, M. (2010). *Spain 1833–2002.* Oxford: Oxford University Press.

Viñolo, V. (2009). *Los años 50 (The 1950s).* Madrid: La Esfera.

Wagg, S. (1995). *Giving the game away: football, politics and culture on five continents.* Leicester: Leicester University Press.

10 Orwell's progeny

The British left in an age of austerity[1]

Philip Bounds

Whenever there is a whiff of austerity in the air, many of us on the British left set our sights on Wigan Pier. Written in the middle of the deepest depression that Western capitalism has ever known, George Orwell's *The Road to Wigan Pier* (1937) still powerfully conditions our sense of how austerity should be portrayed.[2] Its searing and mordant images of overworked miners, whey-faced proletarian housewives and quietly desperate dole claimants have long since acquired archetypal status. Each new generation of British socialists has sought to update them in an effort to evoke the economic and social problems of its own times. Indeed, there is now a lengthy tradition of books, articles and pamphlets in which the conditions described in Orwell's masterpiece are explicitly compared with those of the present. The most substantial recent addition to this body of work is Stephen Armstrong's *The Road to Wigan Pier Revisited* (2012), a deft travelogue which comes close to concluding that conditions in the North of England are almost as bad now as they were in Orwell's day.[3]

Most latter-day attempts to revisit Wigan Pier focus on the first half of Orwell's book, which deals with such matters as housing, working conditions and unemployment. The focus of the present chapter is slightly different. In the second half of *The Road to Wigan Pier* – especially in Chapters XI and XII – Orwell tries to explain the distressing failure of the inter-war left to win much support for a socialist solution to the crisis. His emphasis is not so much on structural or objective factors as on the *cultural* deficiencies of the various left organizations. The contemporary relevance of this part of his book scarcely needs underscoring. Although there were many people on the radical left in Britain who thought that their time had come when international capitalism lurched into crisis in 2008, there has been no revival of socialist politics over the last five years. The innumerable small Marxist parties and the radical wing of the Labour Party are still weak, fragmented and marginalized. To what extent does *The Road to Wigan Pier* help us to understand the modern left's lack of effectiveness? Does its diagnosis of the left's cultural malaise still speak to our contemporary political practices, or should we be seeking new explanations? These are among the questions I shall try to answer.[4]

Orwell's attack on the left

George Orwell was not a political theorist and never claimed to be one. When he tried to account for the failure of the socialist left to capitalize on the crisis of the inter-war period, he made no attempt to deploy the heavy philosophical artillery of a Gramsci, a Korsch or a Lukács. His approach was that of a highly intelligent, unusually independent-minded journalist who based most of his conclusions on his personal observations of the left. He was not interested in analysing the deep structures of capitalist society or the forms of consciousness to which they give rise. Instead he focused on those comparatively superficial aspects of socialist politics which too often induce a neuralgic response on the part of ordinary working people. His superficiality was at once his biggest strength and his greatest weakness. Aware of the importance of first impressions, he had an unrivalled ability to understand the ways in which the surface characteristics of the left 'drive[s] away the very people who ought to be flocking to its support' (Orwell, 2001: 159). By the same token, his big drawback as a socialist thinker was that his obsession with political surfaces prevented him engaging in sufficient depth with issues of structure, organization and ideology. If we look to him for help in trying to understand the weaknesses of today's left, we have to realize that his ideas can only provide a starting point for the debate. Other and weightier writers will also need to be consulted.

The circumstances in which Orwell launched his attack on the left are well known.[5] After being commissioned by the publisher Victor Gollancz to write a book about the contemporary working class, Orwell spent nearly eight weeks in early 1936 travelling through the so-called 'distressed areas' in the North of England. His exposure to such harrowing levels of poverty, unemployment and industrial dereliction went a long way towards crystallizing his exasperation with the left. Given that the deepest crisis in capitalism's history had inflicted such misery on ordinary people, why was it that 'Instead of going forward, the cause of Socialism is visibly going back?'[6] Orwell's most famous answer to that question was that the left had alienated potential recruits with its sheer crankiness. His searing attack on the fruit-juice drinkers, nudists and sandal wearers of the organized socialist movement is still widely quoted. Less famous but probably more important were his discussions of three other things which served to limit the left's appeal – its officiousness, its ambivalent commitment to achieving real change and its uncritical embrace of modernity.

Orwell's attack on the left's officiousness was rooted in a contrast between the socialist movement's working-class sympathizers and its more articulate middle-class spokesmen. Although he always believed that working-class socialists had sound political instincts, not least because they realized that socialism was ultimately about 'justice and common decency' and 'nobody bossing you about', he also believed that their commitment to the left was neither 'complete' nor 'logically consistent' because of their lack of interest in political doctrine (Ibid.: 164). His real target was the sort of intellectually sophisticated middle-class socialists who represented the public face of the left. His main concern about the 'mingy little beasts' who populated the Communist Party, the Independent Labour Party and the Labour Left was that their radicalism seemed wholly devoid of libertarian impulses. What attracted them to socialism was not a love of freedom but an overdeveloped desire for order. Offended by the unpredictable and chaotic nature of free markets, they embraced the idea of economic planning because they thought it enabled governments to subject every last aspect of people's lives to precise administrative control. Their vision of socialism had nothing to do with workers' self-management and everything to do with the subordination of the masses to enlightened but essentially bloodless officials. Orwell even suggested that their 'hypertrophied sense of order' had its roots in a sort of visceral dislike of working people. Their desire to abolish poverty arose not so much from a sense of compassion as from the feeling that the poor were 'contemptible and disgusting'. The politics of the middle-class left were ultimately an expression of the desire for social hygiene.[7]

After pouring scorn on the vision of socialist society to which his contemporaries subscribed, Orwell went on to question whether the middle-class left really wanted socialism at all. He strongly suspected that its desire to change society was at best somewhat ambivalent. Although many middle-class radicals nursed an almost pathological hatred for the bourgeoisie, they could not be relied upon to support a challenge to capitalism when the chips were down. This was partly because so many of them were slaves to political fashion. According to one of Orwell's less accurate predictions, many of the young men and women who called themselves socialists in 1936 would cheerfully go over to fascism when the pendulum of political opinion swung to the right. Their tendency to equivocate also arose from a highly recognizable species of old-fashioned snobbery. Usually reasonably affluent and addicted to the status which their professional positions conferred upon them, middle-class radicals secretly regarded the socialist idea as a grave threat to their wealth and prestige. Hence Orwell's devastating judgment that the 'typical Socialist' was 'a prim little man with a white-collar job, usually a secret teetotaller and often with vegetarian leanings, with a history of Nonconformity behind him, and, above all, with a social position which he has no intention of forfeiting' (Ibid.: 161).

Perhaps the most interesting symptom of the middle-class left's insincerity was its attitude towards political doctrine. Implicit in Orwell's description of left-wing culture was the belief that bourgeois radicals used socialist theory as a means of symbolically asserting their superiority to their working-class comrades. Whereas working-class socialists engaged only superficially with the rarified world of theory, the 'intellectual, book-trained Socialist' mugged up on Marx, Engels and Lenin in order to shore up his sense of entitlement and establish his right to lead. Orwell was especially suspicious of what he regarded as the socialist intellectual's deeply inhumane quest for absolute consistency. On the assumption that Marxism and other radical ideologies provided an integrated explanation for every last aspect of human existence, intellectuals often supposed that there was a distinctively socialist way of seeing everything and doing everything. Their horror of inconsistency tended to transform them into aridly cerebral creatures, secure in a sense of their own intellectual eminence but utterly divorced from the humanizing passions of everyday life. Like his great Tory contemporary Michael Oakeshott, Orwell clearly believed that nothing erodes common decency quite as badly as too much thought.[8]

When Orwell was writing *The Road to Wigan Pier*, British socialism was closely associated with a deep faith in the liberating power of science and technology. J. D. Bernal, J. B. S. Haldane and other members of the so-called Social Relations of Science movement had popularized the idea that socialism's main function was to free scientific research from the constraints imposed upon it by capitalism. As long as the market system prevailed, or so it was argued, the potential of science would be held in check by a debilitating divorce between pure and applied forms of research. Only socialism could revive the intellectual vitality of the sciences and renew humanity's dream of imposing its will on nature through the use of advanced technology.[9] This was the context in which Orwell accused the intellectual left of associating itself too uncritically with the forces of modernity.

Unlike Bernal and his co-thinkers, Orwell believed that there was something *intrinsically* dehumanizing about advanced technology. The ultimate effect of the cutting-edge machinery to which socialists attached such significance was to rob work of its creativity, erode the human capacity for heroism and generally make life insipid, complacent and soft. While accepting that nothing could prevent the onward march of science and technology, Orwell insisted that the left had made a tragic error of judgment in embracing the vision of a 'completely mechanised, immensely organised world' (Ibid.: 175). The main duty of a socialist intellectual was not to worship technology but to warn against its dangers. The culture of a socialist society would somehow have to brush against the grain of its technological base, seeking to preserve the most vital human qualities by continually drawing attention to the dire cultural consequences of machinery. It was not simply officiousness and insincerity which had prevented the left from winning much support. The effete technophilia of men like Bernal had gone a long way towards alienating a working class whose culture was altogether less anaemic and deracinated.[10] It is here, perhaps more than anywhere else, that Orwell's attack on the left speaks most powerfully to the contemporary world. Its pertinence to a culture positively saturated in ecological dogma scarcely needs underlining. This provides us with the cue we need to turn our attention to *The Road to Wigan Pier*'s relevance to the modern left.

Sectarianism and the contemporary left

The politics of the radical left in Britain have been dominated over the last few years by the theme of austerity. After the international financial system came close to collapse in the autumn of 2008, Gordon Brown's Labour administration spent trillions of pounds in an effort to underwrite the solvency of Britain's banks. By the time Brown was ousted from office in 2010, there was something approaching a consensus among politicians that Britain's most urgent task was to reduce the size of the national deficit by cutting public expenditure. The responsibility for introducing a rolling programme of cuts has fallen to David Cameron's Conservative-Liberal government, which argues that public spending has to be driven down if Britain is to retain its creditworthiness and embark on a new cycle of economic growth. Opposition to the cuts has been spearheaded primarily by the trade unions, several of which have taken industrial action in defence of their members' living standards. Opposition of a less visible but more explicitly political kind has come from Britain's dense network of Marxist organizations and parties. Although British Marxists are as fragmented now as they ever were, they all tend to agree that the cuts pose a massive threat to Britain's public sector and need to be resisted *in toto*. The most energizing contributions to the campaign against the cuts have been made by the Socialist Workers Party (SWP), the Socialist Party (SP), the Communist Party of Britain (CPB), the Scottish Socialist Party (SSP) and Counterfire. Some of these groups have tried to reach out to ordinary members of the public by working through front organizations such as The Right to Work Movement, the National Shop Stewards Network and Coalition of Resistance. Members of the various groups have often displayed a heartening willingness to work with each other. Activists from all parties and none have come together to form broad anti-cuts movements in many towns and cities. The most important symptom of this cautious desire for unity has been the establishment of the so-called People's Assembly against Austerity in 2013.

Marxist campaigners against the cuts have acquitted themselves honourably and have notched up a number of minor victories. The Right to Work campaign's success in forcing several large companies to withdraw from a government workfare scheme is particularly impressive.[11] Nevertheless, only the most purblind activist would deny that the left has had a very small impact on public opinion in the years since the crisis began. Recent opinion polls indicate that a clear majority of the British people accept the need for cuts. The left is no nearer to sinking deep roots in British society now than it was in Orwell's day. So let us return to the questions with which we began. To what extent can Orwell's attack on the hard-left of the 1930s help us to come to terms with our own predicament? Have we learned any lessons from the failures of the inter-war period, or must we conclude that our latter-day campaign against austerity is tainted by all the old errors of officiousness, ambivalence and technophilia?

Officiousness

At first sight, the contemporary left seems to have little enough in common with the left depicted by Orwell. The typical activist is no longer a 'prim little man' whose Nonconformist background conspires to make him officious and insincere in equal measure. Modern hard-leftists bear all the hallmarks of the cultural revolution that has swept traditional morality aside over the course of the last fifty years. Shaped by the hedonism of the consumer age as well as by its countercultural alternatives, their structure of feeling is characterized by a very distinctive combination of studied informality, post-hippie authenticity and down-at-heel defiance. Ours is an age in which the seller of *Socialist Worker* or the *Morning Star* seeks to endear himself to his comrades by going unshaved and conveying an air of having slept in his clothes. On the other hand, the waning influence of nonconformity does not mean that officiousness has disappeared from the left. The authoritarian reflexes to which Orwell drew attention are still disturbingly prevalent. Sometimes they take the form of gross intolerance towards dedicated activists who refuse to accept every dot and comma of the party line. At others they manifest themselves in contempt for parliamentary democracy, a bovine determination to have the spokesmen of the far-right excluded from the media or sycophancy towards fake-revolutionary *caudillos* like Hugo Chávez or Fidel Castro. One of the most interesting things about the current crisis is that the hard-left's officiousness is increasingly taking a novel form. These days, in a way that was rarely true in the past, activists have reinforced their illiberal reputation by identifying themselves with the patterns of authority associated with the welfare state.

It is not difficult to understand how this situation has arisen. Convinced that the cuts represent the first stage in the dismantling of the welfare state, activists have felt obliged to launch a fairly simplistic defence of collective provision of essential goods and services. For the last five years, their propaganda has pivoted around the claim that the state is infinitely better than the private, voluntary or charitable sectors at allocating such things as healthcare, education and unemployment relief. In itself this claim is perfectly justified. At a time when the right is seeking to exploit the crisis to advance the neoliberal agenda, there has certainly been a need for an energetic public defence of collective provision. But what is remarkable about the hard-left's recent interventions is that their attitude towards the welfare state has seemed so uncritical. The necessary defence of state provision has long since been drowned out by trite, sentimental and disingenuous tributes to the workers and officials who run the welfare system. Teachers, nurses, social workers and even policemen and welfare bureaucrats have increasingly been portrayed as selfless public servants, heroically serving the indigent and the needy in appallingly difficult circumstances. The following passages are entirely typical:

> 'Stand up for education – Gove must go!' is what hundreds of teachers were chanting as they marched through Nottingham on the day of their strike. The well supported march and rally was applauded by passers by as it made it's [sic] way through the streets into the city centre. This made a big difference to the teachers who were saying 'it's good that parents realise we're striking for their children'.
>
> (Socialist Party Nottingham, 2013)

[Care workers] work very hard. They are helping disabled and elderly people. We are understaffed and yet we go above and beyond to help the residents.

(Socialist Appeal, 2013)

Cuts are hitting women at their most vulnerable and when support is most required. ... Humberside police force planned to replace five constables specialising in rape and child sex abuse cases with civilians as part of its scheme to save £2 million by 2013. The volunteers have five weeks training instead of the two years the police undergo.

(Sachs-Eldridge, 2011)

The problem with sentiments like these is that they overlook the highly contradictory nature of the welfare state. It is one thing to acknowledge that teachers, social workers or claims advisers provide an essential service and work hard on behalf of the people they serve. It is quite another to elide the fact that they sometimes exercise their authority in such a way as to reinforce support for the status quo. As countless radical analysts have pointed out, the welfare state in Britain has 'always been regulative, coercive and oriented towards the imperatives of the labour market' (Pierson, 1999: 180). The relationship between the providers and the users of services is often an extremely hierarchical and intrusive one, intended to reconcile people who rely on the welfare state to their subordinate status in society. The existing patterns of authority also go a long way towards reinforcing patriarchal ideology and undergirding the oppression of women by men.[12]

A long tradition of working-class suspicion of the welfare state suggests that ordinary people are better attuned to this aspect of capitalist hegemony than the middle-class ideologues who claim to represent them. If the left becomes too closely associated with the welfare bureaucracy, it risks creating the impression that it is less interested in the self-liberation of the working class than in the shoring up of existing structures of power. It also makes it very difficult for the left to make a meaningful contribution to the current debate about the proper balance between collective provision and what is sometimes called 'self-help'. Since the crisis began in 2008, many conservative right-wingers have justified the cuts by claiming that the welfare state has sapped society's moral fibre. By coercing people into helping the needy – or so the argument goes – the state has coarsened their moral outlook by depriving them of the opportunity to provide voluntary assistance to their fellow men and women.

Although this argument strikes many people as a peculiarly blatant piece of special pleading, it has prompted some activists on the left to argue for the revival of the old traditions of working-class self-reliance. Their argument is that the welfare state has penetrated too far into the lives of working people and robbed their culture of at least some of its initiative, leaving no room for the sort of mutual aid that was once provided by trade unions, credit unions and friendly societies.[13] Whether or not this perspective is correct, it is clear that the left can do little to revive the tradition of working-class self-reliance while it identifies too closely with the interests of the welfare bureaucracy. The instincts of activists are simply too out of step with those of the constituency they aim to convert.

Ambivalence

A certain officiousness is by no means the only characteristic that modern leftists share with their counterparts in the 1930s. The two lefts are also linked across the decades by their ambivalent attitude towards achieving real change, though here again it is necessary to update Orwell's analysis. As we have seen, Orwell believed that leftist equivocation was primarily a function of the elevated social position enjoyed by socialist intellectuals. If this argument no longer seems very persuasive, it is perhaps because the class composition of anti-capitalist parties has changed radically over the last forty years. The radical left of Orwell's day was largely composed of a mass of working-class adherents and a smaller but highly influential fraction of middle-class professionals. These days there are fewer workers and professionals but more members of the educated lower-middle class. Indeed, one way of understanding the culture of the modern left is to see it as a by-product of the post-war expansion of higher education. As has often been pointed out, not least by historians trying to explain the periodic outbursts of rebellion among students, the labour market no longer works to the advantage of university graduates in the advanced capitalist world. People with degrees often struggle to find the sort of well-paid, prestigious and stimulating positions for which their education equips them. This is the sort of constituency to which the modern radical left overwhelmingly appeals. Excluded from the professional world to which they aspire, disaffected graduates join Marxist parties in order to find an outlet for the skills acquired over twenty or so years of formal education. It is hardly surprising if some of them come to regard political self-advancement as intrinsically more important than the advancement of the socialist cause. The acquisition and retention of a prominent position in the party takes precedence over the creation of a non-hierarchical society. To a degree that would have seemed unthinkable even forty years ago, the political effectiveness of Britain's Marxist parties is stymied by the fact that so many of their members regard activism as a sort of alternative career.

There is also a sense in which the radical left's ambivalence towards changing society is reflected in its approach to ideas. It sometimes seems as if organizations like the SP or the SWP use ideology primarily for purposes of internal party management. One way of putting it would be to say that Marxist organizations frequently operate under the sign of Durkheim rather than Marx. Beleaguered by a deep sense of alienation from their fellow men and women – hollowed out by precisely the sort of *anomie* to which Durkheim attached such significance – many people join radical organizations in the hope of finding a close-knit community in which their human sympathies can flourish. The overriding importance of this quest for community often has a distorting effect on the collective beliefs with which particular organizations are associated. Many Marxist parties use the party line as a means of distinguishing between what a Durkheimian like Mary Douglas might have called the pure and the polluted.[14] In embracing a particular set of ideas, activists bind themselves into a distinctive community by marking themselves off from the horde of unenlightened folk who fail to share their wisdom. The political dangers of this are clear enough: if the most important function of an ideology is to unite an organization by sustaining a sense of 'us' versus 'them', there will always be a powerful if unconscious temptation to make the ideology as controversial as possible. To the person in search of a community to which she can belong, political ideas matter less for their persuasiveness than for their capacity to unite a self-appointed vanguard around the defence of the party line. Telling the truth takes second place to the goal of keeping a small but fervent band of true believers in business.

The present crisis has thrown up its own examples of Marxist parties using ideology as a form of organizational cement. One in particular illustrates the sectarian temper of many sections of the left with considerable clarity. When anti-cuts movements were being formed across Britain in the wake of David Cameron's election victory, there was a lively and sometimes fractious debate about who should be eligible to participate in them. According to a vociferous group of activists – many of them associated with the Socialist Party – the movement should embrace only people who opposed *every last cut* in public expenditure. People who opposed certain cuts but accepted others were condemned for their divisiveness and their woeful lack of militancy.[15] Judged on purely political lines, this position was clearly absurd. If activists choose to associate only with people who reject the government's cuts programme as a whole, they lose the opportunity to influence the hundreds of thousands of people whose opposition to the cuts is sincere but more limited in scope. They also create the misleading impression that activists have a duty to defend every last piece of public expenditure, whereas the left's historic position has always been that savings made in certain areas – defence is the obvious example – should be used to boost spending on health, education and other socially beneficial aspects of the welfare state. But to say all of this is ultimately to miss the point; the real function of the oppose-all-cuts shibboleth is not to build a mass movement but to create a sense of political belonging. By drawing a rigid and highly tendentious distinction between principled militants who reject all cuts and wishy-washy dilettantes who reject only certain cuts, activists in organizations like the SP are engaging in a shamelessly sectarian exercise in political bonding. The fact that they are not fully conscious of what they are doing should not absolve them from criticism.

Technophilia

Although officiousness and ambivalence are still prevalent on the British left, it is equally clear that technophilia has long since been jettisoned from radical culture. It would be quite impossible for a latter-day Orwell to claim that modern socialism is suffused by a naïve faith in the possibilities of science and technology. These days, even in those parties and organizations which ostensibly retain a belief in the principle of economic growth, there is a widespread assumption that technology is imposing an intolerable strain on the environment. Suspicion of science and technology has been central to the left's response to the current crisis, not least because cuts in public expenditure are seen as a grave threat to environmentally responsible forms of government. An especially striking example of this occurred in January 2014 when various coastal areas of Britain were affected by severe floods. Looking on with a certain apocalyptic relish as ordinary people were evacuated from their water-logged homes, many anti-capitalists argued that the floods would never have happened in the first place if the government had not cut spending on flood protection:

> The worst flooding has been based in those rural areas which always tend to vote Tory or Liberal Democrat. The people here have carried on believing that austerity was for other people in inner cities far away. Now they can see the truth and the Coalition can see its votes disappearing under water. Despite rescue

authorities, Environment Agency (EA) staff and many other services and local authorities working non-stop night and day to salvage the situation, against terrible odds, the truth is that they have been left underfunded and ill prepared to deal with such a situation.

(Lighter, 2014)

The Department for the Environment, Food and Rural Affairs (Defra) has already had its budget slashed by £500m, with a further £300m to be cut by 2016. Such cuts can only mean that, faced with extreme weather or natural disasters, Britain will be less prepared and less able to deal with the tasks at hand, with working people inevitably hit hardest.

(Anon, 2014)

Arguments such as these reflect British Marxism's gradual rapprochement with Green politics over the last twenty-five years. Nearly every Marxist party now seeks to justify its hostility to capitalism by claiming that the environment can only be saved by the transition to socialism. One of the more surprising aspects of this engagement with Green politics is that it has not always been adequately thought through. Although eco-Marxists such as John Bellamy Foster, Fred Magdoff and James O'Connor have made a highly sophisticated attempt to synthesize Marxism and ecologism, activists in Britain have often seemed to absorb ecological arguments in a curiously unreflective manner. The tendency has been to accept the tenets of Green ideology without first assessing their compatibility with more traditional socialist assumptions. Nowhere is this more obvious than in the debate about economic growth. Many left-wing activists now take it for granted that continued industrial expansion will inevitably lead to irreparable despoliation of the environment. As such, their socialism is rooted in the belief that one of the main justifications for economic planning is that it will bring humanity's feverish quest for growth to an end. Whereas capitalism necessarily stimulates large-scale economic growth through the process of market competition, socialism – or so the argument goes – enables us to impose strict limits on industrial expansion by coordinating production and consumption. Surprisingly few activists seem ready to acknowledge that this modish suspicion of science and industry conflicts with the perspectives of classical Marxism.[16] Insofar as the founders of Marxism addressed themselves to ecological themes, they generally drew a distinction between the creative potential of industry and the destructive powers of the market. In their view, adumbrated with particular force in Engels's great essay on 'The Part Played by Labour in the Transition from Ape to Man' (1876), there is no necessary tension between large-scale industrial expansion and environmental responsibility.[17] Ecological problems are largely a consequence of the market's gravely distorting influence on production, not the result of the intrinsic limitations of advanced technology. Speculating about life after capitalism, Marx and Engels argued that a planned economy would liberate technology from market distortions and thereby stimulate massive economic growth. The purpose of socialism was not to hold production in check but to create the circumstances in which the 'springs of co-operative wealth flow more abundantly' (Marx, 1976: 18).

Many people believe that British Marxism has benefited from its embrace of Green ideology, but it is equally possible to argue that our political culture has been impoverished by it. Although Orwell was right to warn against the dangers of technophilia, there is surely a case for saying that contemporary socialists have gone too far in the opposite direction. British politics is currently in the grip of a sullen, life-denying and intolerant anti-scientific consensus. Even when they purport to favour economic growth, the major parties perpetuate the idea that technology has brought humanity to the verge of outright catastrophe. Given that Marxists have historically evinced a deep faith in the liberating power of science and technology, it is surprising that they have adapted themselves so unquestioningly to the new mood of environmental pessimism. Armed with the idea that environmental problems are precipitated more by markets than machines, British Marxists could have responded to the crisis of neo-liberalism by arguing that a break with capitalism would greatly augment human wealth. They could also have served as cheerleaders for the various techniques which science has already devised to counter the environmental crisis, ranging from carbon sequestration schemes on the one hand to enhanced sunlight reflection schemes on the other.[18] Instead they have chosen to reinforce the mood of national gloom by parroting the idea that ours is an age in which human beings have no choice but to reduce their expectations. The environmental obsessions of the day have thrown up a series of questions which urgently need answering. Does the Green agenda necessarily result in a collapse of faith in humanity's creative powers? Is there a danger that the attempt to restrain industrial production could effectively put our economic evolution into reverse? Can we even be sure that a phenomenon such as global warming is caused by economic activity? So far – and in spite of the sterling efforts of a number of maverick left-libertarians – the most sustained and stimulating critique of Green orthodoxy has come from the right.[19] This means that the defence of economic growth is now largely associated in the public mind with support for free markets, deregulation and globalization. The left will only be able to make the progressive case for growth if it recovers some of the technological enthusiasms for which Orwell once attacked it.

The catastrophe of catastrophism

It is a testament to Orwell's skills as a journalist that his attack on the British left still holds water, *mutatis mutandis*, more than seventy years after it was written. Everything he said about the left's officiousness, ambivalence and technophilia serves to focus our minds on the problems of contemporary radicalism. Nevertheless, it would be wrong to regard Orwell's talent for skewering the left as a sign that he was free of political weaknesses himself. Although his understanding of socialism compares favourably with that of most of his contemporaries – and although his personal integrity cannot reasonably be doubted – he shared some of the left's faults even as he tried to distance himself from them. Here, too, his example is an instructive one. By scouring *The Road to Wigan Pier* for evidence of the flaws that Orwell shared with his left-wing contemporaries, we can once again dredge up material that exposes the limitations of today's anti-austerity left.

The principal weakness that disfigures Orwell's (2001) book is a species of catastrophism. Writing in the middle of the worst recessions in history and tormented by the growth of fascism, Orwell took it for granted that capitalism had entered a period of radical decline from which it could never recover. All would be for the worst in the worst of all possible worlds until working people were won over to socialism:

> It hardly needs pointing out that ... we are in a very serious mess ... We are living in a world in which nobody is free ... For enormous blocks of the working class the conditions of life are such ...[that]... there is no chance of those conditions showing any fundamental improvement (Ibid.: 158).

Orwell's absolute conviction that capitalist civilization was beyond redemption echoed that of his socialist contemporaries. Virtually everyone in the Communist Party and the other left sects believed that humanity was faced with a choice between socialism or barbarism. The idea that capitalism could ever again embark on a period of sustained growth was dismissed as impossibly naïve. Yet, in spite of the horrors which the world had to endure in the decade or so after *Wigan Pier* was published, history did not unfold according to Orwell's predictions. After the defeat of fascism and the widespread acceptance of Keynesian techniques of demand management, world capitalism entered what Eric Hobsbawm (1994) has justifiably called its 'Golden Age'. Rates of growth increased exponentially, full employment was effortlessly maintained and consumerism flourished. The system's capacity to recover from trauma was greater than anyone on the left had imagined.

The left's taste for catastrophist rhetoric has done a great deal to undermine the appeal of radical ideas. Quite apart from burdening socialists with a reputation for not understanding how capitalism actually works, it has also created the impression that activists positively relish the idea that society is on the verge of outright disaster. The well-known charge that left-wingers are prone to 'scaremongering' resonates so deeply with the public because it so often turns out to be true. This makes it all the more regrettable that catastrophism has played such a central role in the left's response to the current crisis. Right from the start of the crisis, the left has staked its credibility on the claim that government cuts would plunge the British economy into a maelstrom of disinvestment, unemployment and stagnation. The idea that cuts would stimulate economic growth by boosting private investment was dismissed as a neoliberal fantasy, unworthy of being discussed by any serious commentator. Yet the weakness of the left's position is already becoming clear.

Although the British economy is still in a fairly parlous state – and although the possibility of a second recession can by no means be dismissed – the embarrassing truth is that Britain currently boasts the highest rates of growth in the developed world. Predictions of stagnation and widespread social unrest have so far proved wide of the mark.[20] Wedded to an apocalyptic theory of capitalist crisis which has been proved wanting on so many occasions over the last 150 years, Marxists have been caught out by the fundamental Keynesian axiom that 'Things [always] happen, in the country or in the world, to revive business's "animal spirits"' (Skidelsky, 2013). It could even be argued that the left has massively overstated the extent to which ours is genuinely an age of austerity. As a number of Hayekian provocateurs have pointed out, public spending in Britain is currently running at more than 40 per cent of GDP. Spending on the National Health Service has been 'ringfenced' and substantial amounts of money continue to be poured into the education system. It is one thing to claim that the government has introduced a number of cruel and unnecessary cuts, each of which needs to be resisted. It is quite another to claim that the New Right is intent on plunging us into an anarcho-capitalist dystopia. Perhaps one of the reasons why the public remains indifferent to the left is that the times are rather less austere than activists would have us believe.

The left's catastrophist perspective on the cuts is part and parcel of its wider interpretation of the rise of the New Right. Traumatized by the onward march of neo-liberalism over the last forty years, many activists are inclined to reach for the language of the conspiracy theory when explaining its successes. An especially interesting symptom of this taste for conspiracy theories is the enormous popularity on the left of Naomi Klein's book *The Shock Doctrine* (2007). As is well known, Klein argues that the New Right owes its success to its skill in exploiting social crises. Using Pinochet's coup against the Allende government in Chile as her template, she claims that the New Right has achieved power only when people's political judgment has been temporarily warped by a catastrophic decline of the social fabric. Indeed, she goes further than this by implying that the New Right has *deliberately* fomented chaos in order to exploit it politically.[21] It is easy to understand why arguments like these should have gone down so well on the radical left. Portraying the rise of the New Right as a form of political pathology allows activists to ignore the enormously painful fact that Margaret Thatcher, Ronald Reagan and their followers have managed to win so many free elections in conditions of relative social order. Nevertheless, *The Shock Doctrine* throws the terrible dangers of left-wing catastrophism into vivid relief. Ostensibly so uncompromising in their radicalism, its central arguments are more likely to undermine resistance to neo-liberalism than to inspire it. By creating the impression that the New Right has effortlessly manipulated world affairs in the interests of capital, Klein grossly exaggerates its power and discourages those who would seek to resist it. The ultimate message of *The Shock Doctrine* is not that the New Right represents an organized conspiracy against the public interest. Its ultimate message is that catastrophism breeds only disillusionment and despair.

Conclusion

There is clearly no obligation to begin a discussion of the British left's current impasse by invoking George Orwell, but one of the many virtues of Orwell's work is that it stimulates vigorous debate. If we want to understand why the radical left has made so little progress during the present crisis, *The Road to Wigan Pier* is still one of the best places to start. Its capacity to focus our minds on the left's myriad weaknesses remains undimmed. As we have seen, contemporary radicals are both markedly different and surprisingly similar to their counterparts in the 1930s. Separated from the left-wing agitators of Orwell's day by the rise of consumerism and the cultural revolution that accompanied it, they still evince many of the faults which discouraged working people from embracing the socialist alternative during the Great Depression. World capitalism has changed beyond recognition, but the old problems of officiousness, ambivalence and catastrophism still hamstring the opposition.

Having anatomized the weaknesses of the left, Orwell began the last chapter of *Wigan Pier* by asking a simple question: '[I]s there anything one can do about it?'[22] What followed was an earnest but slightly desperate call for the left to overcome its internal divisions, embrace the principles of 'justice and liberty' and forge an alliance between working people and the 'exploited middle class'. It is clear that Orwell held out very little hope that the desired changes would ever occur. He would probably have been even more pessimistic if he had lived to see today's anti-austerity left. Unable to break out of its ideological ghetto, too consumed by political self-importance to ask searching questions about its own weaknesses, the radical left in Britain totters on the brink of outright irrelevance. The internal culture of the various parties and organizations is so stagnant that it serves only to stifle the desire for reform. The left is clearly not going to sort its problems out for itself. The only hope is that it will somehow be galvanized into new life by some profound external shock.

How likely is this to occur? There is perhaps room for a measure of cautious optimism. As the history of the last eighty years goes to show, the radical left has always been very good at responding to the challenge of the radical right. Faced with the insurgent energies of the British Union of Fascists in the 1930s or the National Front in the 1970s, British Marxists forged highly creative, broadly based movements which went a long way towards discrediting right-wing populism in the eyes of ordinary people. There is now an urgent need for the left to respond to another upsurge of the radical right. One of the most startling developments in recent British history has been the rise of the United Kingdom Independence Party (UKIP), a ramshackle but highly effective assemblage of right-wing controversialists which polled more votes than any other party in the European elections of 2014.[23] The radical left has been utterly traumatized by UKIP's success in appealing to disaffected working-class voters. Already there are signs that the trauma is galvanizing the left into new life, prompting activists to engage with precisely those issues of culture, ethnicity and national identity which preoccupy UKIP's supporters. Whether or not this fresh burst of political energy will ultimately rejuvenate the left is anyone's guess, but British anti-capitalists certainly have a lot to learn from the UKIP heresy. Contrary to what many activists like to believe, UKIP is neither a quasi-fascist nor a racist organization. The real source of its appeal lies in its inchoate but invigorating opposition to the anti-democratic orthodoxies which have disfigured European political culture for a generation. The singular gift of its leader Nigel Farage is the ability to popularize the idea that the European elite poses a massive threat to Britain's liberal traditions. If the left can respond creatively to UKIP's libertarianism, welcoming its vigorous support for democracy and individual liberty but rejecting its faith in free markets, it might yet devise a form of radical populism that can appeal to an electorate to which personal freedom matters more than ever before. There is simply no future for a left whose high-minded anti-capitalist rhetoric conceals a base desire to boss people around. Marxism and other anti-capitalist trends will flourish in Britain only if they reaffirm the truth that the ultimate goal of socialist society is to set the individual free. George Orwell knew better than anyone that a desire for 'justice and liberty' lies at the heart of any authentic socialist project. As a writer whose life's mission was jokingly described by his first wife as 'explaining how to be Socialist though Tory' (Colls, 2013: 199), he would surely have relished the idea that the left now has the opportunity to regenerate itself through a creative engagement with the resurgent forces of the libertarian right. His shade will be watching the events of the next few years with considerable interest.

Notes

1 A similar but revised version of this chapter appeared in Richard Lance Keeble (ed.), *George Orwell Now!* (New York: Peter Lang, 2016). The chapter was written in early 2015, before British politics was transformed beyond recognition when Jeremy Corbyn became leader of the Labour Party and the British people voted to leave the European Union. Its arguments about the state of the left are still relevant but some passages are now clearly out of date. The chapter would read very differently if it were written today.

2 See Orwell, 2001. See also Orwell, 2010.

3 See also Taafe, 2010; Sharrock, 2011. Mention should also be made of Beatrix Campbell's remarkable *Wigan Pier Revisited: Poverty and Politics in the 80s* (1984), the most stimulating of the various attempts to update Orwell's book during the deep recession of the early 1980s.

4 I am focusing in this chapter only on the political culture of Britain's anti-capitalist parties and organizations. I am not focusing – except in passing – on the response of radical academics and intellectuals to the international crisis of the last five years. This is because my particular interest is in the failure of the organized left to win support for its perspectives. Like Orwell, I am primarily concerned with those sections of the left which purport to offer a socialist alternative to the capitalist

mode of production. This means that my main focus is on the cluster of Marxist and semi-Marxist parties to the left of the Labour Party. I am aware that these parties are a highly varied bunch and that many of them are associated with distinct ideological positions, but I would also insist that their responses to the crisis have been remarkably homogeneous. I would be the first to acknowledge that my chapter is a highly polemical one, rooted as it is in my own involvement in the British left. I shall be satisfied if it starts some sort of debate.

5 Orwell's trip to the North has been described in detail by his many biographers. See, *inter alia*, Crick, 1992: Chapter 9; Shelden, 1991: Chapter 12; Meyers, 2000: Chapter 7; Taylor, 2003: Chapter 9.

6 Orwell, 2001: 159.

7 For Orwell's belief that the politics of the middle-class left were rooted in a craving for order, see Orwell, 2001: 166f.

8 For Orwell's account of the obsessive intellectualism of the middle-class left, see Orwell, 2001: 162f. For Oakeshott's account of the relationship between rationalism and morality, see Oakeshott, 1981.

9 The single most important text produced by the Social Relations of Science movement was probably Bernal, 1939. Bernal brilliantly summarized the main arguments of his book in 1937. For a useful overview of the ideas of the Social Relations of Science movement, see Roberts, 1997: Chapter 5.

10 For a longer discussion of Orwell's ideas about science and technology, see Bounds, 2009: 50f.

11 See Sawer and Mendick, 2012.

12 To say this is in no way to impugn the honour of the dedicated men and women who keep the welfare state going. It is simply to recognize that they have little choice but to obey the imperatives of the institutions for which they work.

13 Among the only British Marxists who have addressed this issue during the current crisis are the invaluable libertarian polemicists associated with the journal *Spiked*. See, in particular, O'Neill, 2013.

14 For a stimulating survey of Durkheimian forms of cultural criticism, see Smith, 2001.

15 The Socialist Party's position is outlined in Sell, 2011.

16 For the sake of clarity, I have slightly oversimplified my account of the role of Green ideology in modern Marxist parties. It would perhaps be more accurate to say that the perspectives of classical Marxism coexist uneasily with Green ideology in the minds of many activists. Although Marxist parties are often suffused with scepticism towards modern technology, their members can still be heard making the case for economic growth on occasion. Moreover, it is not uncommon for the ideas promulgated by party leaders to conflict with those of the rank and file. Whereas official spokesmen on environmental issues often make the case for 'green growth', ordinary party members tend to emphasize the dangers of economic expansion. For a stimulating defence of green growth by a leading member of a British Marxist party, see Dickenson, 2007. Dickenson is a member of the Socialist Party.

17 See Engels, 1968.

18 For a characteristically cynical eco-Marxist survey of scientific responses to the environmental crisis, see Magdoff and Bellamy Foster, 2010: 20f.
19 The most effective right-wing intervention in the British debate about the environment has been made by the Conservative politician Nigel Lawson.
20 This is not to say that Britain has been entirely unaffected by social unrest over the last few years. The inner-city riots which broke out in 2011 have been widely interpreted on the left as a response to the problems of austerity. For a highly sophisticated account of the political significance of the riots, see Badiou, 2012.
21 See Klein, 2008.
22 Orwell, 2001: 202.
23 For the history of UKIP, see Daniel, 2005; Etheridge, 2014; Ford and Goodwin, 2014; Newark, 2014.

Bibliography

Anon. (2014). 'Cuts, floods and climate change'. *Proletarian*, February.

Armstrong, S. (2012). *The Road to Wigan Pier revisited*. London: Constable.

Badiou, A. (2012). *The rebirth of history: times of riots and uprisings*. London: Verso.

Bernal, J. D. (1937). 'Science and Civilisation'. In: C. Day Lewis, ed., *The mind in chains: socialism and the cultural revolution*. London: Frederick Muller, 185–204.

Bernal, J. D. (1939). *The social function of science*. London: Routledge.

Bounds, P. (2009). *Orwell and Marxism: the political and cultural thinking of George Orwell*. London: I.B. Tauris.

Campbell, B. (1984). *Wigan Pier revisited: poverty and politics in the 80s*. London: Virago.

Colls, R. (2013). *George Orwell: English rebel*. Oxford: Oxford University Press.

Crick, B. (1992). *George Orwell: a life*, New edition. Harmondsworth: Penguin Books.

Daniel, M. (2005). *Cranks and gadflies: the story of UKIP*. London: Timewell Press.

Dickenson, P. (2007). *Planning green growth: a socialist contribution to the debate on environmental sustainability*. London: CWI Publications and Socialist Books.

Engels, F. (1968). *The part played by labour in the transition from ape to man*. Moscow: Progress Publishers.

Etheridge, B. (2014). *The rise of UKIP*. Epsom: Bretwalda Books.

Ford, F. and Goodwin, M. (2014). *Revolt on the right: explaining support for the radical right in Britain*. Abingdon: Routledge.

Hobsbawm, E. (1994). *Age of extremes: the short twentieth century 1914–1991*. London: Michael Joseph.

Klein, N. (2008). *The shock doctrine*. London: Penguin Books.

Lighter, F. (2014). 'UK floods expose Tory hypocrisy and social tensions'. *Socialist Appeal*, February.

Magdoff, F. and Bellamy Foster, J. (2010). 'What every environmentalist needs to know about capitalism'. *Monthly Review*, 61(10): 1–30.

Marx, K. (1976). *Critique of the Gotha Programme*. Moscow: Progress Publishers.

Meyers, J. (2000). *Orwell: wintry conscience of a generation*. New York: W.W. Norton.

Newark, T. (2014). *Protest vote: how politicians lost the plot*. London: Gibson Square Books.

Oakeshott, M. (1981). 'The tower of Babel'. In *Rationalism in politics and other essays*. London: Methuen, 59–79.

O'Neill, B. (2013). 'The great welfare myth'. *Daily Mail*, April 5.

Orwell, G. (2001). *The road to Wigan Pier*. London: Penguin Books.

Orwell, G. (2010). 'The Road to Wigan Pier diary'. In: P. Davison, ed., *The Orwell Diaries*. London: Penguin Books, 23–71.

Pierson, C. (1999). 'Marxism and the welfare state'. In: A. Gamble, D. Marsh and T. Tant, eds., *Marxism and Social Science*. London: Macmillan, 175–94.

Roberts, E. A. (1997). *The Anglo-Marxists: a study in ideology and culture*. Oxford: Rowman and Littlefield.

Sachs-Eldridge, S. (2011). 'Women under siege in the age of austerity'. *Socialism Today*, 152, October.

Sawer, P. and Mendick, R. (2012). 'Tiny band of left-wing radicals bring jobs policy to its knees'. *The Daily Telegraph*, February 25.

Sell, H. (2011). 'The cutbacks and the fightback'. *Socialism Today*, 146, March.

Sharrock, D. (2011). 'The Road to Wigan Pier, 75 years on'. *The Observer*, February 20.

Shelden, M. (1991). *Orwell: the authorised biography*. London: Heinemann.

Skidelsky, R. (2013). 'Osborne may gloat about recovery, but his "hard slog" will leave Britain worse off'. *New Statesman*, September 30.

Smith, P. (2001). 'The Durkheimians: ritual, classification, and the sacred'. *Cultural Theory: An Introduction*. Oxford: Blackwell, 74–96.

Socialist Appeal (2013). SEIU 1199: 'Workers must have a winning strategy!' *Socialist Appeal*, November 21.

Socialist Party Nottingham (2013). 'Stand up for education! Hundreds march in Nottingham on teachers strike'. Available at: Nottingham-socialists.org.uk [Accessed October 1, 2015.].

Taaffe, P. (2010). 'Revisiting the Road to Wigan Pier'. *Socialism Today*, 137, April.

Taylor, D. J. (2003). *Orwell: the life*. London: Chatto and Windus.

Index

For Product Safety Concerns and Information please contact our EU
representative GPSR@taylorandfrancis.com
Taylor & Francis Verlag GmbH, Kaufingerstraße 24, 80331 München, Germany